A History of Charlton Kings

A History of Charlton Kings

compiled by
Charlton Kings Local History Society

edited by
Mary Paget, MA, FRHist Soc

Gloucestershire County
Library, Arts & Museums

First published 1988

Published by
Gloucestershire County Library, Arts & Museum Service
Shire Hall, Gloucester GL1 2HY
Typeset by Alan Sutton Publishing Limited, Gloucester
Printed in Great Britain by
Antony Rowe Ltd, Chippenham, Wiltshire

British Library Cataloguing in Publication Data

A History of Charlton Kings.
1. Charlton Kings (Gloucestershire) —
History
I. Paget, Mary II Charlton Kings Local
History Society
942.4'16 DA690.C4529/

ISBN 0-904950-65-4

Contents

List of Illustrations

The Charlton Kings Local History Society wish to record their thanks to the following for permission to use illustrations:

Mr Eric Armitage (6.18, 6.27, 6.28, 6.29, 6.36, 6.37, 6.49, 6.65, 6.80)
Mrs H. Bennett (6.16, 6.19, 6.20)
Dr Stephen Blake (4.3, 6.67, 12.1)
Mr and Mrs Bone (4.4)
The Revd Graham Bryant (8.23)
Mrs K. Carter (17.1)
Cheltenham Art Gallery (6.7, 18.1)
Mrs Linda Hall (6.12, 6.13, 6.14, 6.51, 6.53)
The Revd Basil Hill (8.29, 8.30)
Mr C. de N. Hill (6.61)
Mr H. Holborow (6.43)

The late Miss E. Holliday (17.3)
The late Miss Annie Hopkins (8.31, 12.7, 12.8)
Mrs James (6.33)
The late Mr Peter Kendall (6.62)
Mrs Kilmister (11.2)
Mrs I. Main (6.82)
Mrs D. Marriott (6.55)
Mrs Beryl Middleton (6.30, 6.38, 6.39)
Dr G. Moore (6.8)
Mrs D. Moxley (6.40, 6.41)
Mr George Ryland (6.3 and the impressions of the Revd Edgar Neale, Tom ('Fishy') Smith, and Charlton pigs on pp. 2, 172 and 188)
Mr Edgar Skinner (19.1, 19.2)
Mrs Eve Stuart (8.25)
Mr Fred Thomas (12.2)
Lady Tovey (6.75)
Mr Ken Venus (8.1)
Miss M. Wilkins (11.4)
Mr John Williams (8.25)
Miss E. Winter (17.2)

Introduction

This is the history of a community in which nothing spectacular ever happened, and even the Civil War which touched us slightly left no more imprint than one grave in the churchyard. For centuries we had no resident lord of the manor and for longer still we had no resident priest, so that our yeomen and husbandmen with a scattering of small gentry, were accustomed to manage their own affairs without interference; and this spirit of independence is still characteristic of Charlton people. Until very recently, and to some extent even now, the same family names continue for generation after generation. Descendants who have migrated elsewhere still remember their roots and believe there's no place anywhere like Charlton. Incomers soon begin to feel the same!

This cannot be a definitive history because there is still much work to be done. For a fuller account of some aspects of our past, we have to refer readers to *Bulletins* already published and those to come, for it will be years before we have exhausted all the material at Gloucester and elsewhere relating to Charlton Kings. But we can be confident that we know the basic facts. *A History of Charlton Kings* is based on more than eight years of research by members of our Local History Society, although it has fallen to me to put it together. I am especially grateful to members of the Wednesday evening Research Group and to other researchers who have given so much of their time and interest. Reference to *Bulletin* articles throughout the *History* show how much I have drawn from the work of others, especially Eric Armitage, Helen Bennett, Steven Blake, Derek Copson, Michael Greet, Bob Hunt, Patrick Love, Harry and Beryl Middleton and Joan Paget. We owe a special debt to Linda Hall who has surveyed houses for us and provided detailed architectural reports on them and their past. We thank Ken Venus for his drawings and maps, George Ryland for his illustrated stories, and all who have allowed us access to title deeds, contributed their reminiscences, or lent old photographs for copying; Dr. Steven Blake for allowing us to use his photographs, Cheltenham Art Gallery for permission to reproduce Thomas Robins's picture of Charlton Park; Gloucestershire Record Office for much help and for permission to use Quarter Sessions plans and other material, and the Librarian of Jesus College, Oxford, for permission to consult the College archives.

Mary Paget

1

Geography

We have to start with a note about the geography of Charlton because this determines all development.

Boundaries

The parish boundary was not altered at all until after 1884 (when the ecclesiastical parish was also split), so in this study of Charlton's past we use the old boundaries. Starting from Sandford Mill, where parish perambulations started, the bounds ran along Hales Road, up Harp Hill and Aggs Hill, along the escarpment above Ham Hill into the valley of the Chelt, up the stream by Lineover Wood, along the escarpment by Wistley Hill, across to Charlton Common on Leckhampton Hill, and down the course of the Pill by Old Bath Road to Sandford Mill again. So it was a large parish, some 3170 acres according to the tithe apportionment. On the north, east and south its bounds were those of the Hundred of Cheltenham already fixed by the eighth century.

Soil

In this area we have lias clay, overlaid by the Cheltenham sands. Clay forms a deep bed at the foot of the escarpment and is exposed wherever streams have cut through lighter soil; elsewhere deep beds of sand and gravel cover the clay and provide well-drained, easily worked land, very suitable for settlement. A little stone is available and has been quarried on Charlton and Ravensgate commons, but the upper beds are soft and the stone is better for lime-burning than for building.

Streams

It is claimed with truth that you cannot leave Charlton by any road or footpath without crossing water (although now it may run in a culvert). The Chelt or Rungebourne rises in Dowdeswell and flows through Charlton, being fed on its way by the Poultbrook or Freeman's Brook, the Hambrook, the Hearne or Crab Brook, the Lilleybrook or Forden Brook, and the Slad (now underground). These streams never go dry, even in such summers as 1976. They can rise very rapidly and the Chelt is much given to flooding, although its flow has been reduced by the building of Dowdeswell reservoir and the water taken out of the Hambrook by reservoirs at the Hewletts and Glenfall. The original force of the Chelt can be guessed from the depth of the valley it has cut, especially in the stretch between Spring Bottom and Cudnall bridge.

Because we have clay under the sand, wells may be dug almost anywhere so there has never been any problem about a good water supply. Many old Charlton houses had wells under their kitchens or just outside the door.

2

Settlement

The Origin of Charlton

Was there early settlement in this district? There certainly was middle Iron Age settlement at Vineyards farm, underneath the Roman 'villa' discovered in 1980; and a burial in the gravel by Sandy Lane shows that men passed through and perhaps lived there. Charlton is near so many Roman sites (Wycomb, Whittington, Haymes, to name a few) that we may guess at a good deal more utilisation of the lower slopes of the hills, even the valleys. The linear dyke near Arle Grove, which starts near a barrow on the brow of Ham Hill and slopes down the escarpment, was presumably a boundary dividing pre-medieval land holdings. With the 4–5 million population now believed to have existed in Britain in Roman times, it is unlikely that any good land would have been neglected, and most of Charlton is well-drained sand and gravel. Neither Domesday book nor our field names suggest dense woodland here in medieval times – Northfield on the hill top and Southfield under Charlton Common are names hinting at open country, and it is just possible that there was a pre-Saxon site near Southfield, now built over.

But until more evidence appears, Charlton must be taken as what its name says, a Saxon *ceorls' tun* established as part of the royal manor and Hundred of Cheltenham (hence 'Kings'). The word *tun* originally meant a fenced inclosure with a dwelling.

The boundaries of that Hundred were in existence by the mid-eighth century and remained unchanged when Norden surveyed the manor in 1617. On the north-east, east and south they continue as our parish boundaries today. By 773 (when there is evidence for a church) Cheltenham was a judicial and administrative centre, with a courthouse, a well-endowed minster and probably a market. It was the focal point of a flourishing royal estate, with a home farm at Leckhampton devoted in the main to growing 'leeks' (the word covering any sort of vegetable) maybe for sale, its pig farm at Swindon, and its ceorls' or labourers' settlement at Charlton to supply labour for the demesne. We use the name Charlton to cover the whole parish, but the simple homestead or homesteads of the labourers – the bond vill to which the term was first applied – probably stood in what we know as Charlton Park (emparked in 1784). That would not have been too far from Leckhampton; men could walk to and from work, and they could cultivate for themselves, in-field and out-field, the land later called Charlton Lower Field (the modern park and Greatfield). This was the only open field land to which the name 'Charlton' was ever applied. It was arable until the mid-eighteenth century.

Growth before 1086

Development from this nucleus came with the setting up of similar homesteads at Bafford (Bassa's Ford), very possibly on the site of Charlton Park House, called The Forden until 1784; Cudnall (Cudda's Hill); Ryeworth (the rye inclosure and farm); and Battledown (Baedella's *tun*). These may be part of a ninth and tenth century extension of cultivation for which there is evidence in other localities. Most of these settlements received and kept the personal names of the men who built up the new holdings, leaders perhaps of family groups. But this expansion does not represent individual initiative so much as deliberate policy on the part of the king's steward in charge of the manor. The whole of a royal manor was the king's, even parts not yet cultivated, and his steward was the man who allocated land and encouraged people to take up new farmsteads. Charlton has never at any time been a nucleated village – indeed, we now know that practically all Anglo-Saxon settlements took the form of scattered homesteads.

The total area of the king's manor was diminished when first Prestbury in the ninth century and then Swindon and Leckhampton in the eleventh century were alienated. The reign of Edward the Confessor must have seen a major reorganisation of the manor, with the creation of three carucates of new demesne to replace the old (a carucate being the amount of land a team of oxen could plough in a season). The loss of ten hides (roughly 1000 acres) was presumably made good by other development in the parts the king retained. That would be normal, to assart new arable and give away old. Sandford and Westall hamlets on one side and Ham on the other were probably started in the 1050s, the new meadow at Ham (OE *hamm*: meadow) balancing the loss of old meadow when Keynsham (the king's *hamm*) and Coltham (the cold *hamm*, that is, the *hamm* which could not be treated as water meadow like the grasslands along the Chelt) were ploughed and divided into strips. A third open field at Whaddon (in addition to Cheltenham's Upper and Lower fields) may date from these years.

Domesday tells us that the two existing mills at Cheltenham had become inadequate for the amount of corn to be ground and that three new mills had been built by the steward during the years 1066–86. Production had more than doubled. Two of the new mills may have been in Charlton. One was Sandford mill, just on our parish boundary as it was to be defined; the other was perhaps Cudnall mill in Spring Bottom. If so, the new tenements mentioned in Domesday – four villein holdings and two bordar holdings (80–100 acres) – could have been at Moor End and the Lye.

This improvement had increased the value of the manor to its lord. Under Edward, Cheltenham had rendered £9 5s 0d in cash and 3000 dog loaves to feed the king's hounds when he stayed at Gloucester. By 1086 the rent had been raised to £20 in money, 16 shillings in lieu of the bread, and 20 cows and 20 hogs as well: the render from the manor was double what it had been. The cows and hogs suggest that part of Cheltenham's prosperity was based on dairying – all those meadows along the Chelt and out at Ham – and part on pig-keeping, as it had been when Swindon (the swine hill) was still the king's.

Extension after 1086

The years after 1086 saw more development, including a new township at Newenton or Naunton in the early 1100s – the number of freeholds here suggests twelfth-century settlement. Shortly after that came the expansion of Cheltenham as a market town by the creation of burgage holdings and freehold tenements. This kind of development was

2.1 Ridge and furrow on Hither Strouds. This was part of an open field system called Strouds.

2.2 Ridge and furrow on the Beeches playing field. This land was levelled in 1931, but the original form was visible during the dry summer of 1983.

typical of the twelfth century, and we know that by the thirteenth century the men of Cheltenham were wealthy enough to buy a seven year lease of their borough from their lord.

The struggle for the throne between Stephen and Matilda resulted in a division of the manor of Cheltenham; her supporter, Walter of Ashley, was rewarded by a grant of £10-worth of land, and this was confirmed by Henry II. About a third of the existing Charlton tenants became Walter's men. But he did not receive his land in a single block; it was made up of a few existing tenements and a considerable amount of undeveloped land. It was probably Walter who gave land for a chapel *c.*1190.

All our Charlton 'Ends' represent new land brought into cultivation beyond the limit of existing arable. In all of them, tenements were planted on one side of the street and well spaced out with 1½-2 acre closes by each house and the rest of the land in strips in the open fields, each new End having new arable. The majority were 'base tenements' (held by work service as well as rent), with a half virgate (here about 12 acres) of field land. (Evidence for the size of holdings will be discussed in Chapter 5.)

One great change took place in 1247. Cheltenham ceased to be a royal manor when Henry III exchanged this and other inland manors with the Norman abbey of Fécamp. He had to recover control of the ports of Rye and Winchelsea and the Sussex estates given to the abbey by Cnut, and was obliged to offer property of reasonably equivalent value. The change of lord deprived the burgesses of Cheltenham of any hope of gaining self-government. However, the thirteenth and fourteenth centuries brought prosperity, the result of a great extension of arable in Charlton. Between Coltham and Battledown was a new field, the Ewen; the lower slopes of Leckhampton were ploughed as Knavenhill field, while Lilleyfield took in what is now the golf course. The slope under Vineyards and Niffnedge (that is, Knife-edge) was Milkwell field. From Sappercombe Lane to Coxhorne was one great field, Strouds, with a smaller Middlefield between it and Castlefield; to the south east above the Blackmoor was Ravensgate field, stretching up to the steep escarpment below Ravensgate Common. It was no doubt this increase in Charlton's arable that produced the wealth we see reflected in the Lay Subsidy Roll of 1327, when Charlton paid a total of 75s 11d, compared with Cheltenham's 81s 4¾d, Westall's 43s 0¾d, Alstone's 33s 10¾d, and Arle's 24s 1¼d. In all, 43 persons in Charlton were rich enough to be paying tax.[1] The 1334 Lay Subsidy shows Charlton's prosperity continuing – the amount due then was £5 0s 0¾d.[2]

Putting together all the evidence available, we may surmise that down to the end of the twelfth century new tenements were being created as fast as new land could be assarted on both manors. But after the division into three tithings for administrative purposes (Bafford, Charlton and Ashley) with the same number of base tenants in each, tenements became relatively fixed, though the amount of land held by some men may have increased. In 1294 it seems likely that 36 of the 126 villein tenements on the manor of Cheltenham were in Charlton Kings[3] and to those we can add the 18 half-virgate Ashley tenements[4] – perhaps 54 base tenements in all. From the twelfth century, freeholds were created too, but these were always more fluid.

1350–1500

We have no evidence to show whether Charlton was affected by the Black Death and subsequent plagues; it is obvious that our prosperity was not gravely menaced. The names of Lucas and Bull attached to land on the escarpment suggests that these late fourteenth-century tenants were clearing the steeper hillsides of scrub, and arable was extended eastwards right up to the parish boundary with the Doles and the Newlands. By the Chelt, one new field was called Barlands or Bearlands (*bare*: cleared land) and across the stream another was Red Wood (the cleared wood). On the slope of Ham Hill was Howbeach or Howbreach field. At this point, there was still moor between Charlton and Ham, the Deepmoors (above Detmore).

The reason for this activity was the demand for grain – very large quantities were being exported from Gloucester in the years 1380–1410.[5] An exporter like Simon Broke collected grain from all the surrounding area, including no doubt Cheltenham market. Consequently our parishioners were well able to contribute to the enlargement of the church tower and the addition of a south aisle, both apparently in the years round 1390, even if the new lord of Ashley, William Grevill the wealthy wool merchant, gave a substantial sum towards the work.

This boom was followed by the usual reaction in the mid-fifteenth century, when the trade of both Gloucester and Cheltenham declined. The recession was just beginning when a new rental of the manor of Cheltenham was compiled for the benefit of Syon Abbey, the new lord – Henry V's delayed gift only came to hand after 1441. The Charlton portion lists all Cheltenham manor tenants, free or base, in the tithings of Bafford Hide and Charlton (that is, the whole parish except Ashley manor tithing and except Ham). John Stubb preserved this rental for us in a careful copy.[6] It names the mid-fifteenth-century tenant, his predecessor, and the tenant before that, so the rental takes us back into the fourteenth century.

There had been eighteen base tenements in each tithing; now there were eleven base tenants in Bafford, holding eighteen messuages (or house sites) between them. Most had been half-virgate tenements; now in some cases two half-virgates had been combined, in others some of the smaller holdings had been added. Of the eighteen base tenements in Charlton tithing, only four had been half-virgate holdings, the others having three or six acres. Now one tenement was reduced to a toft (a house site without a house) and there were thirteen tenants. The economic balance betwen Bafford and Charlton, however, was redeemed by the three Northfield messuages with 45 acres of land. Northfield as a sheep walk was well able to keep its head above water.

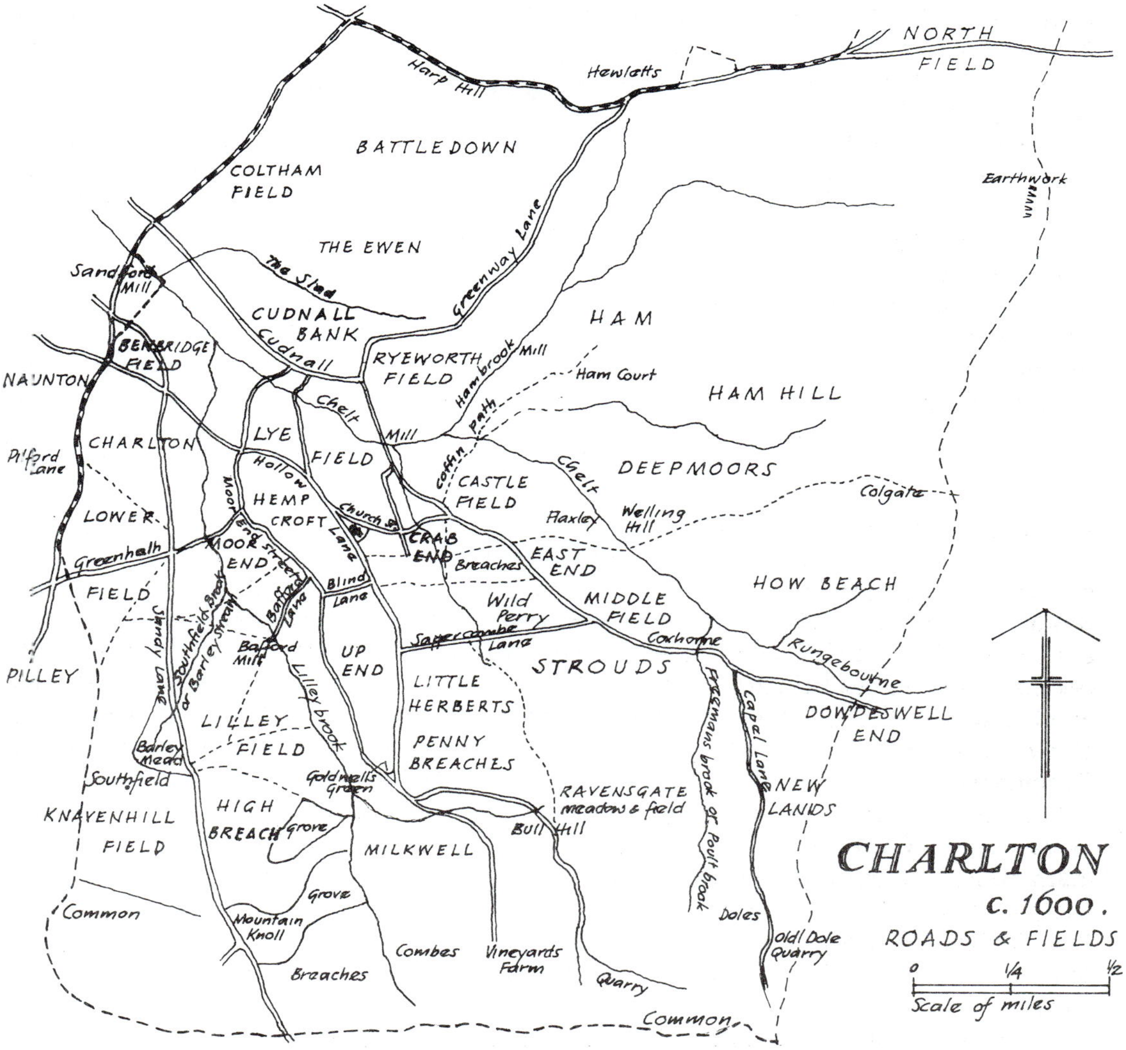

2.3 Charlton roads and fields *c*.1600.

Small freeholds suffered more than base tenements during this depression and those in Bafford suffered most because it had been settled longer and the land was held to be worked out. One Bafford messuage with two virgates (at least two tenements thrown into one), and two half-virgate holdings, were without occupiers when the rental was compiled. But the two-virgate messuage held by Throckmarton and Hopton (previously Hopton and Borowehopis) shows another side of the picture: put together into a larger block, this land had attracted the notice of John Throckmarton, a gentleman of means, and he had thought it a worthwhile investment.

The other Bafford free tenement, a messuage with one virgate, previously Thomas atte Forde's (that is to say, Forden House or Charlton Park), was held by John Grevill;[7] and Grevill also held two freeholds in Charlton with a half-virgate and six acres of land. John's grandfather, William Grevill the Campden woolmerchant, had acquired the manor of Ashley in 1386–7, but these Cheltenham tenements had been bought by his son or his grandson to increase the family stake in this area. So a man with capital could still find it profitable to farm here.

Another Charlton freehold was the Cudnall messuage with six acres held by Wheeler late Hore,[8] also destined to become Grevill property.

Looking at the *c.*1450 Rental, it is perhaps not surprising that amalgamations had taken place; it is more remarkable that so many small units had survived. Six acres or less can hardly have been viable as an agricultural holding. But if the occupier had a handicraft such as weaving to supplement his husbandry, it would do well enough, and Cudnall mill was being used to full cloth.

One Ashley tenement which disappeared between 1327 and 1557 was Robert of Goldwell's. In 1327 he was assessed at 6d, among the least affluent tax-payers. Goldwell's Green was the seventeenth-century name for the Timbercombe Triangle, where the roads from Up End and Little Herberts meet, and between the roads on TM 318 are traces of habitation, perhaps the site of Robert's homestead. It would have been on the very outskirts of settlement in the fifteenth century, if the vineyards on the hill had been given up.

1500–1600

The demand for grain picked up again about 1500, and led to the ploughing-up of the Deep Moors, the last tract of waste below the hills. Now the only common waste in Charlton was 50 acres on Charlton Hill and 50 acres on Ravensgate. Prosperity returned and showed itself from about 1550 in house rebuilding and improvement. But Charlton had used up all its land for arable and had little meadow or pasture and no wood, and by the mid-sixteenth century this was producing other problems. Extensions of cultivation had been pushed to the uttermost.

3

Custom of the Manors[1]

Domesday tells us that in 1086 all land on Cheltenham manor (except the demesne and the glebe) was held by custom; as yet there were no burgesses and no free tenants. But there were seven slaves in Cheltenham and seven more on the two Leckhampton manors. It seems certain from this that the original home farm at Leckhampton had been worked by slaves, supplemented at rush times by labour of customary tenants who paid in this way for their holdings. They may have paid a money rent as well, since there is no evidence for any week-work on this manor, and no one in 1294 paid anything by way of commutation for it.

It has been suggested that the Anglo-Saxons saw each homestead as belonging to all the descendants of the first settler – to the children and grandchildren of Bassa or Cudda or Baedella and their connections – a shared inheritance with shared obligations, not as the property of any individual. But with the twelfth-century demand for clearly defined rights and duties, either the oldest, the youngest or sometimes all the brothers in the family got the right to inherit the whole or part. An alternative theory is that before the Conquest, land was either divided or went intact to the youngest son, because a man's greatest ambition was to fight with his lord. So in war it was the woman and younger children who were left to manage the farm while the man and his older sons fulfilled their military obligations with the fyrd. This attitude would have been reinforced as long as there was a Danish threat. Without evidence, we can only balance probabilities. Primogeniture seems to have come in after the Conquest and so the new freeholds always went to the eldest son.

In the case of Cheltenham, our custom may show a link with Gloucester, for in both places it was the youngest son who inherited customary tenements as far back as we have any knowledge. And Gloucester, like Cheltenham, was a royal manor, so that 1066 did not involve any violent change.

It is true that custom, though persistent, was not immutable; cases are on record where lord and tenants agreed to make a change. But this is unlikely to have happened where the lord was an absentee and his representative very often a local man with his own local interests. The manor of Ashley was an offshoot of Cheltenham and had the same custom, suggesting that ultimogeniture or Borough English here goes back to the mid-twelfth century at least, though no early court rolls survive. On both manors, the youngest son was heir to the whole, or, if there were no sons, the youngest daughter; in default of children, the holding went to the late tenant's youngest brother or sister or their youngest son or daughter.

What, then, happened to elder sons? While new tenements were still being created they could be settled. After that, they could turn to crafts, to trade or to service, and perhaps in time save enough to be able to buy up some free land or a small base tenement. Compilers of the *c.*1450 Rental[2] expected that most would work on the family holding or for some other tenant; if they stayed at home they would not be liable for bederipes (harvest work or payment in lieu) as customary tenants, nor would they be liable if they were employed by a free tenant. So any Charlton boy who worked for a Cheltenham burgess was exempt.

Custom at Cheltenham favoured the woman. A tenant had the right to make a twelve year grant to run from the date of his death and by this means could raise money to pay his debts or make provision for elder children; but, subject to this, all his land was the widow's for her lifetime and she too could lease it for twelve years from her death. The youngest son might have to wait a long time for his inheritance but he would eventually receive it whole, without partition. The problem arose where the widow married again and had children by her second husband, for custom allowed her to make her youngest son heir to her first husband's estate. This was the main objection raised against our custom in 1625.

Cheltenham was ancient demesne of the Crown and benefited from that status even after Henry III had given away his manor. The 1450 Rental states plainly that our tenants were only tallaged (taxed) if the king tallaged his demesne. Cheltenham had been taken into the king's hand so often during the fourteenth century, and in the mid-fifteenth had only just been passed to the Abbey of Syon, that it cannot have seemed impossible that one day it might become royal demesne again.

What about labour services? The 1294 extent of the manor,[3] taken when Cheltenham was temporarily in the king's hand during war with France, shows that there were then 126 villeins on the whole manor, each paying a few pence for the day's ploughing, weeding, hay-making, reaping and carting they ought to have done. The amounts vary, suggesting that commutation began early for some tenants and was the rule for all before Henry III handed his manor over to Fécamp. For 70 of them it was three pence a day for ploughing or carrying, a halfpenny a day for weeding, 1 shilling a day for reaping, a halfpenny a day instead of hay-making (but twelve pence were deducted from the total for this because on the hayfield they would have received food or drink). These were normal thirteenth-century day-wages. The 70 also paid two pence instead of bringing a cart for carrying and three pence for each of the five loads which that cart should have taken to the barn or stackyard. But no one owed more than ten days a year. The 25 tenants who owed only six days a year paid one penny a day instead of carting, one penny instead of hay-making, one penny instead of reaping – the wage rates of a century before. The 22 tenants who did no work, except at harvest time, paid 3½d each for the harvest period. The ten who paid hens and cocks as rent now gave one penny each for them. These figures suggest progressive commutation; the 22 and the 25 had exchanged their work for money at an earlier stage than the 70. The total amount received was £3 11s 10d. In addition, 12 shillings a year was paid instead of the work of an unspecified number of boys and girls.

By 1294 there was, of course, no need for anyone to do any actual work; all the demesne (home farm) was rented out, 149 acres of arable at four pence per acre, 30 acres of meadow at eighteen pence an acre, 16 shillings-worth of pasture, and a mere 2 shillings-worth of wood. These were very moderate rents for the late thirteenth century, so perhaps they were fixed about 1247 when Fécamp first took over as lord. The Abbey needed money, not produce. The last stage in commuting work services and the letting of the demesne had probably happened about the same time. So work services, or money in lieu of them, imposed no great burden on the tenants. Furthermore, as the value of money dropped, so did the value of the fixed commutation. Tenants in 1617 were still paying the same work-silver and still doing or offering to do one day's free or 'bede' reaping.

Labour was commuted early; but even earlier than that, the number of plough-teams and carts the tenants were to bring with them had been fixed. In 1294 these are said to be seventeen ploughs and sixteen carts. But there were eighteen ploughs for customary tenants in 1066, nineteen in 1086. Was the number seventeen laid down at the time of Edward the Confessor's reorganisation? It seems very possible. When he gave away the old home farm at Leckhampton and the new demesne of 1086 was cleared to replace it, and when Swindon too ceased to be part of the manor, all the old manorial obligations must have been reviewed.

Either the king or the abbot collected Peter's Pence for the church, a penny per household (excluding the poorest) when the tax was frozen in the twelfth century. Cheltenham manor paid 5 shillings representing 60 households. Few Ashley tenements were liable, for the majority were created after the tax was fixed for good. But six tenements in Charlton Kings were still liable in 1617, and Norden's survey commented: 'Peter's Pence yearly paid to the Bailiff and not discontinued.'

One custom mentioned in the 1450 Rental was binding on tenants who held as Walter Brevill did – that is, on a number of base tenants but not on all. Walter had to pay a fine if his children, boys or girls, married outside the hide or tithing of Bafford. The amount is not stated and may have been negotiable. Most manors demanded merchet if a girl married outside the *manor* but it was not usual for boys to be limited or for marriage to be restricted to so small an area, and the custom may not have been much observed in practice. Norden remarks: 'Customary tenants may marry son or daughter and a widow may marry without the lord's licence out of the manor.' All in all, few manors had customs as light as those of Cheltenham.

By the sixteenth century, there was no real distinction between base and freehold tenure except in the matter of inheritance; this was why the Grevills and a few gentry families wanted to change the custom. A man like Thomas Lynnet who died in 1548 had found himself obliged to divide his property, the freehold going under his will to his elder daughter Joyce and her husband Richard Stewe, but the customary going willy-nilly to his younger daughter Elizabeth who had married Walter Pates;[4] and there was a real problem when a widow remarried and had more children. So all tenants agreed to make a change, some not very whole-heartedly. Willing or not, however, the tenants of both manors paid for a private Act in 1625. Primogeniture was in future to replace ultimogeniture, and the widow's portion (if not settled on her at marriage) was to be a third of her husband's estate as allotted by a jury. Thus customary tenure was brought into line with freehold. But this Act could not become effective all at once. Women married before 1625 were still entitled to the whole for life and twelve years; and any father who wished his youngest son to have the property could defeat the Act by a surrender to uses of his will, followed by a devise to that son. In the same way, customary property could now be divided among several children. Many did use the surrender to uses in just these ways. It is interesting to note how many Charlton tenants were still leaving the dwellinghouse to the youngest son, even in the nineteenth century. The Act came into operation if a man died without children, even if he had been born before it passed. Richard Pates (grandson of Walter) was a fourth son who died in 1634, and his three messuages in Alstone passed to his eldest brother Thomas. Had he died ten years earlier, his heir would have been the fifth son, his younger brother Lynett.[5]

The 1625 Act did not interfere with payment of heriots except to regulate the amount of commutation if the lord were willing to take money instead of the best beast or best good. Normally, after 1625, money was accepted; though on the death of Giles Grevill in January 1632 'one Roaneish or reddeishe gray Mare and one Blackeishe or darke gray younge gellding' were claimed as heriot but detained from the lord of Cheltenham by John Dole, Mr Grevill's man.[6] Work-silver, bedereap money, tithing silver and Peter's Pence were still demanded from tenements liable to pay them. Norden in his 1617 survey noted 28 Charlton holdings liable to work-silver and six to Peter's Pence, and the sums were duly collected thereafter. Thus a Cudnall tenement (perhaps Ryeworth farm) owed ten pence for work and a Peter's Penny; and the tenant of the two Sandford mills paid 2 shillings work money for them, and four pence for the messuage on which he also paid a Peter's Penny. Among Ashley tenements, Elborough Cottage was said to owe a Peter's Penny, and the Ashley tithing man at the end of the eighteenth century was collecting work-silver and bedereap money from nearly all tenants, to judge by his notebook.[7]

Both manors had pounds in Charlton Kings and could distrain for non-payment of rent, heriot or fines; both had the right to impound animals found trespassing on tenants' land but Cheltenham had the right to impound strays found on the roads. The Cheltenham pound was and is in Horsefair Street (though by 1633 there were complaints that it was being turned into a garden). Ashley's was at Pound Piece at East End, beside the Ashley Court House which stood there until 1868.[8] All tenants, both of Cheltenham and of Ashley, had to attend the Hundred courts held in the court house in Cheltenham, the Great House on the site of St Matthew's church.

One curious feature of Ashley manor were its beedle messuages. There were three of them, one in Bafford and two in Cudnall. These were the longest settled parts of Charlton, and Ashley messuages there may have been allotted to manorial beedles at the time of Walter's grant; summoning tenants to the courts, collecting fines, and other items of court business (perhaps undertaken in rotation) may have been part of the rent due. Down to the end of the nineteenth century, these properties are described in surrenders by the phrase 'being a beedle messuage', though by then they were no different from any other Ashley tenement.[9]

4

Roads and Footpaths

The Road to London

Scarcely any of our roads now run where they did in 1600, and this problem has to be grasped before we can understand Charlton Kings. The road to London has varied more than any.

(a) The oldest road may be the one that forms our parish boundary up Aggs Hill. It is part of an ancient track which ran slightly north of Cheltenham High Street and so may predate it. In a thirteenth-century deed it is called the king's highway, when Walter Hawlf gave Cirencester abbey an assart of land below 'Rodewey',[1] and in 1733 the parish was indicted for not repairing it.[2] Under the 1755–6 Turnpike Act for Cheltenham roads[3] it was turnpiked from Cheltenham market house, up Aggs Hill, through Brockhampton, and so to Puesdown Ash, where it joined the road from Gloucester. The surviving pike house at

4.1 Aggs Hill – turnpiked in 1754.

4.2 Turnpike house at Hewlett's Gate.

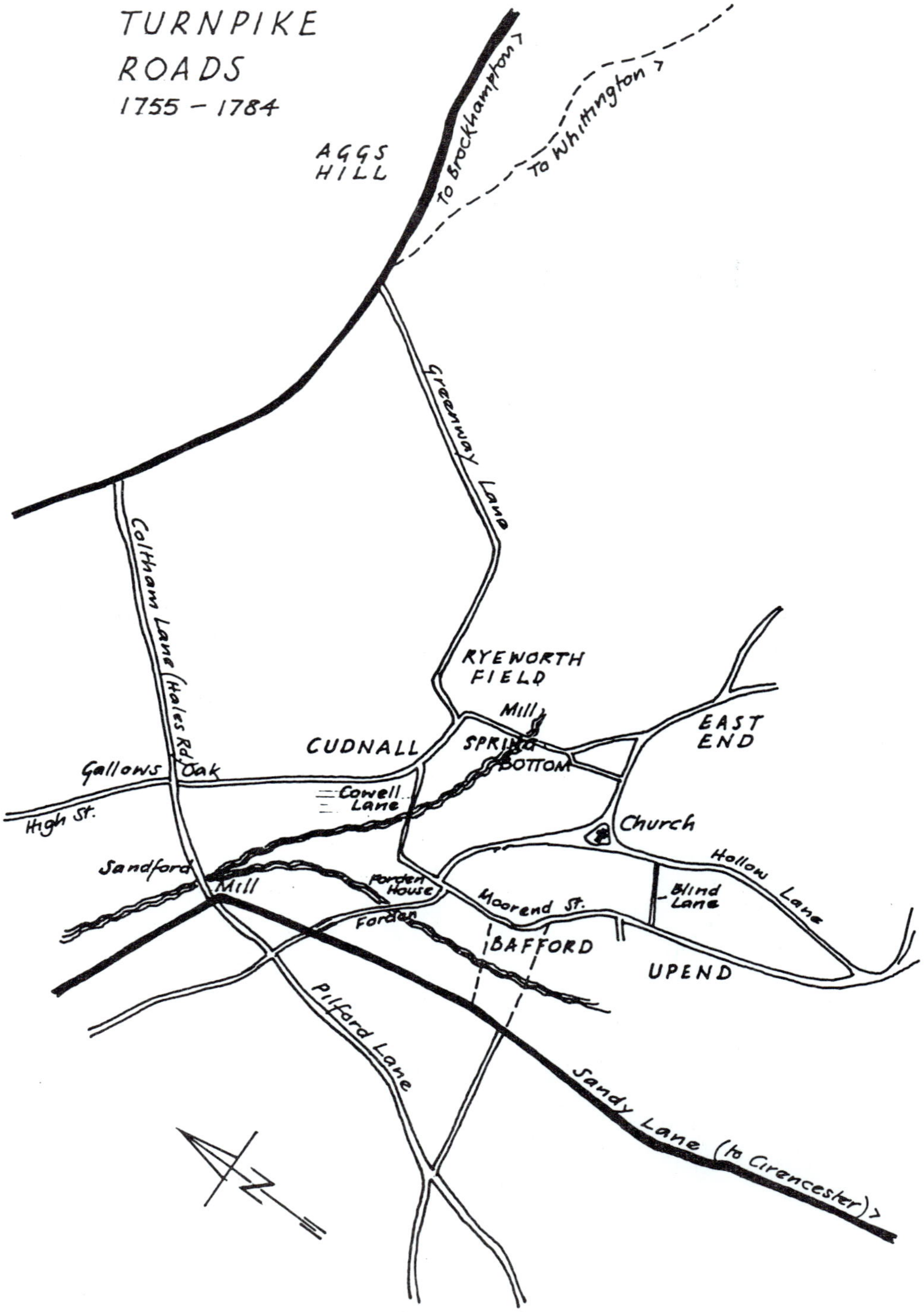

4.3 Turnpike roads, 1755–1784.

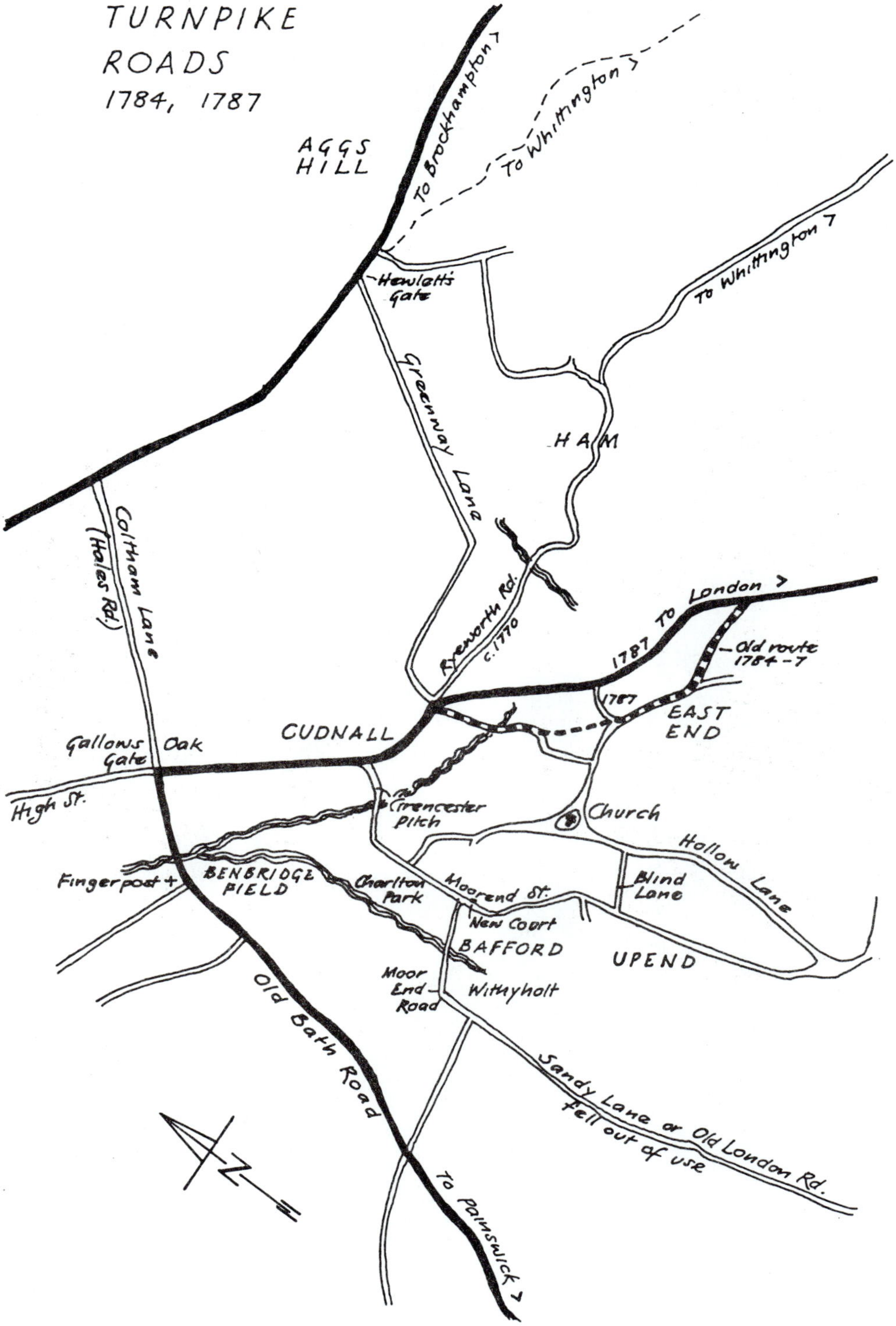

4.4 Turnpike roads, 1784, 1787.

4.5 Spring Bottom (old London road).

4.6 The line of the old London Road (from Six Ways to Spring Bottom) in the garden of Grove House. This photograph was taken in 1980 before building work started.

4.7 Another part of the old London road from the top of Balcarras Lane looking towards, Coxhorne (January 1979).

the junction of Hewletts and Greenway Lane was built there after the reservoir caused the road to bend round it. The road is shown as turnpiked on a map of *c.*1860; however, there was a new Cheltenham Roads Act in 1863 and under the provisions of this Act the road was disturnpiked and the toll house sold in 1864.[4]

(b) Another old track passed south of Cheltenham, crossed Sandford field and Charlton Lower field to become our Sandy Lane, the road to Cirencester and on to London. It was turnpiked in 1755–6, and in 1773–4[5] a stretch from the Churn to Elkstone church and out on to the Gloucester road at Beech Pike was substituted for the original line beyond Cowley.

The 1784 Turnpike Act[6] allowed the trustees to negotiate with Dodington Hunt of Charlton Park. He gave land for a road between the Withyholt and New Court, part of our Moorend Road, and they allowed him to close Sandy Lane from Withyholt corner to Old Bath Road. At the same time, Quarter Sessions sanctioned the closure of a parish road from Hunt's house to Old Bath Road – these two operations enabled him to create Charlton Park and stock it with deer.[7] As late as 1806, Mitchell's map marks Sandy Lane as 'Old road to London'.

(c) Cheltenham High Street continued eastwards past Gallows Oak (at Hales Road). The 1777 map of Cheltenham roads[8] shows an open space here, with a tree in the middle of the road. Then it went on eastwards through Cudnall Street and down the slope alongside Grove House to Spring Bottom. It crossed the ford (as the lane still does) and ascended the bank where the Hearne Brook is culverted, coming out by The Hearne. It continued up East

End Road and Balcarras Lane, swinging left at the top of that lane along the narrow field called the Lancett and south of Coxhorne, crossing Freeman's brook or Poultbrook at Stannett's Ford. Then it followed the present line of road to Salt's Farm and beside the Chelt through what is now the bed of the reservoir to the foot of Dowdeswell Hill. Originally this road was a link between Cheltenham, Dowdeswell and Withington; but by 1700 it had become an alternative way to London, joining the Gloucester–Stow road at The Garricks Head. About 1750 the stretch up Balcarras Lane and south of Coxhorne House was abandoned in favour of improvement of the rest of our East End Road and a new length of main road through Middle field to run between the two Coxhornes and join the old road at the ford. This was the road turnpiked in 1784.[9] But the trustees were given power to divert, and so in 1787 they submitted a plan to Quarter Sessions for a new road from the end of Cudnall Street to the end of East End Road, through the middle of Castlefield. A link between the old and new turnpikes was provided by Hearne Road, cut on the line of an existing footpath.[10] Thus the road to Dowdeswell became the main road from Cheltenham to London. The final stage (so far) was the 1825–6 bypass, cutting out Cudnall Street. This was a last-minute addition to Telford's scheme for a new road continuing from the foot of Dowdeswell Hill,[11] and was completed in 1836 by a short steep cut to link Spring Bottom and London Road[12] so that the road down the slope past Grove House could be abandoned.

The Road to Cirencester

The old Cirencester road was the one up Sandy Lane, first turnpiked in 1755–6. Walking up it now, it is hard to imagine the lane past Southfield as a main road! When the stretch across Charlton Park was closed in 1784, and part of Moorend road substituted, those coming from Cirencester had to proceed by the new road and down the old road past Charlton Park house (now the back drive), then into Cudnall Street by a narrow, winding track called Cowell Lane – this track is marked on Isaac Taylor's map of 1777.[13] About 1784 the road was improved by a new cut from the Chelt going steeply up into Cudnall Street between Charlton House on the left and what is now Langton Lodge on the right (the line of the road before it was modified in 1904 and 1948).

In 1826–7, a new Cirencester Road was made from the crossing of the Chelt, south through the Lyefield to Up End. From the junction with Bafford Lane to the Lilleybrook it followed the old Up End Street. Then it crossed the stream and drove straight up the hill to meet Sandy Lane at the top. This road was still turnpiked *c*.1860, with a pike house by the Lilleybrook.

The Road to Bath

The Old Bath Road was created under the 1784 Act which allowed the trustees to improve Pilford Lane 'from the Direction Post in Bembridge Field near Cheltenham through Birdlip to join the Turnpike Road from Gloucester at or near the Town of Painswick'. There was a toll gate just below Claypit Path (hence the name Charlton Park Gate for an entirely new cul-de-sac of the 1920s). The old Pilford Lane, like several other roads round Cheltenham, had never headed directly for the town. Instead it had continued north to Gallows Oak and along Coltham Lane (Charlton's parish boundary) to Prestbury and Winchcombe. Coltham Lane was improved in 1846 by Charles Hale, Cheltenham's Surveyor of Highways[14] to become Hales Road.

4.8 Hollow Lane (now the front drive of Charlton Park).

4.9 Hollow Lane at Timbercombe.

Hollow Lane and Blind Lane (Croft Road)

When Walter of Ashley got his share of the manor of Cheltenham allotted to him, some time before 1154, these two roads were already in existence to serve as boundaries. The Crown retained land west of Hollow Lane up to the Blind Lane turning; then all the land east of Hollow Lane. Walter got land east of Hollow Lane and south of Church Street up to Grange Walk; then land west of Hollow Lane from Blind Lane south to the Timbercombe Triangle or Goldwells Green.

The deep Hollow Lane is still to be seen up Timbercombe, running parallel to a later cobbled track; until recently this could be traced going diagonally up Bull Hill, and then into the length known as Lynch Lane, where the road, much overgrown, still runs between the remnant of stone walls, and comes out on to Ravensgate Common. Until the 1920s this Timbercombe Lane was sign-posted 'To Pegglesworth and Ravensgate'. What is not always realised is that Hollow Lane did not start at the Triangle; it continued down Little Herberts, Horsefair Street, the upper part of Brookway Lane and then turned west into the present front drive of Charlton Park, crossed the stream by 'the Ford' (a bridge is first mentioned in 1623) and so across Charlton lower field into Old Bath Road. This stretch can be seen in Robins's picture of Forden House *c.*1748. From the house to Old Bath Road it was closed in 1784 and from the house to Brookway Lane in 1827.

There are frequent orders in Court books for hedges along this road to be cut back and for the usual maintenance; but there is no order for the road to be laid down in the first place. Yet it was no botched up parish job; large stones have been deeply set and still appear as cobbling, while in a few places, after more than a century of total neglect, there are still traces of the small stones laid to form a surface. This was once a main road. Was it intended to provide a route out on to the Gloucester–Stow road at Pegglesworth and so on to

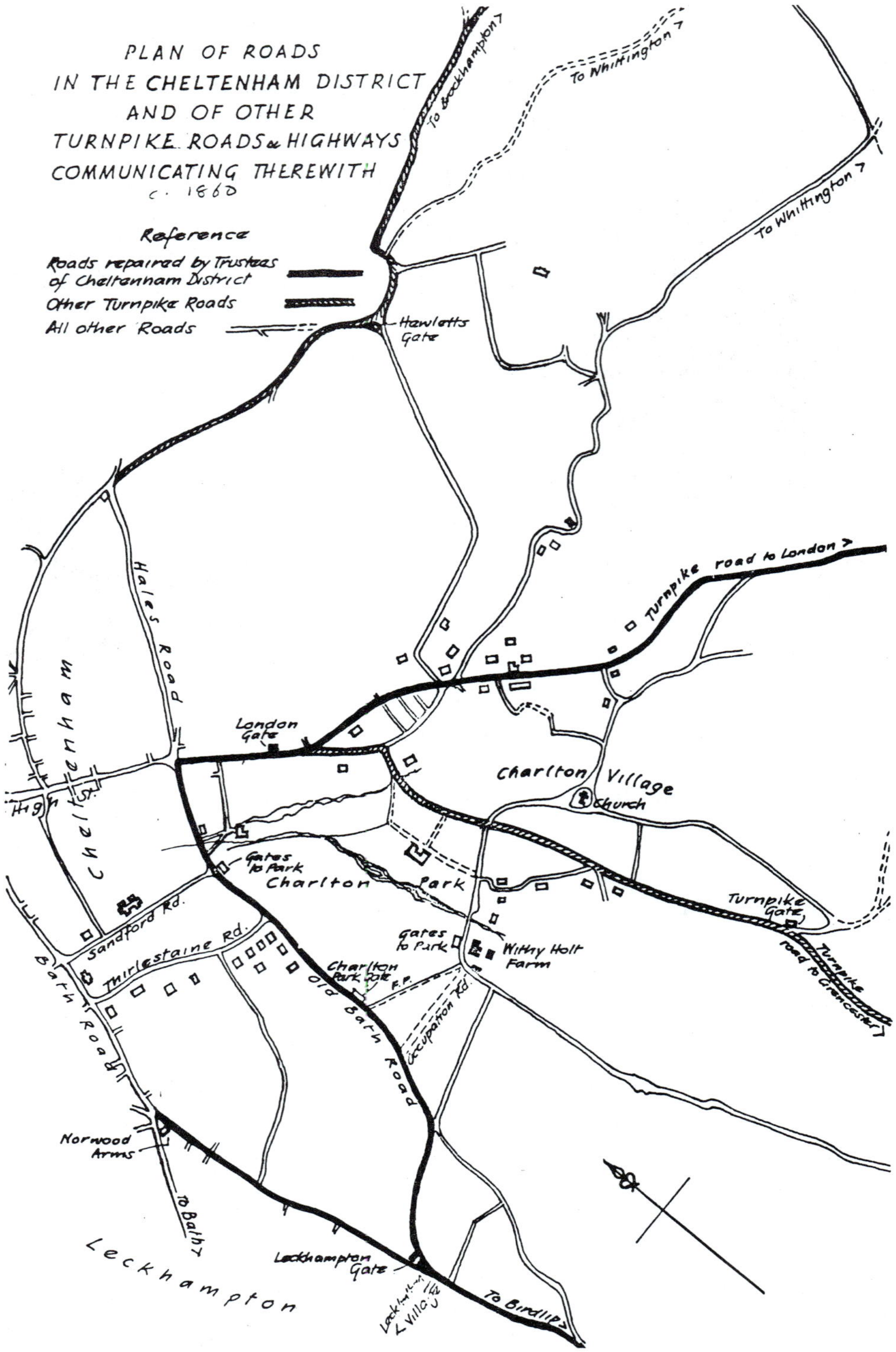

4.10 The road pattern *c.*1860.

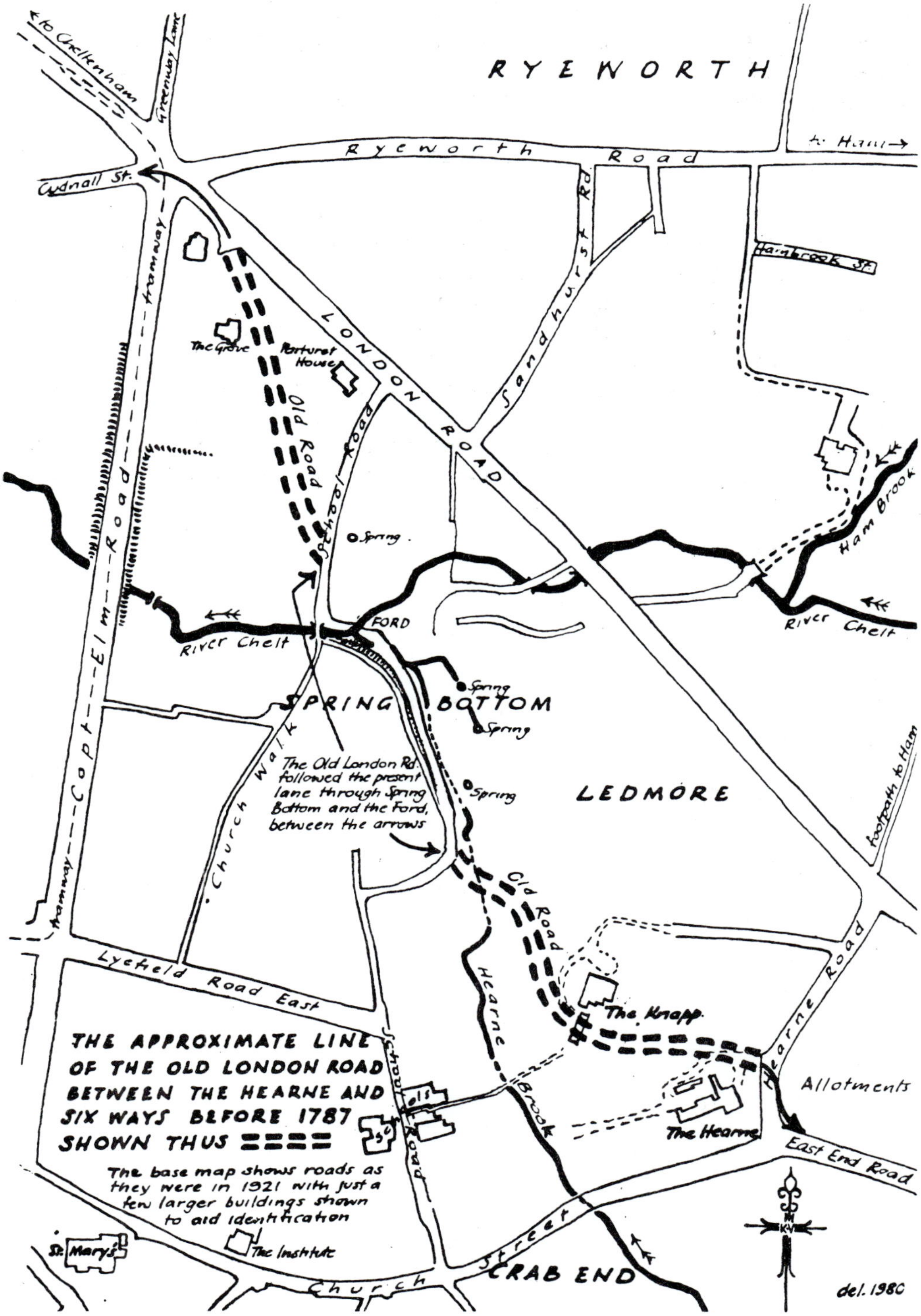

4.11 The roads in 1921 and the line of the old London Road.

London? And if so, is it coaeval with the short by-pass behind New Court formed *c.*1550 as an alternative to twisting, muddy Moorend Street, the by-pass which was abandoned in 1827? Perhaps Hollow Lane ought to be considered as an alternative road to London, not much used after the Balcarras Lane route came into favour.

Footpaths

Charlton is still crossed by footpaths but a number have been closed in whole or part. Several across The Beeches were closed in 1826, together with the continuation of Grange Walk eastward to East End.[15] These footpaths originated as occupation ways through open fields, or as tracks between Charlton, Leckhampton, Dowdeswell and Ham. The 'coffin path' through the Ledmores enabled mourners from Ham to carry their dead to St Mary's, for Ryeworth Road was not cut through the open field until the eighteenth century; that coffin path is further evidence that Ham was developed from Cheltenham and not as part of Charlton Kings, for the two were not linked by any proper road. It was really part of a long-distance trackway from Prestbury, perhaps from Winchcombe, which till 1970 continued across The Beeches and still does continue up Lucas Hill to join Ravensgate Lane.

5

Agriculture

Land Use, Crops and Stock

Field name evidence

Because our settlement extended itself End by End, Charlton Kings never had a three field system as did most of the Vale of Gloucester. At first, each new End appears to have cleared two new fields for itself; later, any waste left between the Ends was cleared (for example, the Breaches or Beaches between Crab End and East End), then the hillsides, and lastly the Deep Moors. By the mid-sixteenth century, a Cudnall tenant would have part of his land in Mill furlong and on Cudnall Bank but he might also have land in Coltham or the Ewen, in Ryeworth or on Battledown, and he would still feel that grazing on the Cudnall fields should be kept exclusively for Cudnall tenants. With land in three, four or five places, there was no problem about arranging fallow years.

Besides the main field agriculture, there are some place-names in Charlton which indicate special uses for some of our land. Hempcroft, Hemcroft or Hencroft was the name of the land between Blind Lane (Croft Road) to the south, Moorend Street (New Court Road) to the west, and Hollow Lane (Charlton Park front drive, part of Brookway Lane, the Horsefair, and Horsefair Street) to the north and east. Hemp was a useful crop. The early ripening (male) plants, pulled first, were made into cloth; the green (female) provided seed and material for ropes. Both had to be retted in water to separate the fibres, a disagreeable process, so if hemp were grown on Hemp Croft, it must have been early when this area was still on the outskirts of habitation. Later this land was divided into strips and Hempcroft became an open field. At the north end of it a medieval Steward of Cheltenham created an artificial rabbit warren, supplying rabbit meat and skins – a coneygrey was a profitable side-line which took up only 2½ acres of land (according to the 1617 Survey). There was still a William Konyger in Charlton in 1423.[1]

After Hempcroft came the Flaxley (*flax leah*) at the eastern end of Castle Field, where flax was grown for linen and linseed oil and again the crop could be retted beyond existing habitation. Flaxley may have been in use until the later Middle Ages, for there was still no development on or near it. John Dowdiswell with a garden by Crab End Way in 1403 was a webber or weaver.[2] A will of 1557 leaves a quantity of linen yarn which is to be woven into cloth and then divided as directed.[3]

Charlton in the sixteenth and seventeenth centuries had a number of weavers. Several were listed in 'Men and Armour' in 1608[4] and though there is nothing to show that they were linen weavers, it seems possible. Linen spinning wheels occur in inventories, as well as wool spinning wheels. Because we once grew flax, Charlton people were accustomed to use linen in their houses. They had sheets, tablecloths and hand-wipes (napkins) in

5.1 Perry pear trees surviving in the hedges on Penny Breaches.

5.2 On Wild Perry – a typical perry pear tree.

abundance, far more than contemporaries in Somerset, though they used treen or pewter, not crockery, to eat from. The only pottery items mentioned in inventories are the shallow milk pans used for separating cream in the dairies. This lack is borne out by the total absence of slipware or old earthenware sherds brought up when digging Charlton gardens: all we find is willow pattern and eighteenth- and nineteenth-century clay tobacco pipes! Early in the fifteenth century, Cudnall mill in Spring Bottom became a fulling mill for a while.[5] Robert and Joan Walker were to have it and rebuild it 'with two stockes called walking stockes', the lord's Bailiff finding the timber. The process of walking cloth was no longer done by human feet: machinery requiring water-power had been invented, so fulling mills were being transferred from the towns to the country. This may be when Charlton had a windmill to grind its corn – the windmill was on Cudnall Bank, roughly where Langton House now stands. The name Windmill Piece survived to the late eighteenth century, long after the windmill had gone and the watermill at Spring Bottom had become a grist mill again. We cannot date this exactly but it had certainly happened by 1500. In the late eighteenth century, Charlton Mill was turned into a leather mill – hence the local name Leather Mill Pitch for a stretch of the London Road cut in 1787 – and in 1801 the mill was rebuilt to grind corn once more.

Grapes may once have been grown on The Vineyards, for there were many vineyards in Gloucestershire between the twelfth and fourteenth centuries. But then imported wine and deteriorating climate made the crop unprofitable.[6] In any case, wine was not our usual

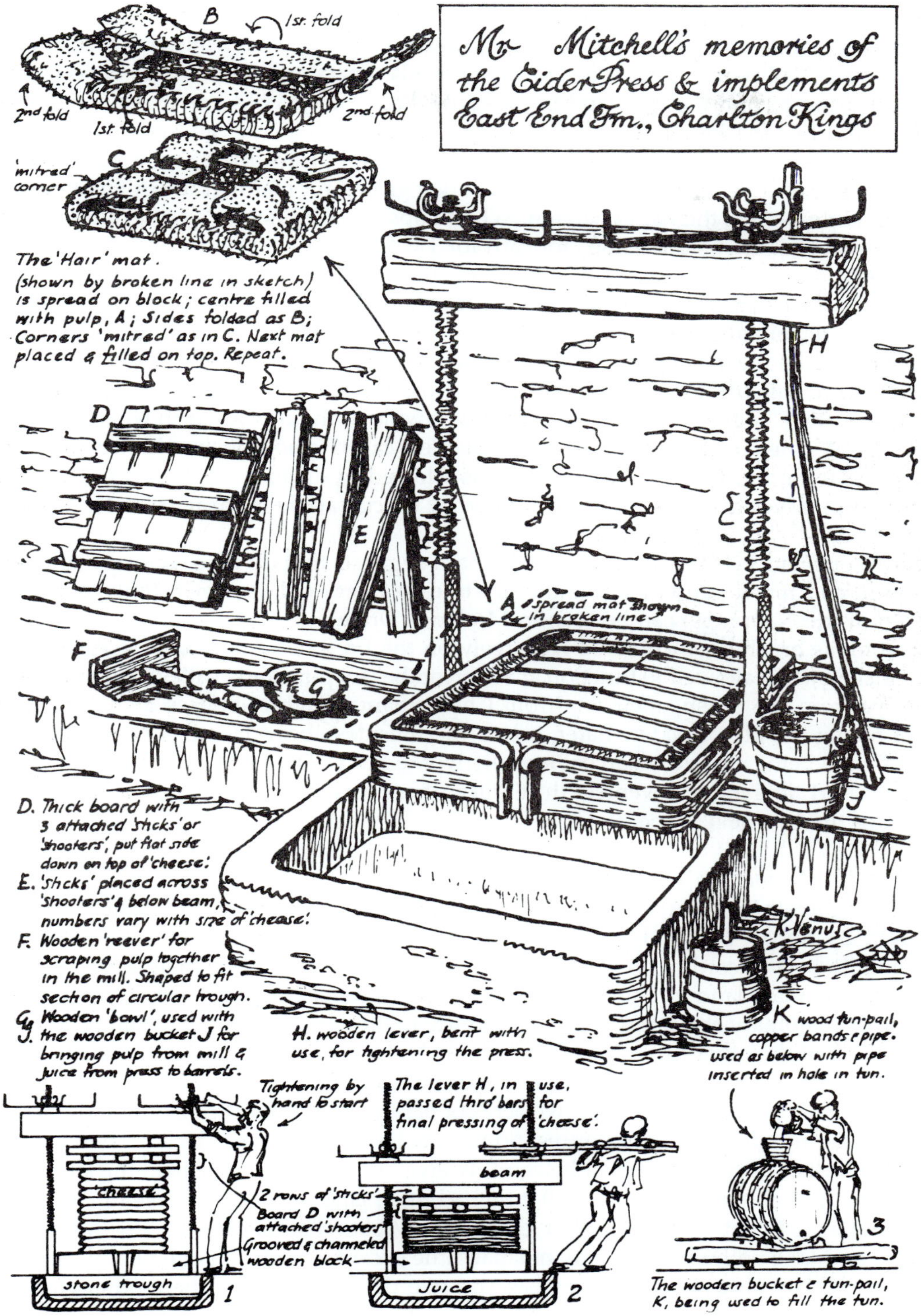

5.3 Cider-making in Charlton.

drink. The name 'Crab End' for an area of sandy soil (developed in the twelfth century) suggests the growing of crab apples for verjuice and cider apples, while crab wood, being tough, made flail swingles and cogs for mill wheels. Pears do better on heavy soil so it is not surprising to find the clay land by Balcarras Lane called Wild Perry and a close near Coxhorne called the Pearmonger's Plot.[7] Perry (locally called cider and made from either apples or pears or both, without the addition of any 'brook-apple' or water) was our traditional drink.[8] Beer was drunk too and barley grown for malting; the original name of Southfield Brook was the Barley Stream. When hops replaced nettles as a flavouring, some were grown in Ham, as the name Hopyard for TM 89 suggests. But it was only a two acre plot just across the Chelt, and we never had extensive hop yards like those in Herefordshire. There were several malthouses in the parish and maltsters were among our wealthiest inhabitants, often living in Charlton but operating in Cheltenham or Gloucester. Malt provided a means of sweetening food when honey was not too plentiful.

With land suitable for apples, we were growing named varieties by the sixteenth century. In 1557[9] Margery Taylor, alias Ruggdale widow, thought it worth while to leave to Richard Gale 'the profit of one apple tree in Stanley' called 'a nonesuch or hard apple' for 12 years (the term which she, as a widow, was allowed to dispose of). Down to the 1900s, brides were advised to ask for the profit from special apple or pear trees for their pin money!

The frequency of closes called Cherry Orchard suggests that cherries were once grown in quantity, and many gardens had mulberry trees – a very old specimen (once part of the garden of the Nappings) can be seen in Morlands Drive.

As long as brushwood could be had freely on the Breaches and along the escarpment, soap makers were allowed to function at Sapercombe (soap-makers' valley) – they could get their lye from the brush, their fats from Cheltenham slaughter-houses and there was a never-failing supply of water. Later, when the hillsides above Howbeach and the Deep Moors were being cleared, charcoal burners worked at Colgate or Colpityate.

For a short time in the seventeenth century, there was an attempt to grow tobacco on a corner of the Lye field, Tobacco Close .[10]

A Charlton farmer in 1552

We know something about crops, stock, and husbandry problems in 1552 from a tithe case brought by Robert Symonds or Symons of Charlton who thought he was being over-charged. Robert (according to the 1557 and 1564 lists of tenants and their acreage) had 83 acres of customary land in Charlton and six acres of freehold in Ham – whether these were statute or customary acres makes little difference to the case. It is possible that he also held land in one of the other townships of which we know nothing; if he did, he was better off than any other man in the parish and as it was he ranked third. Symonds was being asked to pay tithe on two acres of wheat, two acres of barley, four acres of pulse and four acres of oats. He did not dispute these figures. So he was having to redeem by a money payment the full produce of twelve acres of his land, twelve out of 89 if he only held the land in this parish; but possibly twelve out of 120 if he had more land in the area liable to pay tithe to Cirencester. It is not impossible that Cirencester Abbey had chosen to tithe some crops heavily and take nothing in the way of small tithe except a modus of one penny per calf or foal. The Abbey always sent two priests and two deacons to serve the mother church in Cheltenham and its chapel in Charlton Kings, and was accustomed to provide communion elements, bell ropes and strawings for both churches, things the parishioners ought to have bought for themselves. There was no vicar permanently attached to either parish for whose upkeep small tithe would normally have been paid. Down to 1539, tithe had been taken in kind and the Abbey had a tithe barn. After 1539 the king leased the tithes to fermours who were expected to pay priests and deacons as before and provide the elements, ropes and strawings; but now the fermours wanted their tithe in money. It was reckoned to be worth £600 a year to them; and this figure also suggests that tithes were paid at an unusually heavy rate. The arrangement, whatever it was, only lasted until the tithes were sold to Sir Baptist Hicks; then each parish was to have a single minister, the parishioners provided necessaries for themselves, and tithe was paid at the usual rate, except for 1½d modus for calves. The important point for us is that we are told what crops Symonds grew and what the produce was per acre, together with the amount he had been accustomed to pay in lieu and the sum he was asked to pay in 1552, presumably the current market price. The crops were wheat, barley, pulse and oats. An acre of wheat produced five bushels (old value 18d a bushel, increased value 2 shillings); an acre of barley twelve bushels (15d a bushel); an acre of pulse four bushels (20d a bushel) and an acre of oats six bushels (20d a bushel). He was not being asked to pay tithe on hay or on the grass his cattle had eaten, both of which were usually tithed.

What annoyed Symonds most was the statement that he had pastured and sheared 160 sheep. He asserted that he had fewer than a hundred, 60 of which were pastured in another parish (where he would have to pay agistment (grazing) tithe on the grass they had eaten). Of his 100, eight had died. He had 45, not 70, lambs (charged at 18d each formerly, now at 2 shillings). One of the witnesses in the case, Thomas Packer, aged 60, agreed that Symonds had less than 100 sheep altogether and only 40–50 ewes (so his tally of 45 lambs was right). Symonds declared that after shearing he had six tods of wool (15–17 fleeces to a tod) and of these he sold two at 12s 6d a tod and two at 12 shillings. For tithe purposes the wool was valued at 18d a fleece. His other stock on which tithe was due consisted of 34 pigs (8d each), a mare and foal on which a customary penny was paid; two barren kine and either eight milch cows with eight calves (according to the fermour) or nine cows with seven calves (according to Symonds), and on these he paid one penny a calf.

The case went against Symonds and he had to pay 25s 3d tithe and 41s 10d costs.[11] The yield from these crops in 1552 was probably average (a bushel of grain was 56lb, but it is pointless to compare modern yields using improved strains and unlimited fertilisers). No one in Charlton can have kept any great flock of sheep, for we had no upland sheep-pasture except Northfield, and very little pasturage of any kind. Symonds's claim that he had had to put half his sheep elsewhere is plausible, and so is his statement about numbers – if he really had 160 sheep, his flock was larger than any we know of in this parish before 1700. Only four of the Bafford tenants had sheephouses, according to the 1617 survey, and they may have had a prior right to put their sheep on Charlton common – there was a driftway through the fields called The Drifts or The Thrifts to the hill. In any case, Charlton common was only 50 acres and Ravensgate common the same. To lose eight sheep by disease was not uncommon. However, the ewes had produced a lamb apiece (if Packer's statement was true) and the profit on two-thirds of his clip did more than pay tithe on everything, leaving two tods (56lbs) for future sale or for the use of his womenfolk. He will have owned oxen for ploughing but on these (as on his barren cows) he paid no tithe. They were shod for ploughing; ox shoes have been found on Penny Breaches and The Croft.

We know a little about Symonds from the parish register. He first married on 5 October 1542 and Alice his wife was buried on 24 July 1544. After a decent interval he married a widow, Jane, on 3 February 1546/7. She was in fact Jane French, for Walter French, son of Jane Simons, was buried just over a month later on 15 March 1546/7. Robert French, a freeholder in 1557, must have been Jane's relative (not a son) and the relationship explains why in 1564 Robert Symonds was French's sub-tenant for his two acres. The only evidence to support the notion that Symonds had land elsewhere, either in the Cheltenham area or outside, is the absence of any entry for the baptism of a son at Charlton. A daughter Jane was baptised here on 19 July 1552 (the year of the case). Did Robert leave Charlton after that, though he was still farming here in 1564? There was a son, one must suppose, for a much later Robert was marrying Margaret Marten (of Charlton mill) at St Mary's on 26 May 1614. If the older Robert did leave the parish he came home for burial on 30 June 1572.

Inclosure 1557–1627

Whatever side-lines there were, Charlton tenants in the early sixteenth century lived by their arable. They could not have fed any cows or horses or sheep through the winter if they had not been able to turn them out on to the open fields as soon as harvest was carried, for every scrap of ploughable land was ploughed. By 1550 there were far too many beasts on the open fields, more than could be fed; until that point there had never been any attempt by the manor courts to regulate numbers. Matters were brought to a head by the Ham tenants who inclosed their own fields very early and then started putting their beasts on Ryeworth. This 'oppression' of the open field system had to be stopped – but how?

5.4 This great oak marks the line of a 1564 inclosure between Catshay and Penny Breaches.

5.5 Pollard oaks between Great and Little Breach.

We are fortunate to have a collection of documents on the open field problem, collected and copied out by John Stubb, who became Steward of Cheltenham manor in 1607 and was himself a Charlton man.[12] He was not baptised at Charlton Kings, as were the other children of John Stubbs senior and his wife Joyce Marten (daughter of the miller of Charlton mill), but he must come between a son Thomas, baptised in 1572, and a daughter Agnes, baptised in 1575. The heir was the youngest son Richard, baptised in 1576, who granted some Cheltenham property to his 'brother John' in 1610.[13] John had a legal training which fitted him to become steward of Cheltenham manor in 1607; and to the income from his stewardship, his Ashley land and town property he added a farm at Wellinghill when he married Jane, widow of Robert Alexander alias Mansell. John and Jane were admitted on 22 June 1615 and immediately surrendered the tenement to Robert's son Samuel who granted it to them for their lives.[14] All this is important, because it means that John was personally involved in the later stages of the open field saga and he must have heard talk about the early stages of the dispute when he was a child, for it all started a good twenty years before John was born and continued until he was a middle-aged man.

In his account, Stubb makes no secret of his belief that inclosure and strict stinting were the only means by which the open field problem could be met. 'Oppression of the fields' had become really acute by 1557 when the first inclosure was suggested. As a preliminary, it was necessary to discover who had and who did not have common rights in the various fields, for grazing in the open fields was not available indiscriminately. To quote John Stubb:

> it appeareth that although some of the tenants who have messuages and landes lying in every ende of the towne, have common the length (through) out the whole towneship, yet such as have noe landes lying in Howebech feild, ought to have noe common there, and soe on the contrary such as have noe landes lying in Cuddenhill feildes nor Bafford nor Nupend feildes, ought (not) to have any common in any of those feildes, where they have noe landes, for that our commons are recyprocall, we have common in other mens landes, bycause they have the lyke Common in ours.

It was not a single field-system but a very complicated one. The new arable that had been won from the waste when Bafford and Cudnall and Upend were created remained appropriated to those settlements, not to be shared with tenants holding land in other parts of the parish.

So there had to be an accurate survey by Commissioners appointed by the Council in the Marches to measure what each man held in the open fields. This is the first document Stubb copied out for his own guidance. The acreages (whether statute or customary) must be correct, otherwise there would have been an outcry, but naturally they do not include any land around the houses (gardens, orchards and home closes) to which the tenant had sole right. The 1557 survey and the one which followed seven years later, were meant to include only *commonable* land.

The first agreement was for limited inclosure for five years from 1557. Permission was given to fence one acre for every ten acres held in any of the open fields. But inclosures were to be made in the places allowed by the Commissioners and not anywhere else. Almost without exception, inclosure was to begin on the escarpment. The main fields – Coltham, Lower Field, Cudnall Bank and so on – were not to be touched. The total arable involved was 1657 acres (470 held of Cheltenham, 747 held of Ashley, 340 held of both).

The five years ended; some hedges were removed, others remained; and there was a great deal of quarrelling. So two years later, in 1564, a second scheme was drawn up.

Northfield and the greater part of Robert Goodrich's Ham Court estate were still excluded. But this time Ham 'under the hill' and parts of Battledown were brought in, making the overall total of arable 2044½ acres. Permission was given to inclose rather more: three acres for every 20 held; so that under this more generous allowance 291½ acres would in future be held in severalty. For that is what it amounted to. Freeholders were told in 1564 that they might make permanent inclosures, while base tenants could inclose for the life of the living tenant and twelve years after. But the Commissioners 'being gentlemen of wisdome and discrecion' foresaw that eventually all inclosures would be permanent. However, there was still a long way to go and stubborn opposition to be met. The Ham tenants and some others by their 'frowardness and obstinacy' persuaded their neighbours for the sake of peace to lay their inclosures open. Stubb (writing it up later) accused them of malpractice, that they

> besides this unreasonable kinde of common, did drawe many that had stocks of money to hire houses in Charleton, in hope of keeping sheepe and horses upon the common groundes, and within short tyme by the rotting of their sheep did lye upon the charge of the parish. And all neighbour townes about did put their cattell into the common fildes of Charleton, yea, and did buy ricks of hay, of purpose to winter greate flocks of shepe there, so careless was everyone of the common good.

Stubb was partisan but he knew very well that too much winter grazing trampled and ruined the soil, especially in a wet season.

Stubb became Steward of the manor of Cheltenham in 1607 and from then on, as Steward and as tenant under both manors, he was deeply involved. He could not persuade the majority to keep their sheep out of Howbeach, though it was common knowledge that sheep on that land always got rot. But the first April after he became Steward 'having sworne an indifferent Homage we procured with much adoe a stynt, thought it were but for one yeare'. For every twenty acres held uninclosed, a man might put 30 sheep, six beasts and two horses on the fields in winter, with the option of putting two beasts or eight sheep instead of one horse, or five sheep instead of a beast; and 'if any will keepe only sheepe it amounts by this stynt unto 71 for 20 acres'. Stubb added 'although by this stynt a farre greater proportion of cattle was allowed than the grounds could beare, yet it did worke some good effects and made the Inhabitants more pliable to yelde to some reasonable condicions'.

He was backed in his fight by William Norwood as fermor of Cheltenham and Giles Grevill as lord of Ashley, with the result that in the following September it was agreed that

> Free and base tenants may inclose and keep in several all lands within the vill except all arable lands lying in the common fields underwritten, viz Midlefeild, Barlands, Beach, Castlefeild, Lower Feild, Hencrofte, Lylly, Milfurlong, Longfurlong, Pycked Land, Coltham, Yewyn Breach, Bancke, Ryworth, and le Lye.

Inhabitants were to hedge their closes or be fined 10 shillings; the penalty for putting cattle into lands held in severalty was to be 20 shillings. It was assumed that all closes would become meadow or pasture.

> Having procured this order for the keeping of all the grounds of the towne (saving the arrable fieldes) in severall, we thought the victory had byn wonne, and laboured to keep up our groundes accordingly, and soe we of Nestend did, although our hedges were

> dayly throwen open, yet we made them up againe. And to give neighbours the better encouragement I did sowe Newbreach in the fallowe years and did mowe The Hale and did set the hay in a reeke in the said close and tooke the profitts of all my groundes, affirming constantly, that if any did put any cattle into my groundes or pull up my hedges that I would bring my accion against them, yet many of my hedges were secretly broaken, but none durst doe it openly.

His chief opponents were Mrs Ann Grevill (widow of William Grevill) who held Rogeresland at East End, his own brother-in-law, Samuell Rudgedall, and Walter Higgs. Several lawsuits ensued, one in particular against Mrs Grevill who had sent her brother Mr Moore and some of her servants to drive three oxen into The Hale. Stubb had passed them in the road and was given the news while he was at breakfast.

> I sent them backe word, that he was to blame to eat up my grasse with his sisters oxen and that if I had knowen that he had byn going thither I would have gon backe and ympounded them.

However, Stubb did not hurry himself, he rode into Cheltenham and then to Leckhampton on business and only after that did he go up to his close, where Moore had been kicking his heels all morning awaiting him:

> He tould me that he had stayed a greate while for me, I answered that the fault was his, If he had acquainted me with his purpose I would have gon backe with him, then he asked me what I would doe with the oxen, I replyed that I would ympound them, he asked where, I said in Ashley pounde. He willed me to give him my hand, I answered that it should be needles, his eyes should see it . . .

and the oxen were duly driven to the Ashley pound at Pound Piece beside the Court House at East End.

The case went on for several years, Mrs Grevill maintaining in her petition that all inclosure was 'to the express and manifest wronge and greate hinderance and damage of your poor oratrix and the undoing of thother poore tenants there, the benefitt of their said comons being a speciall and principall parte and stay and meanes of their liveinge and sustayneinge of their wyves children and families there', in saying which she truly expressed the feelings of many Charlton people, who could not envisage any husbandry which did not include commoning on the open fields in winter and was not mainly arable. Stubb said a majority wanted to inclose, following the example of the tenants of Ham and Northfield who 'did keepe in severall their pasture and meadow ground to the very great wealth and quiett of the same places'; 'the greatest parts of the tenants of Charleton aforesaid had not sufficient meadows and pastures in severall to finde their plowe catle and milch kyne for the necessary maintenance of their families'.

Charlton, in fact, was beginning to see a change from arable to mixed farming, with increasing emphasis on dairying. This was a general trend in many parts of the country, a reaction to a series of wet summers. Over and over again one reads in seventeenth-century deeds the words 'formerly arable, now meadow or pasture'. One consequence of the Stubb/Grevill quarrel was a schedule drawn up in 1610 to show how many acres each tenant had uninclosed in the common fields and how many sheep, cattle, or horses should be allowed. It is not surprising to find Mrs Grevill at the head of the list, with 66 acres open. Richard Pates had 70 acres and Roger Holder 68. But most tenants had much less, some

5.6 Snow reveals evidence of ridge and furrow cultivation (*left*) on Lower Penny Breaches, and (*right*) on the Deepmoors.

very little. Cudnall tenants were keeping their land open to oblige Mrs Badger or Badghott, the Impropriator, for tithe of grain was worth more to her than agistment or grazing tithe. But after Mrs Grevill's death in 1612, and in part thanks to the influence of William Norwood, the inclosers got their way. In 1627 Stubb could write:

> Sithence which Tyme all the said enclosed groundes have byn kept in severall accordingly, without the gainesaying of any person, and many other groundes have byn lykewise taken up in severall, to the greate profitt and quiett of the inhabitants.

Early inclosure and laying down to grass has preserved for historians evidence of pre-seventeenth-century ploughing. When we walk up Timbercombe today we see on the Lower Penny Breaches the unmistakable marks of old plough-curves in the ridge and furrow. The big oak, once part of a hedge between that field and Catshay, is about 400 years old; the boundary line between them must be a result of the 1564 inclosure. The pollarded oaks between Great and Little Breach (between the former allotments and the football field) go back to that date too.

Inclosure alone did not solve the open field problem, although it went a long way. While any land remained to be commoned, stinting was necessary. This was done by court order, reinforced by the yearly appointment of four men to 'drive the fields' and check the number of animals actually on them – tenants who had too many were then fined. Driving was done regularly until 1638 and occasionally thereafter, and as late as 1695 the order was yearly repeated that

> none of the inhabitants of Charleton Kings shall pasture or feed any horse beast Cow beast sheepe or Pigg within the said Parish within any of the Corne Feilds until the said Feilde bee ridd.[15]

Farm buildings: evidence from Norden's Survey of 1617

Norden's survey of the manor of Cheltenham made in 1617 shows how far inclosure had proceeded – by then most tenants had some two-thirds of their land in closes and one-third in strips. The survey does not deal with crops or stock as such but it does mention the principal farm buildings, at least in those cases where they were in good condition and consequently of value.

Out of the 22 base tenants in the survey, twelve had barns. All the larger tenements were equipped with a barn for storage of crops, but some of the smaller men had one too. William Cleevely in Horsefair Street had at most fourteen acres including his home close, but he had a barn behind the house; some of its foundation stones have recently come to light. There were eleven stables as against eight oxhouses, suggesting a slight tendency to use horses instead of oxen for ploughing and carting, and there were thirteen cowhouses. Besides the sheephouse at Northfield, only four tenants (all Bafford men) had sheep-houses. Keeping doves or pigeons was a manorial privilege and the medieval culverhouse at Bafford may have belonged to the lord, but in 1617 Thomas Cartwright and Robert Machin had dovehouses and no one questioned their right to have them. Cartsheds and small buildings such as pigsties must have been plentiful but were not considered worth a mention.

Stock and crops, 1660–1700: evidence from inventories

We have 27 inventories during these 40 years which mention stock and crops. This gives a rough idea of what the better-off Charlton husbandmen or yeomen possessed at death – the very poor were automatically excluded from probate; widows, the very elderly and craftsmen often possessed no more than a pig. But the valuation process gave scope for a certain amount of fiddling before the appraisers arrived. The tally of crops in the ground or in the barn is likely to be accurate, but stock and implements were easily removed and in a number of cases demonstrably had been. Actual values are likely to have been on the low side, for appraisers were neighbours; and with an old man or woman the beasts may have been of poor quality. Katherine Bastin,[16] besides her five good cows, had two old ones worth scarcely anything, and William Churche[17] had 'one little old mare' worth £1.

To illustrate the difficulty of interpreting inventories, take Thomas Cartwright's as an example. He farmed in Ham and had one of the better farms in the parish, perhaps 100–150 acres. When he died in December 1663[18] he had fifteen cows and young beasts valued at £40, 60 sheep £20, two hog pigs and four stores £5. Yet he owned, if we are to believe the inventory, neither horse nor ox, no plough, harrow or implement of any sort, no cart or wain. In spite of having no means of cultivation, he had £8-worth of corn in the barn and £10-worth of hay. The chances are that his heir had taken away as much as he could before the appraisers got there, to reduce the amount he would have to pay on probate, and the valuers let him do it. From the last clip Thomas still had 9½ tods of wool unsold, value £9; and he had butter, cheese and apples in store value £5 1s 0d. So the milk from his herd of cows was turned into butter and cheese and much had been kept for sale when prices rose after Christmas. He must have had a large orchard of good keeping apples to have enough to be worth mentioning by late December (cider apples would not have been stored but would have been milled in the autumn or early winter, according to kind). Even without any implements of husbandry, Thomas Cartwright's moveables were valued at £126 18s 0d. – he was really worth a good deal more. His inventory shows how difficult it is to postulate a rising/falling standard of living from this material. It is remarkable, taking these 27 inventories, how many men with corn growing in the ground had no means of ploughing or harvesting, even allowing that some people may have shared their equipment.

A more accurate inventory in this respect was Thomas Whithorne's.[19] He had three mares and a stallion, three pairs of 'old geares'; a long cart, wheels and ropes: a 'donge cart and thrills', a plough, three harrows, and a 'a seed lopp with iron thereto belonging' – the value was £3 5s 6d out of £94 2s 10d. Thomas Mansell's total goods were valued at only £69 19s 10d but they included two carts, two pairs of wheels, a plough and two pairs of harrows, altogether worth £3 10s 0d, slightly more than Whithorne's.[20] Lynett Pates 'gentleman' still used oxen, but his farm was well equipped. He had two long wains, two dung wains and a pair of wheels all worth, with two yoke of oxen, £20; two ploughs, a pair of harrows, a roller, horse gear, ox yokes, and plough string, five saddles, a pad and panell [?pannier], put down altogether as £10.[21] These examples tell us what *ought* to have been on the premises to be appraised.

Oxen were becoming less common; Anthony Webb[22] had two yoke worth, with his bullocks, £30; and Richard Whithorne the elder, one yoke valued at £11,[23] about the same price. Men who had horses usually preferred mares so that they could breed from them; colts are valued in a number of instances; Thomas Whithorne in 1664 and Daniel Ellis in 1684 kept stallions[24]. Unspecified horses were presumably geldings, and Daniel Ellis's gelding described as such sounds like a riding horse rather than a cart-horse.

Everyone had cows and most had more than would be necessary to supply a household. Inventories differentiate milking cows, barren cows, heifers, three-year-olds, two-year-olds, yearlings, and calves. John Cook[25] had eleven milkers, John Ruck[26] had nine, Thomas Cherington[27] had eight. Lynett Pates's twelve cows were without calves although that inventory was taken in April[28] – perhaps he had been too unwell to see about mating them; and Charles Boyear[29], besides three cows with calves, had four that were barren in March. Most men had young stock they were bringing on.

Dairies, cheese presses or wrings, and earthenware milk pans are frequently mentioned, a churn appears in only one inventory, and it seems likely that more cheese was made than butter because it could be kept for future sale. Many had cheese in store. Daniel Ellis[30] had six cows and 1000 cheeses worth £10 in his house. It was generally accepted that 'the same land rarely makes very fine butter and remarkably fine cheese', to quote that notable housewife Mrs Rundell.[31] Theophilus Brereton with three cows had a hundredweight of cheese, valued along with other things[32]; and Arculaus Humphris with seven milkers had 60 cheeses worth £4 10s 0d.[33] The values indicate that the cheeses were small and sold for around twopence per pound. Almost everyone had some cheese for domestic use, but it seems likely that most men sold their cheese during the summer months to raise cash before the harvest came in.

There was no market for beef cattle. The only man to have bullocks was Anthony Webb.[34] Bull calves were usually slaughtered young, which accounts for the numerous recipes in eighteenth-century cookery books (such as *The Compleat Housewife* of 1728) for veal pies, chine of veal, collared breast of veal, 'ragoo' of veal, and the like. Nearly everyone kept some sheep; the numbers varied from Samuel Harris's three, worth 15 shillings[35] to Daniel Ellis's flock of 138 worth £28.[36] Lynett Pates had 37 ewes with lambs, 50 hoggs, and 67 dry sheep, total value £68 7s 6d[37]. But the normal flock was between 30 and 60, as allowed by the 1608 stint for the uninclosed open fields, and most of these sheep were still wintered on the common arable; only Daniel Ellis had sheep hurdles.

Three Charlton men kept bees. They were Thomas Mansell in1669[38] whose two stocks were worth 5 shillings; John Ruck yeoman in 1685 who had six stalls of bees and a pot of honey worth together £1[39]; and Charles Boyear the elder yeoman whose three stalls were worth 10 shillings.[40]

Arable land was no concern of the appraisers except when the inventory was taken in the spring, after crops had been sowed. Thomas Whithorne, dying in April 1663[41] had two acres of wheat and rye, ten acres of pulse, twelve acres of barley, two acres of vetches, or 26 acres arable, valued at £25. Pulses included peas to be dried for eating in the winter and horse beans for fodder; most of the barley was for malting. Lynett Pates in April 1685[42] had 46 acres planted, fifteen acres of wheat, eight acres of pulse, seven acres of oats, sixteen

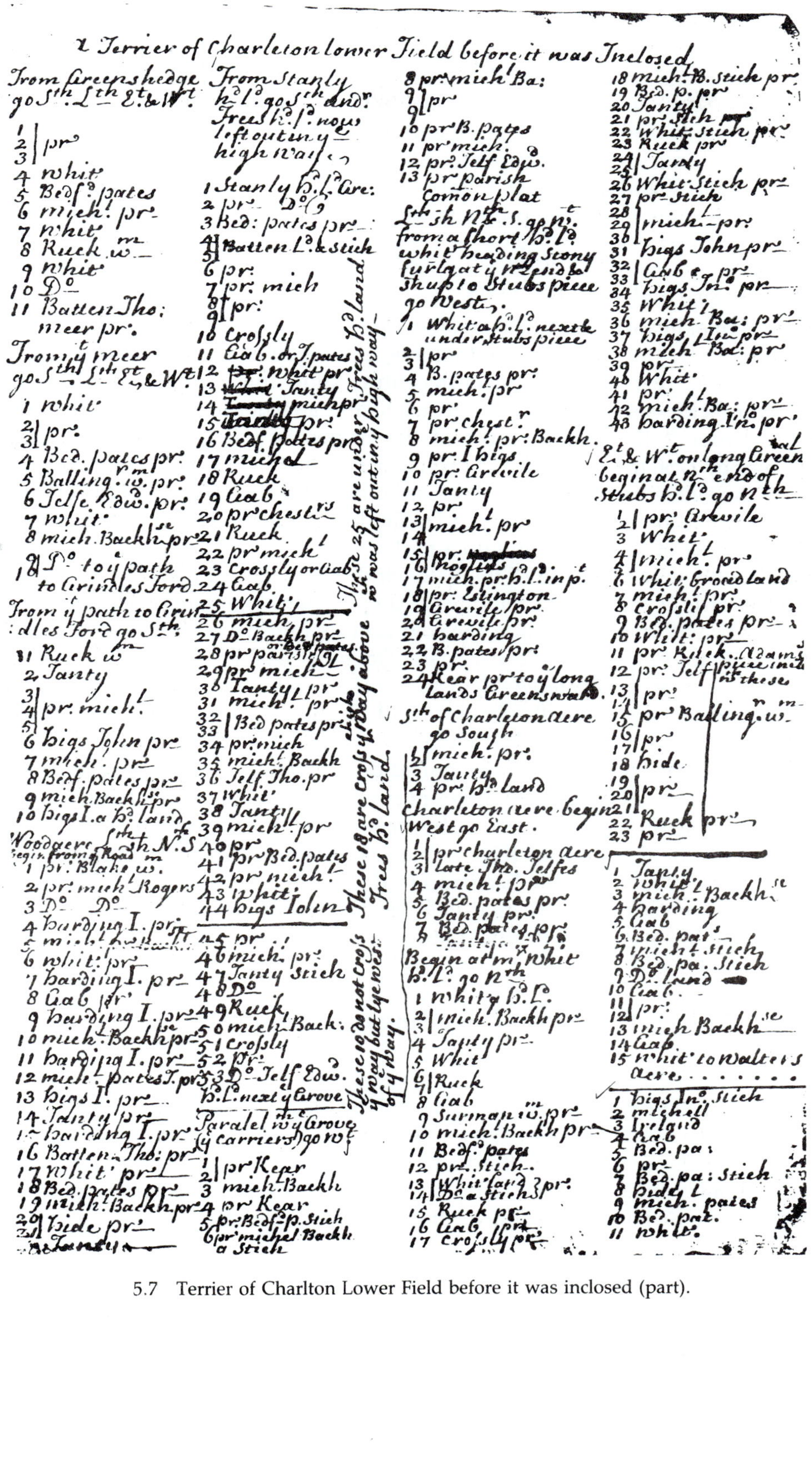

A Terrier of Charleton lower Field before it was Inclosed

5.7 Terrier of Charlton Lower Field before it was inclosed (part).

acres of barley, total value £33 1s 0d, and his meadow was reckoned to produce £9 10s 0d worth of hay. Richard Whithorne the elder[43] on 10 March had £10 10s 0d worth of winter corn on the ground and £3 15s 0d worth of pulse. He had not yet done his spring sowing, but we may guess what else he would have planted from the store in his barn -- wheat and maslin thrashed, pulse and barley thrashed and unthrashed, and two loads of vetches and oats. Maslin or muncorn is not uncommon. Most Charlton men were growing barley for malting, some wheat and pulse for themselves, and a good deal of cattle feed; but everything goes to show that dairy products were now more profitable on the whole than wheat.

The end of the open fields, 1700–1800

There was no formal inclosure in Charlton after 1627. The fields were inclosed piecemeal as strips were bought by the wealthier landholders, put together and exchanged. The court books for the first 50 years of the eighteenth century show this going on rapidly. In 1700, Charlton Lower Field was still cultivated in strips, and a terrier (copied later) lists tenants and strips in order.[44] But against most of the names is a note indicating change of ownership, and by 1750 the majority had been acquired by the Prinns. At first they wanted land to create the extensive meadows we see in Thomas Robins's picture of the environs of Forden House (Charlton Park): then when Dodington Hunt succeeded to the property in 1784 he turned most of this meadow into a park.

One result of the slow inclosure of the fields and the change to dairying was a gradual movement outwards as farms were relocated. Dairying means milking twice daily, so farm buildings must be within easy reach of the cow pasture otherwise there will be a problem getting the milk to the dairy. We can date Detmore (Ashley) to 1545,[45] Wellinghill (Cheltenham) to *c.*1600, Colegate (Ashley) to *c.*1650, Southfield (Cheltenham) and Vineyards (Ashley) to late seventeenth century, Old Coxhorne (Ashley) to 1685, Coxhorne House (Cheltenham) to 1715, Old Dole (Ashley) to *c.*1780. But among others, Gab's and Green's farmhouses on Sandy Lane were pulled down when Prinn acquired their land.[46]

Thus the Charlton of 1800 was very different from the Charlton which John Stubb knew in 1600. Yet some strips remained: the tithe map shows them on Coltham, The Ewen, Ryeworth and Lilleyfield. As late as 1835, Ashley court was asked whether people still had a right to turn their ploughs on the headland in Ryeworth, and it was stated then that no commoning had been exercised on that field for the last 30 years.[47] So a vestige of the practice remained in 1800. The Lilleyfield strips were still open in part and still arable in 1848.

The Size of Holdings *c.*1154–1900

Ashley manor, c.1154–1450

We can say more about holdings belonging to Ashley (alias Charlton) manor in this period than we can about those still held under Cheltenham, because though the 1274 Fécamp survey must cover the tithings of Bafford and Charlton, we cannot disentangle them from the rest of the manor of Cheltenham (Arle, Alstone, Westall, Sandford and Naunton). The land of Ashley manor became the third tithing. Walter of Ashley was rewarded for his support of Queen Matilda by a grant of £10-worth of land out of the royal manor of Cheltenham, and this was confirmed *c.*1154 by Henry II. Walter was given only one tenement in Bafford, the beedle messuage in Moorend Street. He was given land on the west side of Little Herberts Road over to Up End, and may have received one existing tenement in Up End. In Crab End he was given Broadcroft furlong from Hollow Lane

(Horsefair Street) to the Hearne or Crab Brook – this was arable out of which he seems to have given the site for a church – and land beside in the Lye Field. In Cudnall he received four tenements, allotted to him as every other holding on the south side of the street (Charlton House; no. 6 and Ivy Cottage which became beedle messuages, and 'the ancient messuage' next to them, all one holding; Elborough Cottage, and a tenement on the site of that part of Hetton Lawn lately called Little Hetton). Some of his demesne land was nearby. He also got much waste land east of Hearne Brook and south of the Chelt, which he began at once to develop as East End – the first of his base tenements was the one by Lower Castlefield known for some reason as 'the Nap and Pen'. Walter intended East End to be his manorial centre, so he reserved for himself a site for a manor house (never built) with a court house and pound, altogether twelve acres of demesne, the rest being scattered. Most of Castlefield and most of Middlefield was Walter's, and as cultivation later extended into the waste, much land regarded in 1154 as worth little became new Ashley arable.

An inquisition post mortem of 1246 speaks of a virgate of demesne but no manor house, and nine virgates of customary land. This appears to have been divided into eighteen base tenements of a half-virgate each, so that Walter's Ashley tithing matched the two other tithings that each had eighteen base tenements.[48] By the fourteenth century, that virgate of demesne and some new land had been divided into freeholdings, for the lord needed free tenants to represent Ashley at Cheltenham's Great Courts. We know of three freehold tenements belonging to Ashley manor in the fourteenth and fifteenth centuries. One was Over House at East End – Lucy atte Noverhowse was assessed at 2s 7d in the 1327 Lay Subsidy. Another was held by John Freme in the later part of the fourteenth century and when he died, three men (apparently his sons-in-law) conveyed the messuage and two virgates of land to John Coppe of Charlton Kings in 1391.[49] John had some land across the Slad and his name became permanently attached to the messuage Cops Elm and the land, Cops Edge. This freehold seems to be the one settled in 1477 by the Balle family.[50] It was certainly the freehold for which John Gale the elder and John his son did fealty in turn in 1751 and 1771.[51] Robert Danger held another Ashley freehold with half a virgate in 1404, when he got a re-grant of it from John Grevill, lord of Ashley, paying 26s 8d fine, twelve capons and twelve pullets for it.[52] So if we postulate four virgates of freehold altogether we shall not be far out. All the rest of the Ashley waste as it was cleared seems to have been put with old customary holdings or used to make new ones.

Cheltenham manor c.1450: tenements in Charlton Kings

We are fortunate to have details about Charlton holdings in the mid-fifteenth century preserved for us in John Stubb's book.[53] In preparation for Norden's new survey of Cheltenham manor in 1617 Stubb copied out the survey compiled when Henry V's grant of the manor to Syon Abbey at last took effect. It had been delayed until after 1441 when various Crown leases ran out. The rental did not include the Ham Court estate which was regarded as a sub-manor, and it did not give acreages for demesne land leased out in small parcels, so that in effect we are given no information about the greater part of Ham and Battledown. What is helpful to us is the division of the manor into its tithings and the separation of free and base tenements within the tithings. We are told the name of the *c*.1450 tenant, his predecessor, and the tenant before that, which takes us back to the late fourteenth century.

Bafford tithing covered the area from the Chelt south to Up End and east to Hollow Lane, plus tenements on the east side of Little Herberts. Charlton tithing included the Cudnall tenements interspersed with Ashley's and much of Ham, with any land elsewhere not given to Ashley.

One complication about all rentals and surveys is the absence of any firm division between Charlton and Naunton in the Benbridge, Charlton Lower Field and Pilley areas. Some Charlton tenants had land in Naunton which went with their Bafford holdings, but the amount was not sufficient to make any great difference. Another problem is whether in 1450, 1557 and 1617 the areas set down were statute or customary – there are sufficient similarities to suggest that in 1557 and 1617 certainly, and in 1450 probably, the same measure was used. As Norden's survey was made for the Crown, his acres may be presumed to be statute, and there is reason to think that on royal manors 'royal acres' were normally used. An abstract of all the Charlton Kings entries in the 1450 rental and of the 1557, 1564 and 1617 surveys has been published elsewhere[54] so they need not be repeated in full, though they contain material for a complete volume. Here there is space only for a few comments bearing on the question of the size of holdings.

Table 5.1: Bafford and Charlton tithings, 1450.

Tithing	2v	1½v	1v	¾v	½v	¼v	24a	7a	6a	5a	3a	2a	1a
Free holdings													
Charlton	–	–	–	–	1	–	–	–	2	–	–	–	–
Bafford	3	1	–	–	2	–	–	–	–	–	–	–	1
Base holdings													
Charlton	–	–	–	–	5	–	1	–	9	1	3	–	–
Bafford	–	–	–	1	10	1	–	2	3	–	1	1	–

Key: v = virgate a = acre

An overall picture of Bafford and Charlton tithings in 1450 can be gained from Table 5.1. So there were four major tenements, all in Bafford and all freehold, a total of 4½ virgates. Below them comes a gap, not a single virgate holding, free or base. The 24-acre tenement was shared by three men; it represents the customary portion of Northfield farm, our only sheep farm, and that explains the high rent of 30s 2d paid for it. Leaving it out of consideration and also the odd one-acre freehold and two-acre base tenement, the smallest holdings were normally three or six acres – four holdings of three acres and twelve holdings of six acres below the fifteen half-virgate base tenements. This seems to indicate a 3–6–12–24–48 pattern in the twelfth century rather than anything larger. It fits in with what we know about Cheltenham's demesne: land for three plough-teams in 1086, 149 acres of arable in 1294; and it fits in with what we guess about Ashley: two virgates for Cop's Elm, half a virgate for Danger's freehold and something like 1½ virgates for Over House, a total of four virgates or 96 acres (98 acres freehold in 1557). It fits in, too, with John Grevill's 1½-virgate freehold, previously his father's and before that Thomas de la Forde's, which was the one called The Forden or Forden House – our Charlton Park house. At 24 acres to the virgate, more or less, this was 36 acres. Giles Grevill the younger was holding it in 1564 with 37 acres. We shall not be far out, then, if we postulate about twelve acres as the normal holding of field land in 1450, with 48 acres as the maximum. A survey of Prestbury in 1575 states categorically that the half-virgate there was twelve acres.[55]

Cheltenham and Ashley tenements, 1557 and 1564

When the survey of field land was made in 1557, as a preliminary to the first small measure of inclosure, Ham and Battledown were again omitted. By now the very last of the available waste had been ploughed, so there was considerably more arable and consequently larger holdings; by definition, the acreages given represent land held in the open fields – closes around the houses which were never open to common grazing were naturally left out. But we do have the *total arable* of each tenant, whether held of Cheltenham or Ashley manors. There were now four tenants who held between 80 and 110 acres.

Giles Roberts and Robert Alexander in partnership (with John Alexander as sub-tenant) had 109 acres; Nicholas Holder (farming himself in partnership with Richard Rogers) had 105 acres; and William Keeke and Robert Symons had 83 acres apiece. Below that came a gap, with no one having between 66 and 80 acres (just as in 1450 there were no virgate tenants). Below that, with 50–65 acres, there were four tenants, seven holding 40–47 acres and five between 30 and 39. We might call these the well-off middling men.

Under 30 acres, there were thirteen having between 20 and 29 acres; then eight with between ten and nineteen acres. Last came the very small tenants: four with seven acres, two with five acres and one with only two acres.

As we have seen, there were four major holdings in Bafford and Charlton in 1450 and two in Ashley, all freehold, but the largest was probably not more than 48 acres. Now in 1557 there were four outstandingly large tenements in the three tithings – more than double the 1450 maximum in two cases and nearly double in the other two; but not one of them was a freehold. The extra land gained by the last clearances of waste had been added to customary tenements.

The only large freehold in 1557 was John Rogers's 63 acres held of Ashley, and it would appear that he with the East End demesne had engrossed a major part of the old Ashley freehold, leaving 28 acres for Richard Goodrich (Over House) and no more than five and two acres respectively for Hicks and French. Rogers still had these 63 acres in 1564; then it was held by William Grevill gentleman who died in 1604 and his widow Ann who died in 1612, after which it was broken up into three tenements.

The biggest Cheltenham freeholds were Thomas Wye's (37 acres) and Thomas Dowdeswell the younger's (20 acres); next came one of thirteen acres and one of seven acres (part of Sir Henry Compton's estate in Cheltenham, now split up). Altogether Charlton was prosperous. There were sixteen tenants with 30–65 acres and thirteen with 20–29 acres, more than in any other range. This comfortable condition was reflected in house improvement between 1560 and 1617.

The second inclosure list of 1564, taken as a whole, differed little from that of 1557 but as it included 'Ham under the hill' and Battledown, the total arable involved was now 2044½ acres and there were more tenants in the upper ranges. Giles Grevill the younger had come of age and had taken in as sub-tenants five men shown in 1557 as independent 'copyholders' (by which term the surveyors seem to mean men whose customary tenements were being turned into leaseholds). Consequently with his own 37 acres, Giles Grevill's total was now 139 acres. Edmond Cartwright of Ham had four sub-tenants and a total of 109 acres. William Pates with additional land at 'Badleton' now had 85 acres, and Robert Symons's six acres at Ham brought his total to 89. Walter Goodrich and Robert Goodrich of Ham Court had 67 and 48 acres 'under the hill' which qualified them for common rights – other land on the hill was excluded. Thomas Higges had 55 acres of glebe on Battledown, John Blycke of Ham had 30 acres 'under the hill' and fourteen acres besides, a total of 44 acres.

A few tenements had changed hands in the seven years between the surveys, but most changes in name represent fathers and widows dying, or sons coming of age – all natural developments. What we do see as starting in the years between 1557 and 1564 is the building up of large estates with tenant farmers, the common pattern of agricultural holding down to 1900.

Cheltenham manor, 1617 (Charlton tenants)

Norden's survey of the manor of Cheltenham in 1617 is copied into the court book.[56] He dealt first with freehold tenants and demesne land, then base tenants, and noted each parcel of land held, though he did not bother to measure some very small closes or woodland. Any total we can deduce understates the real figure; but for the first time the acreage of arable and the acreage of grass can be distinguished, even though there were still closes described as 'arable or pasture' which were in process of conversion.

Points that are immediately striking are the continued fragmentation of freeholds; the amalgamation of medieval base tenements into sizeable farms, very often with a cottage or two as well as the main house; the increase of grassland in every part of the parish, even at Ham which was to remain down to 1900 the area of Charlton with most arable. Finally, we see the continued build up of the estate with subordinate farms, as noted first in 1564, and observe the way in which the Packers at Ham Court and the Grevills at The Forden were breaking down the old manorial framework.

Norden's survey gives us our first real look at the Ham Court estate. By 1617 this consisted of the manor house with 122 acres of arable and 81 acres of grass, a mill, four messuages, a small house, and another 57 acres including orchard. With pieces not measured, the total was over 260 acres. Ham Court was already a modern estate. Its area had been much increased by the Packers since their purchase in 1574; their predecessor Robert Goodrich in 1564 had only claimed 48 acres 'under the hill', though that phrase implies that he also had land on the hill which he was not willing to throw open to general grazing – Ham (according to John Stubb) being the first part of Charlton to inclose its arable. The estate would have been larger still had Alexander Packer been able to buy the freehold portion of Northfield from Richard Phelps in 1615; he was outbid by Thomas Nicholas, shown here as holding 65¾ acres besides 200 acres of the 300-acre sheepwalk. The other third of the sheepwalk with 40¾ acres held in base tenure was Robert Hawthorne's. Nicholas's part of Northfield did come into the Ham Court estate later, but it soon passed out of it again, so what we have here is the basic estate, then and always predominantly arable.

Giles Grevill is noticed next by Norden. Grevill was lord of Ashley and himself held much land in that manor in addition to his Cheltenham tenements. Norden credited him with a messuage called Smithes at 4s 10d rent; this appears to be the same as the Nether House of 1450, though by 1617 there were two houses and two cottages on the land. He also held what had been Wheeler's or Dowdeswell's, with about fifteen acres instead of the twenty acres of 1557 (this accounts for a slight reduction in the rent from 3s 2½d to 3s 1d). Norden apparently accepted the Grevill contention that The Forden (which appeared in the 1450 rental) was no longer part of Cheltenham manor. As far back as 1541 a witness had said that the Grevills had two manors 'throne cald Ashley Cowt & thother cald Forden Cowrt'.[57] So on the basis of this survey no useful comparison can be made between Giles Grevill's agricultural holdings and those of Ham Court or any other Charlton tenement. Grevill is not shown as holding any customary land of Cheltenham in 1617 but as two heriots were paid for him at his death in 1632, he must have acquired two later on. With his Ashley land, Giles Grevill probably held as much land as Packer, in his case roughly the same acreage of arable and grass to judge by later settlements.[58]

The tenant with the next largest total acreage was Thomas Cartwright who inherited from his father Edmond Cartwright in 1600. Thomas held five base messuages in Ham and Charlton and one base messuage in Westall. With the first five he had 88 acres of grass and 81 acres of arable; with the last, six acres of grass and twelve acres of arable. So taken as a whole, his farming was pretty evenly divided between dairy and corn, and his total holding was 187 acres. The Charlton messuage was Churchend House which his widow Isabella afterwards had and passed to her son Thomas in 1625.[59]

After Cartwright came Roger Holder of Cudnall's Mease (successor to Nicholas Holder of 1557 and 1564). Roger had the old base messuage and a house occupied by his brother John, with an orchard and an acre of garden; rather more than fifteen acres of grass and 24 acres of arable in the fields. Besides that, he had three Bafford messuages with three houses and three sets of farm buildings, two orchards and three gardens containing four acres. Grass and arable together came to 76 acres. So in all Roger held 115 acres. The court books show him mortgaging his land very freely, perhaps because he was careless and hot tempered (he spoke opprobrious words in court), perhaps because he had three daughters and no son to plan for.

The third tenant in this category was Edmund Goodrich with two messuages in Charlton and in addition a homestead called Coltham. Land near the houses came to two acres; he had 30 acres of grass, sixteen acres of arable and 60 acres described as either arable or pasture: he seems to have been in the process of changing over. Altogether he had 106 acres, mainly in Ham.

No tenant fitted into the 85–105 acre range – the same gap noticed in earlier surveys between the top men and those in the middle range. But by 1617 the split between top and middle range tenants was somewhat more pronounced than before because there were only three men holding between 60 and 85 acres. Richard Pates gentleman had two mills at Sandford with several closes there or on Battledown, apparently all grass; he also had a messuage in Charlton with an acre of garden and close, a half-acre coppice, sixteen acres arable and eleven acres grass, his total, excluding garden, coming to 83 acres. Thomas Horwood had three messuages in Bafford and so 9½ acres of garden and orchard and an acre of coppice; his field land (not always clearly differentiated) seems to have been 51 acres of grass and 28 acres of arable. Robert Machin had 3½ messuages in Charlton with a little cottage as well as his house, three acres in his two gardens and two orchards and 37½ acres each of grass and arable. In addition he held 5½ acres of freehold land in Charlton and Naunton.

In the 20–50 acre bracket were nine tenants, nearly all holding more than one ancient messuage, and there were sixteen tenants with less than fifteen acres. But it is clear that no one in Charlton depended on such a small acreage for a livelihood. Some we know to have been craftsmen, one (Samuel Deighton) was a doctor of medicine, and many others held Ashley tenements. We have no Ashley court books to say exactly what, but we can make a rough guess by looking at the amount of rent they were paying under each manor in 1625, when they were assessed on the basis of their rents for their contribution towards the cost of the new Act.

Looking back 70 years from the new Act of 1625, we can see considerable change in the pattern of farming; this, more than any special grievance, was the reason for altering the custom. When inclosure first began, practically all land was ploughed. By the third decade of the next century, half was under grass. In 1557, most men held and farmed their own tenements; by 1625 organisation into estates with tenant-farmers was well advanced and was to be the norm before another century had passed.

Holdings in Charlton Kings, 1800–1900

The eighteenth century saw the consolidation of farms by purchase and exchange of strips and closes, and the virtual abolition of open fields. By 1800 most farms were grouped into estates; and though a few remained outside this system in 1848, at the time of the tithe commutation, even those were not occupied by their owners. When the government compiled a list of landowners in 1873 there were six estates in this parish, just one owner-occupied farm lately bought from an estate, and no smallholdings.

THE CHARLTON PARK ESTATE[60]

When the Grevills sold The Forden to John Prinn in 1701 for £725, it consisted of the house and grounds, home farm and 70¾ acres. The next four generations built up the estate and when William Hunt Prinn inherited in 1803 he owned (besides land elsewhere) eight farms in this parish. Our first view of the estate is in 1809–10, when Prinn redeemed the tithes; the largest unit was just under 259 acres and only one farm, at Ham, was still mainly arable. The rest had more grass and one had no arable at all. Arable, by this period, need not imply corn-growing; root crops for feeding cattle were an important part of good husbandry.

The farm which Bradshaw rented at Ham from W. H. Prinn consisted of Wadleys, Ham

Table 5.2: Charlton Park estate (1809–10)

Tenant	Arable	Grass & wood	Total
	a r p	a r p	a r p
Thomas Ballinger (i.e. Northfield Farm)	20.0.26	57.2.14	77.3.0
J. W. Bradshaw (Ham)	121.1.30	73.2.0	194.3.30
William Finch (i.e. Vineyards)	102.1.20	136.2.17	258.3.37
John Joy, late James Humphreys (i.e. Southfield Farm)	83.2.30	90.2.5	174.0.35
Edward Greenwood late William Humphris (i.e. Home Farm)	30.3.32	63.1.22	94.1.14
Widow (Mary) Howman late James Howman (i.e. Bafford Farm)	54.1.39	176.1.20	230.3.19
Betty Lea	0.1.23	17.2.9	17.3.32
Joseph Timbrell (i.e. Old Coxhorn Farm)	–	62.3.0	62.3.9

Total arable: 421.3.18; total grass: 889.0.10; whole estate: 1310.3.28

Key: a = acres r = rods p = poles

North and Stone Barn (Ham South). He himself owned and farmed Ham Court, 74a. 0r. 2p (13.1.31 arable, 55.3.17 grass) – his widow put it up for sale in 1838.[61] So in all, Bradshaw was farming just under 269 acres, a little more than Finch.

William Hunt Prinn died in 1821 without children and without any near relation. Under his will, the estate went first to George Bragge Prowse (Prinn) who also had no children, and then to Jane Eliza, wife of Sir William Russell, for life, and her son Sir William, the second baronet (1833–1892). When he came of age in 1843 the estate was re-surveyed.

One might have expected extra arable because of the Corn Laws, but in fact the balance was much the same, and Ham was still the only farm with more arable than grass. Charlton Park now accounted for 113a.0r.30p and 'groves etc in hand' for 73a.3r.15p. The Home Farm by the house had gone altogether and had been replaced by a new farm house in Horsefair Street. Old Dole Farm had been acquired. The total acreage was 1334.3.12 in Charlton Kings, besides 102.2.8 in Naunton and other land outside this area.

This survey was said to be more accurate than that of 1810; consequently all farms are shown as a few acres smaller than before, except Ham (up from 195 acres to 204½ acres); Vineyards Farm was down by 46 acres now 'in hand'.

The Charlton Park estate was disentailed in 1851 and vested in Sir William Russell absolutely. The census of that year tells us that he had reorganised his Ham farms, in part because the two Burrows tenants were 67 and 70 years old respectively, in part because he

Table 5.3: Charlton Park estate (1843).

Tenant & farm	Arable	Grass	Other	Total
	a r p	a r p	a r p	a r p
Thomas Pates Withyholt Farm	69.2.23	145.2.9	2.1.37	217.2.34
Mrs Margaret Nicholson Southfield Farm	76.0.31	90.0.18	1.1.4	167.2.13
Thomas Finch Bafford Farm	48.1.18	172.3.22	1.2.16	222.3.16
Thomas Ballenger Vineyards Farm	80.1.20	128.2.37	4.3.3	213.2.20
Thomas Ballenger Northfield Farm	19.0.6	53.2.21	4.3.21	76.2.8
John Rowland Old Dole Farm	46.2.2	18.3.18	0.1.36	65.3.16
Charles Dowle Coxhorn Farm	1.0.15	44.1.3	0.3.4	46.0.22
John & William Burrows Ham Farm	119.2.6	85.2.11	3.0.14	204.2.6
Joseph Karn	–	17.3.0	0.0.33	17.3.33

Key: a = acres r = roods p = poles

had acquired land at Northfield and Ham Villa (the mid-nineteenth century name for Ham Court). Now William Burrows was at Ham Old Farm with 26 acres and John Burrows at Ham Villa with 48 acres, so that between them they were farming the 74 acres which had been Bradshaw's. Thomas Fry had taken over at Ham Farm with 280 acres.

Just before another estate map was made in 1865, Russell bought the two small farms at Little Herberts, and in 1868 he bought land from the Agg family. He was a good landlord, his cottages (such as the two pairs marked WR which he built in School Road and which were demolished in *c.*1974) and his farm houses (such as Old Dole which he rebuilt *c.*1870 and Old Coxhorne) were very well built. He was out-and-away the biggest landowner in Charlton Kings in 1873, when he had 1466a.3r.6p. The following year he was obliged to begin selling off property, starting with the farms at Ham.[62]

THE LAWRENCE PROPERTY

In 1824 'the Charlton Estate' of the Lawrence family (so described in the sale particular) was offered for sale by Walter Lawrence Lawrence and his mother, Mary Morris, who had a life interest. This was Elborough Cottage in Cudnall and land on Cudnall Bank, the Slad and Copsedge, previously Ellis's or Cook's. In the sixteenth century this farm had been reckoned as 40 acres; rearrangement to bring the fields together had reduced the total to 37a.2r.13p., all pasture. The house was bought by Pruen for £1750, the land sold for £2631, and with the cutting of the new London Road in 1825–6 much of it became available for building.[63]

THE OAKLANDS

One of the building sites across the Slad was bought by Alexander Ogilvy and a house called Woodlands was built in a commanding position. He sold this in 1837 to Nathaniel Hartland for £3500, and the name was changed to The Oaklands – in 1846 an estate map shows it as having 30a.0r.3p., including all the Lawrence estate which did not adjoin the old or new London roads. Hartland added to house and estate so that by 1873 he and his wife had between them 106a.2r.39p.

THE HIGGS ESTATE

In 1810 Charles Cooke Higgs while still a minor inherited properties that had been accumulated by the Wager, Cooper, Sloper, Cooke and Higgs families. He owned Charlton House and the whole of Mill Furlong down to Old Bath Road; a house and land on Cudnall Bank; land at the Ewens; Glenfall; land on the London Road near East Court; Wellinghill Farm; and East End Farm (Wager Court). After he came of age in 1818 he sold Glenfall to Iggulden, and acquired Sturmys on Balcarras Lane by exchange with Lovesy. But otherwise his estate changed little during his long lifetime – he did not die until 1884. All his land was tithe free by 1848. In 1873 Charles Cooke Higgs had 159a.1r.20p. in Charlton Kings.

SAMUEL HIGGS GAEL

By 1873 Samuel Higgs Gael (or Gale) had built up an estate of 131a.2r.17p., partly by inheritance and partly (it would appear) by purchase. He himself lived on Battledown.

THE LOVESY ESTATE

The last of the Whithornes, by will proved in 1816, left his property to his sister Elizabeth Lovesy and her two sons, but since one son died unmarried and intestate, the whole, together with tithes throughout the parish, came to the survivor, Conway Whithorne

Table 5.4: The Lovesey estate (1848).

Tenant	Arable	Grass	Wood	Other	Total
	a r p	a r p	a r p	a r p	a r p
In hand (Coxhorne and Knapp)	15.2.25	21.1.36	18.1.33	5.1.25	67.2.19
Alfred Townsend (nr Coxhorne)	–	–	32.3.24	–	32.3.24
Richard Burrows (nr Coxhorne)	15.0.8	96.3.14	–	0.1.3	112.0.25
Gabriel Ballinger (Ashgrove)	–	40.2.25	–	0.1.2	40.3.27
Charles Yeend (at Little Herberts)	1.0.8	43.1.31	–	0.1.0	44.2.39
William Pates (Timbercombe)	–	8.1.20	–	4.0.14	12.1.34
Emma Powell (Ham)	–	30.2.7	–	1.0.20	31.2.27
William Burrows (Ham)	–	55.1.0	–	1.0.30	56.1.30

Key: a = acres r = roods p = poles.

Lovesy. His property consisted of Coxhorne House and farm, Whithorne House, The Knapp House, and land in Castlefield and Cudnall (ripe for development as building land, especially after the new London road was cut in 1825–6). He had a small farm at East End called Sturmys, the malthouse in Moorend and other property there, and he acquired Ham House and Ham Days farm. By exchanging Sturmys with Higgs he acquired more land on the escarpment. His estates in that area stretched from Hill Farm (California) to Little Herberts Road, and altogether he held well over 300 acres. When Lovesy died in 1846 this property was divided among his children, the greater part going to his son Conway Whithorne II. In 1848 (leaving out tenancies of less than 10 acres) C. W. Lovesy's estate was divided as shown in Table 5.4.

At Ashgrove there was a cottage; but no dwelling is mentioned in connection with Richard Burrows's land at Hill Farm (now California). This agrees with Mr R. E. Davis's information that the present farm house was created during the nineteenth century out of two small cottages, although the barn is much older. All these holdings were almost entirely grass.

In 1866 and 1868 parts of this property were offered for sale, including Whithorne and Coxhorne houses, Hill Farm, and Ashgrove Farm.[64] Colonel Holmes bought Whithorne with 6a.3r.0p., and Richard Burrows bought Hill Farm with 114a.1r.8p.; but five members of the Lovesy family still held between them 181a.3r.20p. in 1873.

JAMES WILLIAM AGG AND JAMES AGG GARDNER

The tithe map shows the first named as holding 19a.1r.7p. including the Radways and land at Oakley; and the second as holding 13a.1r.23p. On 8 April 1868 the Aggs sold to Sir William Russell 26a.1r.30p. freehold and 23a.2r.38p. copyhold land, besides the free and copyhold thirds of 2a.2r.27p. part of Northfield Hill.[65] However, Russell's affairs were already in a bad way and in 1874 he put up for sale his Ham property including 52a.3r.15p. 'late Aggs'.[66]

ABRAHAM HATHERELL, HAM

In 1848 Hatherell held altogether 55a.2r.12p. of which he himself kept the woodland in hand (3a.2r.11p.) and the rest was let to four tenants. Only one acre was arable.

GLENFALL

The tithe map shows Edward Iggulden as owning no more than 4a.2r.29p., occupied by Thomas Fry, the pasture land called Freeman's Ground and Little Iron Moors. After the Glenfall property came to the Molyneux family this must have been greatly extended, for sale maps of 1868–1874 show Mrs Molyneux as owning land adjoining property offered for sale all over Ham. Yet no figure for her estate was included in the 1873 return.

Table 5.5: Single farms in 1848.

	Arable	Grass	Wood	Other	Total
	a r p	a r p	a r p	a r p	a r p
Colegate Farm[(a)]	6.2.18	29.1.22	4.0.36	1.0.0	41.0.36
Little Herberts Farm[(b)]	30.2.1	21.3.7	–	0.0.32	52.2.0
Dowdeswell Mill[(c)]	–	23.0.39	–	–	23.0.39
Home Farm, Little Herberts or Cherington's[(d)]	–	8.3.24	–	3.3.32	12.3.16

(a) Owned by the Reverend Stephen Middleton, and occupied by William Dobell.
(b) Owned by Sarah Taylor, and occupied by William Pates.
(c) Owned by John Saunderson, and occupied by Robert Kirby.
(d) Owned by William Chapman, and occupied by Edwin Chapman.

Key: a = acres r = roods p = poles.

SINGLE FARMS IN 1848

Of these, only one, Little Herberts Farm, had arable in excess of grassland. Before 1865 Sir William Russell had bought both this farm and Chapman's Farm in Little Herberts. This last, with 12a.2r.36p. was offered for sale in 1874 but withdrawn.[67]

That was the state of Charlton holdings when the agricultural depression struck. All farms were of moderate size, not one reached 300 acres and most were dairy farms; those two factors helped them to survive because there was still a market for milk in Cheltenham which had turned from a fashionable spa town to an educational centre. No farm went out of cultivation, but labour was cut, sometimes drastically. Thomas Fry of Ham Farm (280 acres) had employed twelve men in 1851. His successor, John Neather, in 1881 was managing with the help of a son-in-law. The farm with the biggest labour force in 1881 was Ryeworth (137 acres) employing eight men and a boy; Ham Days (235 acres) had five men; Northfield (125 acres) one man, one boy; Glenfall (76 acres) with Mary Fry 'farmeress', one man. It is noticeable that most of these 'men' were in fact under 21 and many of them had come from other parishes, not Charlton Kings.

So a great many Charlton men were unemployed, dependent on their wives' earnings. Even the construction of the railway between 1879 and 1881 affected only a few of the younger men, for most of the labour came from outside; and the same was true when Dowdeswell reservoir was built.

One new estate was created after 1873. This was Lilleybrook, which in the ten years before 1900 acquired a stretch of land from Southfield Farm in the west to The Vineyards in the east. But Mr and Mrs Lord were not primarily interested in farming. What they wanted was an estate for hunting and shooting, with coverts like Mountain Knoll and Jennings Grove and the small wood at Timbercombe which they extended. All the coverts that once belonged to Lilleybrook are marked by laurel trees, now of considerable size. The farm at Little Herberts which had been Chapman's became their home farm to supply the house with milk and eggs.

6

'A Bit of Old Chorlton'

Charlton was 'a one-sided village' – that is to say, for a long time all the houses were built on one side of a street with arable on the other. This was true, for instance, of Cudnall Street (houses on the south side), Moorend Street or New Court Road (houses on the west side), Church Street (houses on the south side), Trigmerry Lane or School Road (houses on the east side), Upend Street, now part of Cirencester Road (houses on the east side), and Hollow Lane or Horsefair Street in the section opposite Hencroft (houses on the east side). All had large gardens and home closes of 1½–2 acres.

In the fourteenth century, settlement was spreading up Little Herberts where the west side of the road belonged to Ashley manor and the east to Cheltenham; so new holdings were created on both sides. The name Herbert seems to come from OF *herberge,* a lodging or harbourage – for a long time the name was spelt Harbour or Harbord.

With the sixteenth-century demand for extra dwellings, new houses were built opposite the old ones on the ends of common field strips: by 1600 they seem to pair off down the street. Most of the older houses were upgraded or rebuilt between 1550 and 1650. Such was the demand that Elizabethan legislation did not stop people building cottages without the statutory four acres of land; they merely paid a yearly fine in the manor court.

In this area timber was the normal building material. All our older houses were timber-framed with thatched roofs, the space between the timbers filled with wattle and daub (cow hair and clay or lime). The base timbers rested on stone foundations to prevent rotting. Chimneys were frequently inserted into existing houses *c.*1608–13, when Cheltenham manor and Hundred court began to insist on this as a fire precaution.[1] Stone tiles gradually replaced thatch. Stone as a building material was rarely used above foundations

6.1 Old Church House in 1824. (Note also the old houses east of the church and beyond Church House.)

6.2 Old Church House from the east.

until the nineteenth century, and with stones, as with timbers, we have to remember that they may be old stuff.

Towards the end of the seventeenth century bricks began to be made. Some houses received a brick skin and sash windows to bring them up to date. The name Claypits Path is a reminder that bricks for Forden House (Charlton Park) and New Court were probably made from clay pits at the Old Bath Road end (as shown on the 1811 estate map), which means that they were being worked about 1700. Old houses rebuilt and new houses erected after 1750 were all made of brick, and there were many small brickyards in the parish, some at work until the end of the nineteenth century. These new houses were the 'nice villas and genteel cottages' noticed by the Reverend F. E. Witts in 1824[2] or the basic cottages being built to meet the acute need for labourers' houses. The eleven **Buckles' Row** cottages were put up in 1808, their bricks burnt on the spot using clay from land by the Hearne brook; the four **Yew Tree Cottages** in School Road, erected about 1833, cost £25 apiece to build.

Most of our old farm houses were divided into two or three dwellings to meet the housing shortage; but by the mid-nineteenth century, there was no longer any demand for 'nice villas': Cheltenham was not expanding. Sir William Russell cut Copt Elm Road in 1865, hoping to sell building plots for good houses, and he erected a pair (**Lyefield Villas**) as show houses. But only two more, **Lexham Lodge** and **Charlton Lawn**, had been built by 1870. He had no better luck with building plots on Pound Piece; only one sold. House sites on the Battledown estate sold very slowly. When development did start again in the 1890s, it was mainly the small three-bedroom semi-detached house that found a market; and this type of development was greatly stimulated by the coming of the electric trams to Charlton in 1903. People still demanded long gardens, for the pig stye at the far end remained an important element in home economy.[3]

Unfortunately, many of our older houses have been destroyed, a number since 1945, without any attempt to survey or record them. This is one reason for including in this section houses which have been pulled down, as well as those which survive. Some were in poor condition and could not have been saved; others were demolished because their gardens and home closes were wanted as building sites. Numbers in brackets refer to illustrations.

Churchend and Crabend

Powell, an artist who visited Charlton in July 1824, has given us a view of a medieval

6.3 Churchend House, the south end which is shown in plans as the servants' hall. This drawing was made from a photograph of *c.* 1900 when the exterior was rendered, with the details of timbering added from recollections of how it appeared after being stripped. The house was demolished in 1933.

house, **Old Church House** (6.1 and 6.2) on the south-west corner of the church before it was lengthened. The house had been part of the chantry endowment. After 1548 it was bought for the benefit of the parish (see page 151) and was pulled down in 1827–8 so that its site might be added to the churchyard.[4]

Churchend House (6.3) afterwards called **Brixton House** and then **The Grange** (Cheltenham) represented the fourteenth-century messuage of a tenant named Lucas, the man who gave his name to a field by Bull Hill. With the house in the sixteenth century went land on the hill and five acres stretching down to the Hearne brook. This was one of five messuages which Thomas Cartwright of Ham inherited in 1600. He rebuilt it soon after as a substantial timber-framed farmhouse with two storeys above ground floor, and was holding it in 1617. We can trace its ownership down to the nineteenth century when Colonel Meall bought it and added to it; the name was changed twice and the house enlarged twice more before it became the Vicarage in 1899. But it was too expensive for most vicars and was pulled down in 1933 – its name survives in the Grange Field (site of its garden and paddock).[5]

Opposite Churchend House was **Churchend Meese** (6.5), Mrs Summers' cottage (on the site of no. 98). This was copyhold of Cheltenham, and was demolished in 1931. In 1598 it passed by marriage from the Reynolds family to the Cleevelys[6] and was still theirs in 1733 when Henry Cleevely husbandman died. His inventory shows that this had been a hall house and he still slept in his 'lower room' in the best bed, though there was an upper chamber with a plainer bed in it. Henry's most valuable possessions were his brewing utensils worth £2. 16s. 0d, and his wood and ladder in the outhouse worth £2. 15s. 0d; yet John Prinn had recently paid him £80 for his field land and his widow was to receive £100 for the house and its 1½-acre close, so they were not poor, just old-fashioned.[7]

The seventeenth century saw several houses built on the end of strips in Hencroft. One was on the site of **no. 130 Horsefair Street**, and its well is still there although the timber-framed house was burnt down in 1901 (there is a smudgy photograph of the fire in the *Cheltenham Chronicle* for 11 May 1901). This was Richard Ruck's cottage on the corner of Blind Lane, mentioned in the 1617 survey. Opposite, on land which is now allotments and

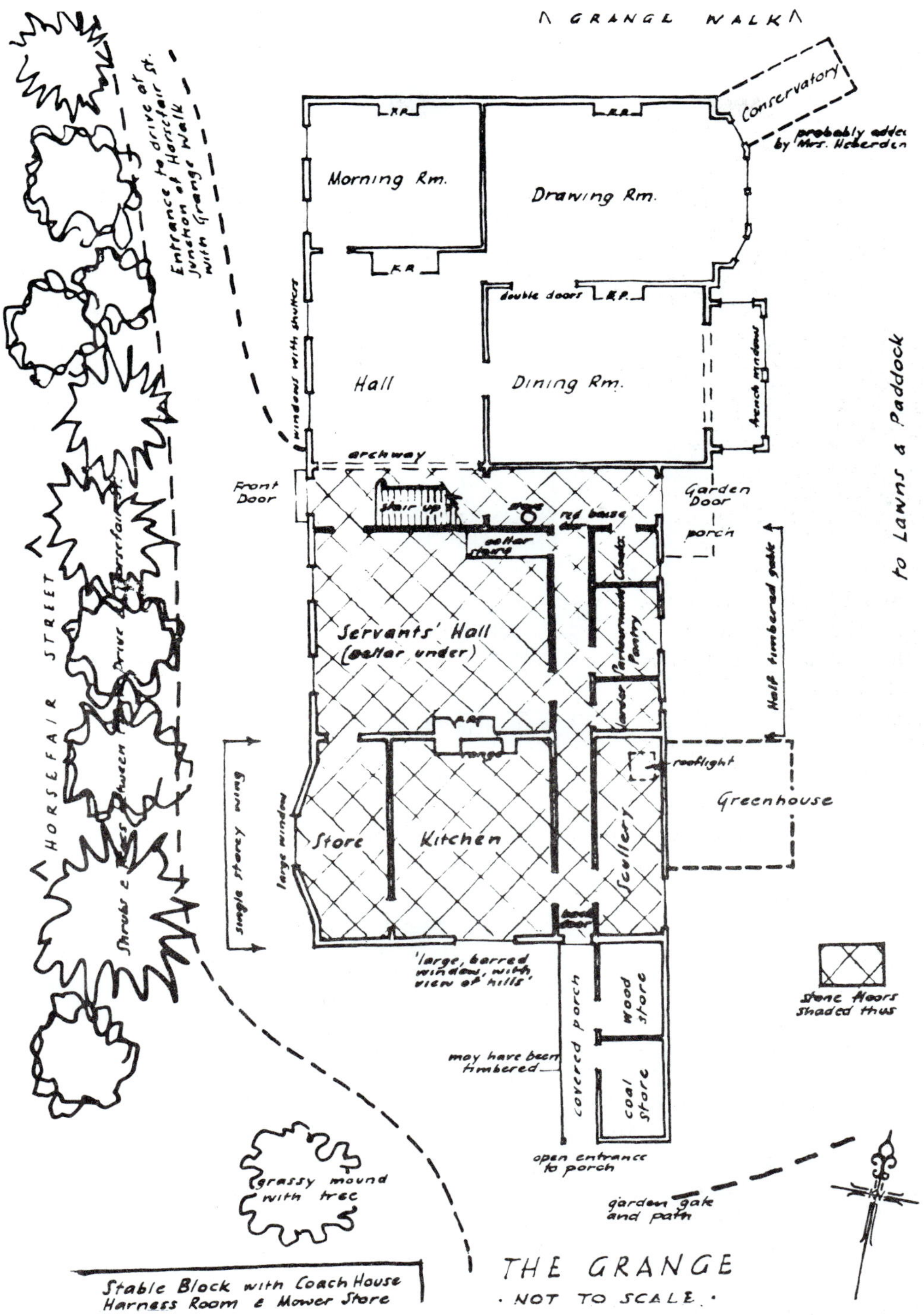

6.4 Plan of Churchend House (later called The Grange).

6.6 These large foundation stones which had formed part of the 1617 barn belonging to the Reynolds and Cleeveleys, were found in the garden of the next-door property.

6.5 Church End Messuage, demolished in 1931. In the sixteenth century this was the home of the Reynolds family.

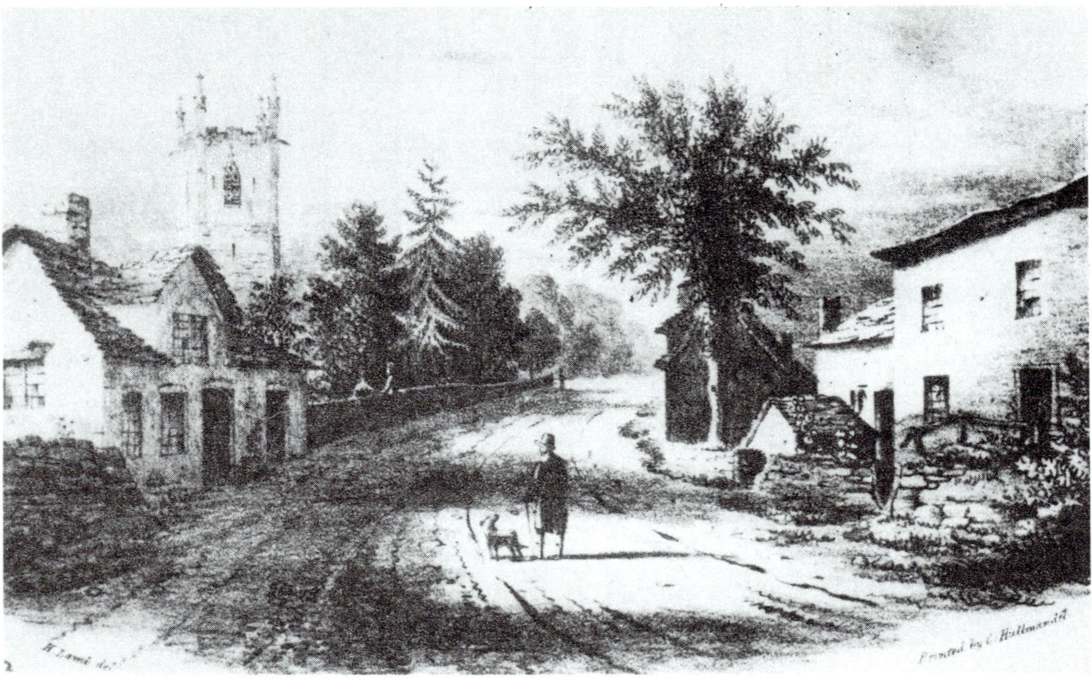

6.7 Forge Cottage *c.*1820. This may have been the Charlton Cottage beerhouse kept by David Denley in 1844.

6.8 Barns Hay. A lithograph from Powell's *Liber Naturalis* of his 1824 drawing of Church Street.

the cemetery entrance, stood Walter Brevel's messuage called **Brevels** (Cheltenham) in 1450. The old house was allowed to fall down about 1640 but the name of the close, Brevel's Hay, preserved the memory of it.[8] For tithing purposes these two Horsefair Street houses were held to be in Bafford.

There were houses on the east side of the church till 1854, when the churchyard was extended, including two entitled to pews in church and so probably there by 1630. One was a timber-framed house with a big porch called **Church Cottage**, which belonged to Anthony Webb in 1698.[9] Further down Church Street (also called Charlton Street or Crab End Way) was **The Forge** (6.7). Francis Crumpe's inventory taken 17 January 1670/1 included 'iron coles and iron ready made, 2 anvils, bellows and shop tools' valued at £28 0s 0d[10] and his widow Grace paid hearth tax on a 'forgearea' in 1672. This forge continued to shoe horses at least until 1922. East of the forge was an Ashley tenement held by the Crumps, on what had been John Dowdeswell's garden in 1403.[11] East of Crump's house and Bobbys Alley was a timber-framed and thatched hall house (freehold) called **Barns Hay** (6.8). In the late seventeenth century this was occupied by the Randalls and after them by the Halls, who developed the land and, in 1875, sold the old house (then divided into three cottages) as a site for the Baptist Church.[12] **The stone cottage** (6.9) in the lane (until recently used as a store-room for Morris's shop) seems to have been built on part of Barns Hay about 1660 (perhaps with re-used stone). It may have been the home of Richard Randall in 1672, when the main house was occupied by William Randall and his

6.9 The Stone Cottage (before the 1985 alterations). East front (*left*), and window in west wall (*right*) with diamond mullions and cast iron window catch.

6.10 Brevels Haye. Worn and bent roof timbers (*left*) strengthened by a strut added in 1924, and (*right*) a detached chimney stack added in the seventeenth century.

children. Morris's house was built on to it in 1831; and in 1985 the stone cottage was drastically altered to fit it for a dwelling again.

One branch of the Brevels were Ashley tenants, and there is a reference in 1557 to Margaret Brevell, a widow, having a house with solar in addition to her 'nether house'.[13] This may be the first reference to the timber-framed house called **Brevels Haye** (6.10), standing in the garden of an older house. When the new roof was put on Brevels Haye in

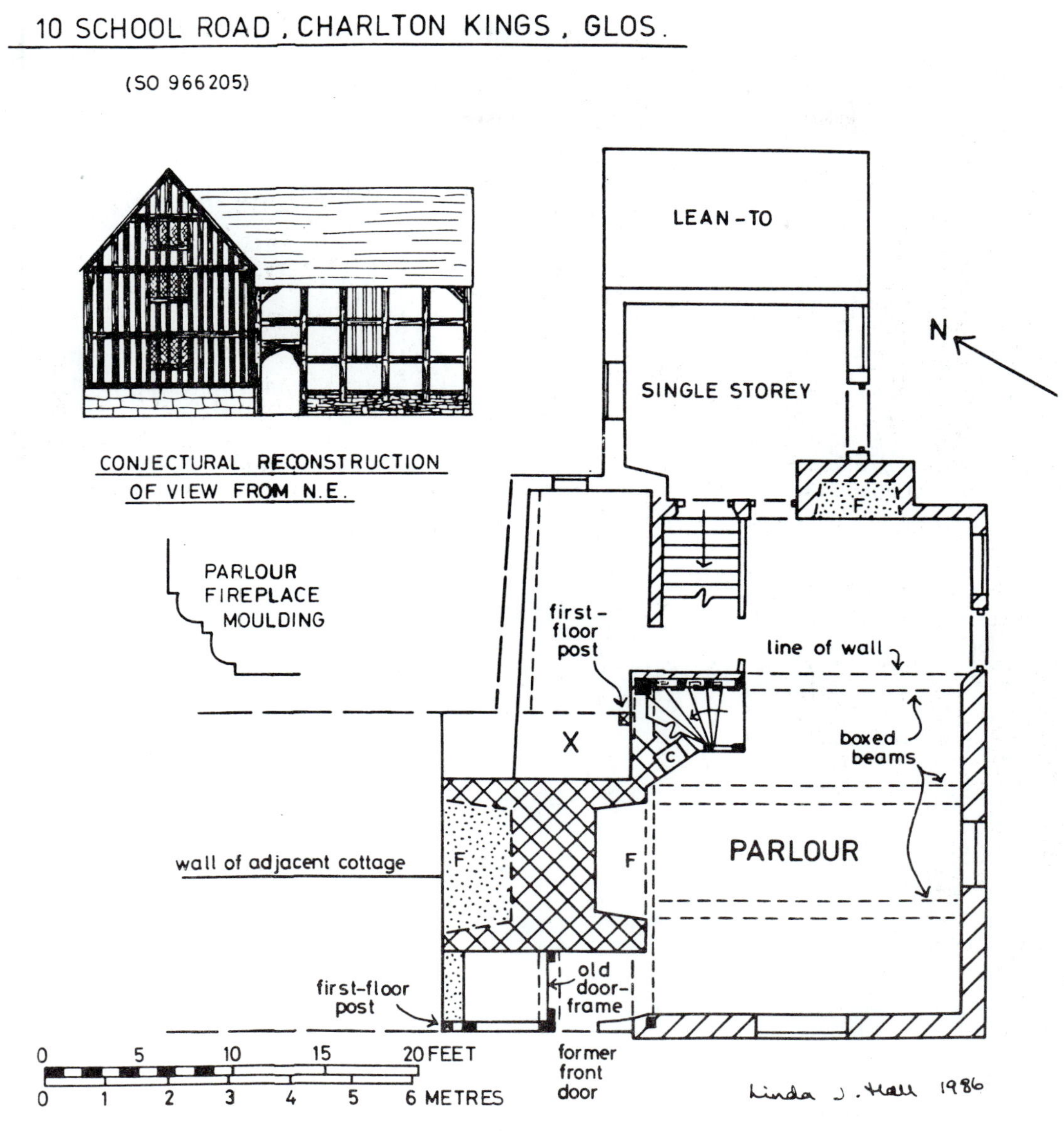

6.11 Charlton Cottage.

1984, the roof timbers still appeared to be of the sixteenth century and it was clear that both chimneys had been added to this three-bay house which is now a scheduled building. Until 1924 it had a stone tiled roof; the outside is plastered and the antiquity of the building completely hidden. Its hay has been reduced to a small garden, but there is still a way out to Church Street over the site of the 'nether house', which became one timber-framed and thatched dwelling in a court of mean houses called **Pruens Row** which were pulled down in 1938.

On the north side of Church Street there was a timber-framed and thatched house, divided into dwellings called **Crab End Cottages**. It stood behind **The Merry Fellow** (which was built in the mid-nineteenth century on its close) and its site is now a car park and skittle alley. Opposite the Barns Hay house, but originally approached from Trigmerry Lane or

6.12 Charlton Cottage. There is a stone base three feet deep to the west and south walls.

6.13 Charlton Cottage. This stone fireplace was uncovered in 1985.

6.14 Charlton Cottage. Chimney breast and timbers.

6.15 Yew Tree Cottage (now demolished). This sketch is by H. V. C. Holman who died in 1880 at the age of 85.

Mill Lane (School Road) was **Ivy Cottage** (freehold), a timber-framed and thatched house built *c.*1600 on a strip in Broadcroft, as that part of the Lye Field was called. It had substantial timbers and for its last fifty or sixty years the thatch was covered by corrugated iron.[14] It was divided into two dwellings but was still sound when it was demolished.

Charlton Cottage (6.11), formerly called **Joyce's**, on the east side of Trigmerry Lane, was originally a sixteenth-century hall-house with parlour and through passage, partly built of large panel timber-framing and partly of close studding. On the west and south sides the timbers rested on huge stone blocks (6.12 and 6.13). In the seventeenth century a stone chimney stack ten feet thick was inserted, the framing either encased or rebuilt in brick, and the roof raised with four steep gables, covered until 1920 with stone tiles. This work may have been done when it came into the hands of a branch of the Gale family. In the nineteenth century the cottage was divided into two, the northern part rebuilt to make a third dwelling and its land reduced by building other cottages on the frontage and by the sale of a plot for the school. After a threat of demolition, it was partially restored in 1954 and more thoroughly in 1984.[15]

The ancient house next to Joyce's was **Yew Tree Cottage** (6.14) (freehold) facing west up a cart track which became Lyefield Road East. This was a medieval messuage. When it was demolished in the 1950s, fourteenth century coins were found under the floor, and it may

6.16 Hawthorne's in 1902.

6.17 Hawthorne's: close studding and diamond infilling on the east front.

6.18 East Court, built 1805–11 with later extensions.

6.19 Wager Court in 1901. The right-hand wing was rebuilt in 1913–14.

well have been a cruck construction, to judge by the south end, though the beams were concealed under layers of plaster (6.15). This was the last thatched cottage in Charlton Kings, and like all the older houses had been divided into two dwellings. In the eighteenth century it belonged to a branch of the Ballinger family. Its barn had been turned into cottages in the early nineteenth century and these were pulled down about 1912.

In 1557 John Hawthorne held an Ashley manor tenement called Partridges Meese with 26 acres of land. It was rebuilt about 1600 as **Hawthorne's** (6.16) (now **King's House**), with close studding on three sides and wide box framing on the fourth. On the east side which faced the main road, part of the frame is infilled with ornamental diamond pattern (6.17). The timber-framing has a deep stone foundation, but the massive chimney breast rests only on the ground. The stone fireplaces here seem decidedly later than those of a similar but larger type at Elborough Cottage and at Joyce's. Until recently, the quarry floor tiles were laid directly on the earth. The kitchen on the south side, part stone, part timber, is a later addition to the main house, but still seventeenth-century. Robert Hawthorne sold this property in 1715. Hawthorne's was one of the old Charlton houses divided by William Flatcher into three dwellings. Luckily, the house was bought by the architect Samuel Holland Healing, of the firm of Healing and Overbury, who in the early 1900s restored it as a single house and it remains a perfect example of this style of building. Its present name was given in 1933 and has no justification. Near Hawthorne's were three other timber-framed houses, all now demolished – one was on the site of the bungalow at the bottom of the hill, one opposite, and 'Nobby Hall's' at the top of the hill.[16]

East End

There was a freehold messuage on the site of **East Court** (6.18). It was held in 1557 by John

6.20 The north wing of Wager Court in 1901.

Rogers with 63 acres of Ashley land, and he was succeeded there by William Grevill and his widow Mrs Ann Grevill (the lady who gave John Stubb so much trouble over inclosing). After her death in 1612, the property was divided into three and a comparatively modest farmhouse was built (though it was entitled to a seat in church). East Court was erected by Richard Pruen between 1805 and 1811, and later enlarged.[17] The old houses had faced East End Road, but the new mansion was built with an entry up a carriage drive from the new London Road.

Wager Court (6.19 and 6.20) formerly called **East End Farm**, stands on a medieval site. The house (as it was in 1901, when Mrs Bennett's photographs were taken) was an early-sixteenth century hall-house with through passage and a parlour wing added *c.*1600; the plan[18] in 6.21 was drawn by Mrs Bennett from an accurate memory. However, in 1913–14, the McLarens rebuilt the older part, so the seventeenth century wing is all that remains of the old house. Edward Wager held this house with 31 acres of land in 1557, and it stayed in the Wager family till the marriage of Jane Wager to Samuel Cooper in 1687. From Cooper it passed to his cousins the Slopers and their cousins the Higgs without ever having been sold until the end of the nineteenth century. Across the road from the old house (near the *c.*1900 East End Farm) was the farmyard with a magnificent seventeenth-century timber-framed barn, burnt down in 1924.[19] A big oak near the barn was killed by the heat; it was the fellow to the dead oak still standing by the entrance to the house.

Balcarras House (6.22) (the name is nineteenth-century) was the Gale family's farmhouse (Ashley) by 1557. In 1775 the holding was broken up; and after passing through several hands, the house and some land were bought in 1844 by the Reverend J. F. S. Gabb, the Vicar, then living at Pear Tree Cottage in Cudnall. Between 1844 and 1858, Gabb sold the farmhouse and two acres of garden and orchard to Walter Parry – the rateable value of the whole was only £24. 5s. 0d. He built another house called Balcarras (now Balcarras Court) on the site of the old stables and coach-house; in 1858 its rateable value with apple orchard

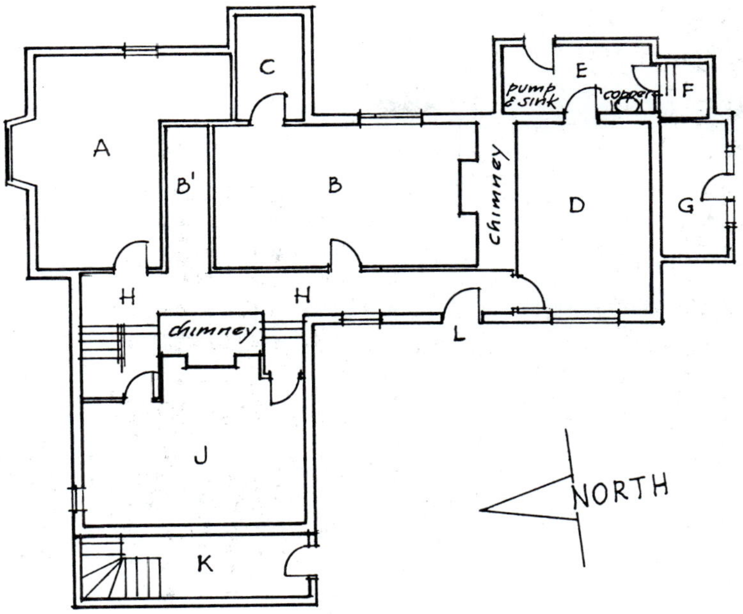

A. Stone-flagged room with no chimney, possibly dairy.
B. Sitting room, board floor.
Bi. Broom cupboard, no door.
C. Small cupboard room, possible original entry when a single gable (A–B) was built.
D. Kitchen with range recessed into large chimney.
E. Lean-to scullery, ceiled, with pump and sink (P) and copper (O).
F. Larder, down 3 steps.
G. Lean-to workshop, unceiled, probably board floor
H. Passage way from kitchen to stairs, with inner door under existing stairs to cellar stair.
J. Sitting-room raised above cellar, board floor
K. Storage shed with very wide stair to cellar, perhaps for casks.
L. Front door, with 'rustic' porch.

The cellars were built of small, thin bricks, less than standard size.

6.21 Plan of Wager Court before 1912.

(5a.0r.17p.), hay orchard (5a.2r.20p.), orchard of unspecified type and cherry orchard amounted to £118 12s 0d. On the London Road, he built Balcarras Lawn, g.e.r. (gross estimated rental) £75, which became a home for his son J. W. Gabb. The *Cheltenham Post Office Directory* for 1880–1 shows J. F. S. Gabb at Balcarras, J. W. Gabb at Balcarras Lawn, and Captain Tonge at Balcarras House. However, no surrender of the old house had been made to Parry, so Gabb's widow was obliged to claim as though the two new houses had not yet been built! Balcarras House then became the home of General William Smith and his daughters (who played such an important part in the parish life of Charlton Kings), and its size was increased. Not long ago, the house was nearly burnt down when unsuspected bacon beams in the ancient farm chimney caught fire.

6.22 Balcarras House.

6.23 Over House.

6.24 Detmore in 1979.

Over House (6.23) (Ashley freehold) in East End Road just stood beyond Steel's Alley. It was the home of Lucy atte Noverhowse in 1327 and in the mid-sixteenth century of Eleanor Hewes widow (tenant of Richard and Rouland Gooderich). In 1709 it belonged to John Walsh and was sold in 1739 to Richard Bastin the younger for £195, a considerable price for a farm house and stone barn without a great deal of field land. The old house and its close were divided between Charles, William, Emily and Sarah Kear in 1844; the barn became cottages (still in evidence) and the timber-framed house was added to and divided into dwellings; other properties including the **Duke of York** and the **New Inn** (now **Linden Lawn**) were built on its close. The old house and cottages were sold to Benjamin Wood in 1860, hence its more recent name of **Woods Cottages**, which were demolished to make way for council flats.[20]

Detmore (6.24 and 6.25) on the Deepmoors started as a single-roomed cottage (Ashley) held by the Dowdeswell family and first mentioned in 1545. This cottage became the kitchen of a house extended in the eighteenth and again in the nineteenth century; a stream ran right under the kitchen floor so that water could be obtained by lifting a flagstone and dipping a bucket! The foundations of this original house gave way and had to be renewed in the early part of this century.[21] For many years this was the home of the Dobell family, first as tenants and then as owners.

There were several closes called Coxhorne, lying in the angle between the Chelt or Rungebourne and its tributary Freemans Brook or Poultbrook. Those nearest the Chelt were Ashley customary land which in the late eighteenth century belonged to a branch of the Ashmeade family – there may have been a house on it by 1685 if the will of Gyles Ashmeade[22] really belongs here; he left a house and standards to a nephew Gyles. The farmhouse and land were sold in 1792 by Margaret Ashmeade and bought by Dodington Hunt for his son William Hunt Prinn, so no surrender was made till 1798 when William had come of age.[23] This is the house known as **Old Coxhorne** and, although modernised by Sir William Russell, some parts are old. Nearby was a one-acre close (Cheltenham) held in 1658

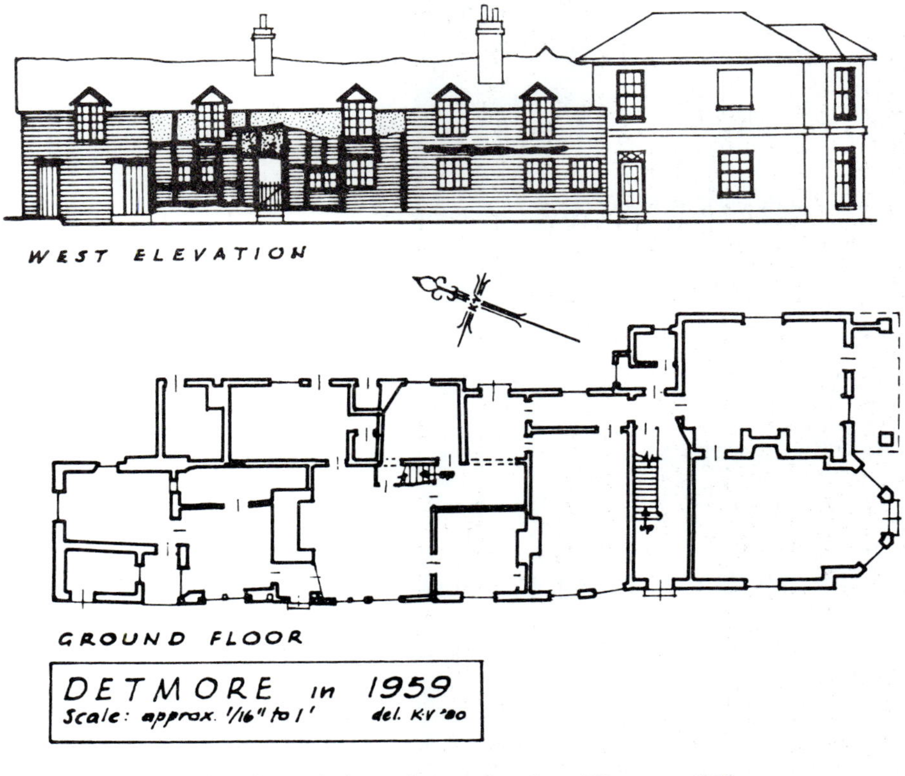

6.25 Ground plan and west elevation of Detmore, 1959.

by Lynett Pates and his wife who sold to Joseph Lewis and his wife Susannah. In April 1715 another Joseph Lewis surrendered to John James and his wife Jane, and after Joseph's death his widow Elizabeth completed the business, specifically mentioning this time a house in the possession of John James called **Coxhorne**.[24] This was added to in the later eighteenth century and became the home of the Whithorne family, rather than their older Charlton houses, Moorend House and The Knapp.

6.26 South front of The Hearne.

6.27 Courtfield (formerly Castleton House). The wing on the left was added when this was Dr Connolly's asylum.

6.28 The Close (formerly Conway House).

6.29 Bridge House (formerly the Hermitage). The stream runs right underneath the house.

The Hearne (6.26) is a Gothick house of *c.*1830–4 built on an old site. We first hear of two copyhold cottages held by Agnes Balle *c.*1450; in the sixteenth century these were replaced by **Balls House**. A moiety of Balls House was settled in 1653 by Richard Sperringe on his wife Elizabeth and a son John; he mentions a hall, buttery, chamber over hall, little chamber over buttery, and cockloft;[25] the remainder was claimed in 1658 by the elder son Thomas.[26] After his death Elizabeth, his widow, married John Moulder in 1660 and the house continued in the Moulder family until 1765 when it was sold to Hugh Bradshaw of Ham.[27] Bradshaw, having no use for the old house, allowed it to fall down, so there was only an orchard and shed on the site when Alexander Nicholson of East Court bought it in 1829 and built the present house; as its land was partly Cheltenham, partly Ashley, there were double surrenders for it.[28] The first occupier was William Baylis, whose daughter married the Reverend J. F. S. Gabb in April 1836. Then the Mercers occupied and owned the house until 1870 and continued to own it until 1919; their tenants were General H. R. and Lady Norman, followed by A. W. Martyn, who became the owner in 1919 and did not sell until 1942.

The Knapp, demolished about 1976, was an Italianate house of the 1840s which had replaced a much older house belonging to the Whithornes. In Ashley court books it is always described as **The Knapp and Pen**; there has been a house on this site since Castlefield was developed in the twelfth century.

After the new London Road was cut through Castlefield in 1787, new houses were built on the north side of it. **Springfield** (demolished to make way for **Nazareth House**) and **Castleton House** (now **Courtfield**) (6.27) were both built in 1820; the latter was added to when it became Dr Conolly's asylum. **Conway House**, now **The Close** (6.28) was built by the Lovesys *c.*1827 as a public house;[29] it is said that fresh horses were put on here so that the London coaches could go into Cheltenham in style. **The Hermitage** (now **Bridge House**) (6.29) and **Hambrook House** (demolished) (6.30) date from the years 1825–35; **Acomb House** (demolished) from *c.*1845.

Little Herberts, Up End and Bafford

Little Herberts Farm (Cheltenham) (6.32), by Sappercombe Lane, was held by the Rook or Ruck family. One of Powell's 1824 sketches shows a sixteenth-century timber-framed

6.30 Hambrook House (now demolished) was the nineteenth-century home of General Burton and the artist Clare Burton.

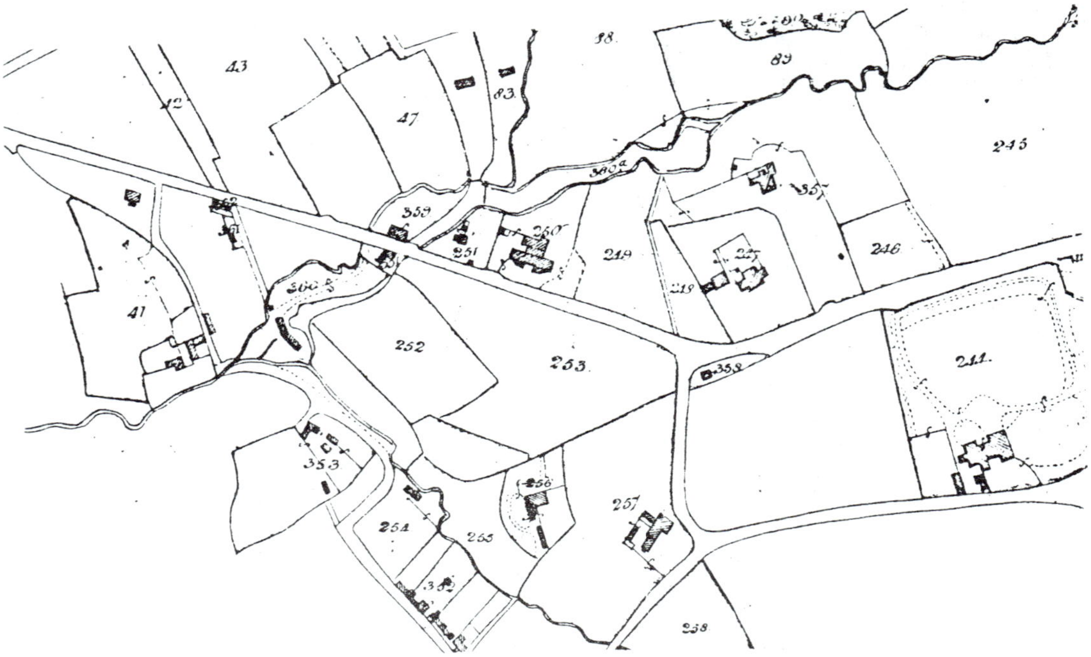

Key:

244 East Court
357 Springfield
83 Hambrook House
257 The Hearne
247 Castleton House
359 The Hermitage
256 The Knapp
250 Conway House

6.31 Tithe map of 1848.

6.32 Powell's 1824 sketch of Little Herberts Farm.

6.33 The nineteenth-century brick barn (now demolished) at Little Herberts Farm. In the background is a pair ot the first council houses to be built by the Urban District Council *c*.1920.

6.34 Cherrington's Farm (or Home Farm, Little Herberts) which was demolished *c*.1963.

farmhouse with Timbercombe ridge in the background; and this must be Little Herberts before it was totally rebuilt in the late nineteenth century. John Tombs's 1826 map of footpaths marks it and Sappercombe Lane, and shows a big barn against the Lane. This must shortly have been replaced by the nineteenth-century brick barn, older than the house, of which we have a photograph (6.33). Now Beeches Road runs slap through the farmyard.

Cherrington's Farm or **Home Farm, Little Herberts** (Ashley) (6.34) probably dated back to the fifteenth century. It had always been divisible, so that two generations of the same

6.35 Vineyards Farm.

6.36 The Nappings, home of the Batten family in the seventeenth and eighteenth centuries.

6.37 Brunswick House (now Glenure) in Cirencester Road was built *c.* 1820.

6.38 The south front of Southfield Farm (before restoration), which is a much older house than it appears to be.

family or a man and his partner could share it.[30] It was restored in the 1920s and might have lasted many more years if it had not occupied so much land. On the same side of Little Herbert's Road, **no. 49** is a timber-framed cottage quite concealed from the casual eye by modern additions. A curious fact about this house and its neighbours is that they are back-to-front, facing away from the road and on to a footpath! If Little Herberts Road was improved about 1550, as postulated, the footpath may represent the old line before a bend was made to avoid a bad stretch; and the farm and no. 49 would predate that bypass.

Above: 6.39 This old barn at Southfield Farm has served a variety of uses. In 1922–6 it was an engine shed for the quarry railway and has now been converted into homes.

Right: 6.40 The Withyholt was demolished during the 1960s. Its Victorian high-gabled front was added to an older farmhouse.

Vineyards Farm (6.35) is a late seventeenth-century Cotswold stone house standing on a ledge just below the top of the escarpment; it is well sheltered from east winds but open to the north and west. However this site found favour with Middle Iron Age and Roman builders, and there may have been a medieval house here, if this slope were once a vineyard. The name goes back to 1599 at least.[31] There was a quarry on the common behind the house, so the builders had no problem getting stone.

The Nappings, Up End (6.36) (Ashley) is said to be medieval and certainly stands on an old site, though the present building looks seventeenth-century. John Batten was admitted 17 May 1659 and in 1706 settled it on his eldest son Francis; however, after Francis and his wife Abigall had mortgaged it in 1711, it was claimed in 1723 by John's other son Thomas. Its land went up to Timbercombe Lane and included a close called Goldwells.[32] The Battens must not be confused with the Bastins who had another Ashley copyhold a little further down the road.

Across the road, **Lilleybrook** stands on the site of a copyhold house (Ashley) held by the Ashmeads. To judge by the print in Griffiths, [33] it had been rebuilt or improved *c*.1700 and again *c*.1816 when it was sold to Robert Mansell RN. This house was destroyed by fire in 1831 and rebuilt, but the stables remained until recent alterations. The present house was enlarged in the 1890s[34] and became an hotel in 1922.

Mitchell's map of Cheltenham (1806) shows a sizeable house in a large close, roughly on the site of Charlton Kings railway station. Perhaps the house of Edmund Welsh gentleman in 1747?[35] Next to that were two copyhold cottages held by members of the Churches

6.41 Note the rounded brick piers of this nineteenth-century cart shed at The Withyholt (now demolished).

6.42 The 'swiss' architecture of Moorend Park (demolished in November 1979). *Above left*: The south front; *above right*: the west end with the conservatory; *below left*: the stable block; *below right*: the dummy lodge.

family,[36] either father and son or two brothers. John as nephew and heir of Edward Churches claimed one cottage (heriot 8 shillings) in 1717; and Richard as son and heir of another John claimed the other cottage in 1728 (heriot £1 4s 7d).[37] In 1820 both cottages were sold to Thomas Barton for £950 and it was Barton who rebuilt them as **Brunswick House** (6.37), now called **Glenure**;[38] the occupier before 1829 was the Countess of Portsmouth. The house was sold in 1837 for £1200.

There was land of Richard Brereton west of the Churches in 1729. This belonged to a modest house which Theophilus Brereton gentleman bought in 1655 from the Reverend William Driver and Elizabeth his wife.[39] It was rebuilt in the mid-nineteenth century as **Brierton House**, now called **Barrington Lodge**.

Southfield Farm (6.38) (now called Manor) was built at the source of the brook originally known as the Barley Stream. The outside, before the latest alterations, looked Victorian with its porch, bay windows and plastered brick; but the brick was not of a Victorian type and the roof timbers are much older. Probably this is a late seventeenth-century farmhouse built on what had been arable – it was certainly there by the early eighteenth century when it was the home of a branch of the Ballingers. The brick barn (6.39) (now altered) was used in the years 1922-6 as an engine shed for the quarry railway.

The Withyholt (6.40 and 6.41) started as a modest farmhouse to which a Victorian high-gabled front was added and a new small farm house built on Moorend Road. It was probably a new farm in the mid-eighteenth century, replacing two old ones pulled down by Prinn. The Withyholt in its turn has been demolished.

Moorend Park (6.42) was built by Frind Cregoe Colmore, a Birmingham business man, between 1835 and 1840. The original design was by J. B. Papworth, but then Colmore opted for a 'Swiss' exterior. *The Handbook to the Environs of Cheltenham* by H. Davis (1843) says 'Moorend – a costly Swiss villa, also attracts much attention for its elaborate architectural arrangements', but contemporary enthusiasm was muted. It became an hotel in the 1920s and was demolished in 1979.

Bafford Farm (6.43) began as a mill; John Packer in 1585 and Thomas Packer in 1597–8 were the common millers.[40] As a mill it disappears from court books in 1600 and re-emerges later as a freehold farm. The old mill pond is marked by Mitchell in 1806 and the site can still be seen; till recently the house bore traces of this distant past in a door below the present ground level (see illustration). The roof timbers still have their bark on them. In spite of additions on the west end, a partial brick skin and sundry alterations, it is recognisably a seventeenth-century house even now.

6.43 Bafford Farm, a sketch from *c.*1890.

6.44 Bafford Cottage was 'Samuel Broad's' in 1734.

6.45 The front of Bafford Grange (formerly Bafford Cottage) built *c.* 1710 was described in 1734 as being 'opposite Samuel Broad's'. This photograph shows the later Victorian verandah.

6.46 Box Cottage; the stone part was originally called Yew Tree Cottage.

6.47 Spring Cottage, once the home of the Pates family.

At the lower end of Bafford Lane is **Bafford Cottage** (6.44), a seventeenth-century house with a substantial part added about 1900. In the seventeenth century this was the home of the Broad family; in 1652 Richard Broade and Mary his wife sold to Thomas Ashmeade (living on the site of Lilleybrook) some parcels of its land including Baffourde Paddock.[41] Samuel Broad was living here in 1734, and Betty Broad spinster in 1763.[42]

Across the road is an early eighteenth-century house (built perhaps about 1710) and described in 1734 as 'opposite Samuel Broad's', a new house on old arable. Formerly known as **Bafford Cottage**, it is now called **Bafford Grange** (6.45). Elizabeth Little claimed her sister's messuage in 1734, and in 1773 she and her husband Miles Astman sold it to Thomas Evans, who improved it – he has left a date stone 1774 on additions at the back.

Next door to Bafford Cottage is **Box Cottage** (6.46), the home of the poet Cecil Day-Lewis while he was teaching in Cheltenham. It is actually five cottages put together; the stone part was once called **Yew Tree Cottage** and may be late seventeenth-century, though it has no dateable features. On to it have been tacked four brick cottages built at different times in bricks of varying colour (three at the front, one at the back). All the cottages were one room up, one down, originally.

At the top of Bafford Lane, at **Spring Cottage** (6.47), lived a branch of the Pates family. This is an early seventeenth-century house, though of course much modernised; the beams in what was once the hall suggest that date, and so does the end next to the road, built of stone up to first floor level and then with narrow seventeenth-century brick with a shaped gable (6.48). This is the house referred to in Lynnett Pates's inventory of 1685[43] as having a hall, parlour, cellar, pantry, closet, parlour chamber, middle chamber, chamber over hall, pothouse chamber, man servant's chamber, dayhouse, old dayhouse and kitchen – that is, three bedrooms over the main house and two others over outhouses. Pates also had an 'old house' (empty in 1685 except for three baking stones but with a corn chamber and barn still used) and this was on the other side of the road apparently on the site of recent houses in Charlton Close, for between the old house and Pates's dwelling was a five-acre close bought by Lynnett in 1626 and then described as 'against a close or curtilage of Richard Pates' his father.[44] Thomas Pates sold this close to William Prinn in 1765 when it was still five acres and said to have Bafford Street to the south, the highway (that is, Moorend Street or New Court Road) to the east, and be 'next adjoining to the curtilage of the said Thomas Pates save as divided from the same by Bafford Street'.[45] John Pates was still at Spring Cottage in 1848 but had left by 1857. In 1826 Pates's five-acre Home Close became the site of a new property, **Bafford House** (6.49).[46]

6.48 The end wall of Spring Cottage, built of stone and narrow bricks.

6.49 Bafford House was built on Pates Close in 1826.

6.50 The Laundry stands on the site of Robins's beedle messuage. (H. V. C. Holman's sketch.) The chimney and the works have now been demolished.

6.51 New Court; John Prinn's east front.

The **Laundry** (6.50) in New Court Road stands on the site of an Ashley manor beedle messuage held from 1709 by William Robins, a maltster (father of Thomas Robins the elder, the painter, who was born here). It remained in the Robins family till 1805 when Henry Robins, a London auctioneer, sold the messuage, malthouse, garden and orchard to John Whithorne of Moorend House. His tenants, the Turks, continued to brew here until 1879 when it was converted to a steam laundry. No part of the beedle messuage survives and only the office part of the laundry.[47]

Below the laundry were the medieval houses, Grimes's and Younging's;[48] the sites have recently been built on again. The high wall from here to the corner of Moorend Road was put up in the nineteenth century when **Moorend House** became a private asylum; a stone built into that wall has some Whithorne names cut into it and presumably came from their

6.52 New Court; on the north wing one panel of close studding has been left uncovered. Note the window to the left where the wood of the frame is almost flush with the stonework in the style which was common before 1710.

6.53 New Court; *left*: attic stair bannisters, probably put in 1614; *right*: John Prinn's bannisters *c.* 1697.

6.54 Charlton Park; a 1922 photograph of Dodington Hunt's west wing of 1784–8.

6.55 The east front of Charlton Park *c.*1922. The sloping line of brickwork covers timber gables.

6.56 Contrasting styles of windows at Charlton Park. *Left*: a seventeenth-century stone mullion looking into the courtyard; *right*: narrow sash windows on the south side *c*.1710–15. Compare the bricks between the windows with those of 1855 in the bay to the right.

old house, another medieval site. The last relic of Moorend House, a gardener's cottage belonging to Moorend Park, was demolished in 1979. It stood across the road from New Court.

New Court (6.51–6.53) (now called Court House) was indeed 'new' in 1557, when it is mentioned for the first time. It was a close-studded timber-framed house erected c.1550 by or for Sir Henry Compton on freehold land called The Horne between two roads. The house was slightly improved in 1614 by the addition of a parlour chimney and perhaps a staircase window which still has seventeenth-century glass. Margaret Rich's will and inventory in 1691–2 gives us a good idea of its lay-out and furnishing, all the furniture very good but a little old-fashioned, for Margaret had inherited it. She had seven pictures, Spanish gilt hangings in her summer parlour, a Spanish table, a clock, and other luxuries.[49] John Prinn acquired New Court in 1695–7, rebuilt the central hall in brick, and heightened the roof over his new dining parlour and the chamber over it. He left the sixteenth-century wings alone structurally, but he panelled the old parlour and may have put in the south staircase. The house was modernised in 1797–8 when it was intended as the dower house for Charlton Park; the north staircase which does not quite fit may even have come from the Park. About 1890 the porch was added, half the windows on the west side renewed, and a bay stuck on a window on the east, which makes New Court look Victorian when seen from the road.

The house we call **Charlton Park** (6.54) was until 1784 **The Forden** or **Forden House**.[50] It was a Cheltenham freehold, with a virgate of land, held until *c*.1400 by the Ford family. Then John Grevill senior acquired it. It remained in the Grevill family until bought by John Prinn in 1701. About 1562, Giles Grevill the younger came of age and set about building himself a new timber-framed house round three sides of a courtyard. This house is still the core of Charlton Park (6.55); some of the beams can be seen on the attic floor. Seventeenth-century mullion windows (still visible from the roof) originally looked into

6.57 Charlton Park; the head of the 'Chippendale' staircase.

6.58 Park Cottages, once the home of Dr John English, a vicar of Cheltenham during the seventeenth century.

this courtyard (6.56). John Prinn gave the timber house a brick skin, starting with the east front in the years 1701–9, proceeding with the south front where the narrow windows are typical of the period 1710–1715 (6.56), the north front (to judge by Thomas Robins's painting) *c.*1720 and finally adding a new western block in 1732. That is the date put on the attic beams and on the gable end. So John Prinn lived to see the whole completed – he did not die until 1735. This is the house depicted by Robins in *c.*1748 (see page 190); the picture hung in the billiard room in 1848 and is now in Cheltenham Art Gallery. Beside the house, Robins shows a farmyard with barns and dovecote, and a little south of the house four public roads met. In the foreground are dutch-style water gardens of *c.*1701 (rather like those in the gardens of Westbury Court at Westbury-on-Severn) and a large walled kitchen garden.

John Prinn's grandson William had an only daughter Elizabeth who died in childbirth in 1772, so when William died in 1784 her husband Dodington Hunt entered into the estate for life. It was Hunt who created the park and stocked it with deer. He rebuilt the west front, giving it an extra storey and making it symmetrical, with large deep-set windows, and put in the superb 'Chippendale' staircase leading to the upper floors (6.57). The courtyard was filled in by building an oval drawing room with Adam-type plasterwork. This was the house George III saw in 1788; the big cedars near the house may already have been planted by that year. Other improvements were the removal of the old stables, and the diversion of one of the four public roads; timber and bricks from the stables and west block may have been used to build the new stables (which contain massive beams) and the high wall surrounding a new kitchen garden north of the house. The water-gardens were replaced by a lake and the park landscaped by Hunt's son when he succeeded to the property in 1803. After the new Cirencester Road had been cut in 1826–7, a dry stone wall was built from the Chelt at Cudnall bridge to the Lilleybrook in Moorend Road, and Moorend Road was extended so that the three public roads near the house could be closed, two becoming the back and front drives. The house was altered somewhat in 1885; but the obliteration of the east and north fronts has been the perhaps inevitable result of its conversion into a school since 1939. The eagle gates which now adorn the Cirencester Road entrance are shown on the Old Bath Road by Robins *c.*1748; about 1784 they were moved to the public road on the east side of the house, and then to their present position in 1940.

On Charlton Park back drive stand **Park Cottages** (6.58), originally a single house. In 1617 it was one of Thomas Harwood's three Bafford messuages and beside it stood a barn of six bays which had originally been the tithe barn. Harwood sold the messuage and some other land to Dr John English, Vicar of Cheltenham, in 1636; in 1638 the court ordered 'that Doctor English shall att his charges cause a gate to bee sett upp at the Lower end of Henncroft over against his house in Charlton', on pain of 6s 8d.[51] As the last of the bishop's appointees, English did not have to be celibate or belong to Jesus College (see page 00). When the Civil War came, English supported the King and was thrown into prison, and while he was thus imprisoned, his wife and daughter died. To their memory he erected a memorial in Cheltenham parish church, with a touching inscription which may be read in J. A. Rawes, *Memorial Inscriptions of Cheltenham*.[52] When English made his will in 1648 he was living in Charlton Kings, presumably in this house. His son John succeeded him here, but after the son's death there was a dispute as to who was the next heir, which was won by Elizabeth Collins, wife of a Stepney victualler. From her it passed to her only daughter Frances who married William Jelfe of Charlton, and in 1709 they divided the house into two. This building appears to date from *c.*1600, though the outside is plastered and we have not yet had a chance to survey it. The roof is stone-tiled.[53]

Cudnall

By the water-splash in Spring Bottom was **Cudnall** or **Charlton Mill** (Cheltenham) (6.59). This was worked for many years by the Martin family. John is named on the Lay Subsidy Roll of 1327 and his descendant Walter sold the mill in 1631.[54] In the late eighteenth century it became for a time a leather mill (hence local people call London Road from Six Ways to the bottom 'Leather Mill Pitch'). In 1801 it was rebuilt as a grist mill and Powell sketched it in 1824; the last miller was 'Peggy' Allen in the 1890s.

On the other side of the water-splash stood a yeoman farmhouse known as **Tantys** (6.60 and 6.61) (Ashley), so picturesque that it has been sketched many times.[55] Once it was on the main road to London! Like Wager Court, it was L-shaped, one part very much older than the other; a photograph taken not so long before it was pulled down suggests that the

6.59 Powell's sketch of Charlton mill in 1824. It continued virtually unchanged until 1900, but has now been demolished.

6.60 Tanty's Cottage sketched by Powell in 1824. It was demolished *c.* 1970. The house on the right, 60 School Road, is older inside than out.

6.61 H. V. C. Holman's 1948 sketch of the south side of Tanty's Cottage.

6.62. North and west sides of Tanty's Cottage.

6.63 Grove House as modernised by Richard Haines in 1763. This side faced the main road.

6.64 Grove House was further up-dated by Clarence Mason Dobell in the nineteenth century. Haines's date stone is on the chimney.

main block could have been medieval, with an addition of *c.*1600. All the photographs and drawings show a change of roof line at the junction of the L. Inside, its timbers were massive, and structurally it need not have been pulled down. But it needed improvement, had not been scheduled, and had a large garden ripe for development. Timbers on the side most often sketched had been covered by brick and the chimneys were brick, but timbers on the north and west were still exposed (6.62). The roof was stone-tiled. The Tantys had brought together a fair amount of land; John Tanty died in 1699 and was succeeded by William, and then by John who claimed in 1730.[56] Another John claimed in 1757 and proceeded to lose all his inheritance.

Grove House or **Cottage** (6.63) (freehold, Cheltenham) had a predecessor; the barrel well in the kitchen which was sealed in 1972 is said to have been of a seventeenth-century type. The first positive information we have comes from 1706, when Thomas Mansell and Anne his wife (who lived in a beedle messuage further down Cudnall Street) with their son Thomas surrendered a small strip of Ashley land to Thomas Lawrence the younger who had just purchased the freehold.[57] His son William inherited in 1713 and his grandson John in 1757. Then in October 1762 John Lawrence conveyed the house to Richard Haynes or Haines, and six months later (with Elizabeth his wife) surrendered the copyhold.[58] The change of ownership explains the date stone 1763 on the big chimney stack (6.64). Richard was modernising the house for himself and his first wife. He improved it again in 1784, on his second marriage to Elizabeth Clay, adding a good sitting-room and building a coach-house and stable. He left Grove Cottage to his five children by Elizabeth and in 1829 they sold it for £900 to the well-known architect Robert Smirke (who designed, among other public buildings, the British Museum, the General Post Office, and the Shire Hall in Gloucester). He wanted a house for his wife's sisters. By the date of his death, 1867, only one sister survived and she decided to live in Cheltenham, so the house was sold, for £500 this time, to John Dobell of Detmore, who added to the garden and also exchanged some land, subjecting it to restrictive covenants to prevent building. After John's death in 1878, it

6.65 Hetton Lawn was built in 1862. The house has been turned back to front so that the main door is now on the south or garden side.

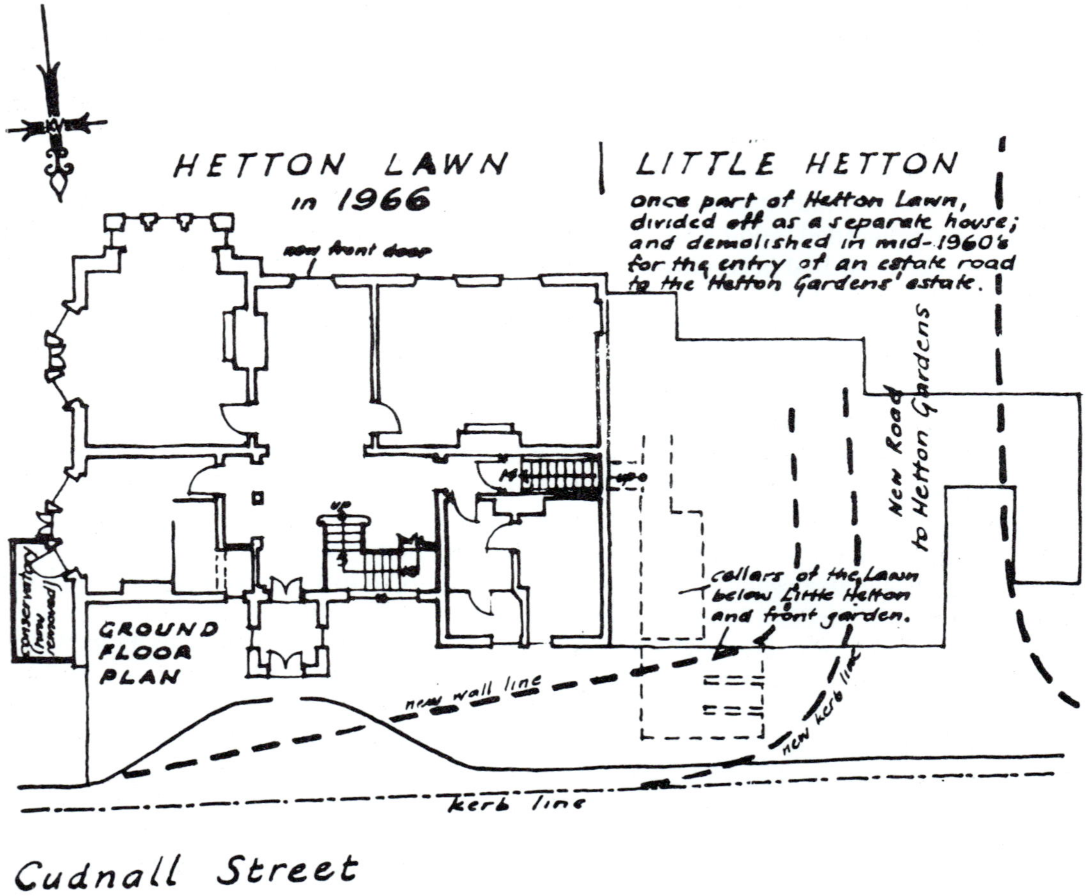

6.66 Little Hetton was the original customary tenement to which Hetton Lawn was added by the Reverend H. G. Liddell in 1862. Little Hetton was demolished in the mid-1960s.

was conveyed by the executors to a son, Clarence Mason Dobell, who lived there and was responsible for the mock timbering on two sides (6.64). He added another two acres to the garden, taking it down to the Chelt for the first time.[59]

Next door to Grove Cottage was an Ashley freehold, **Cops Elm**, so called from its having been conveyed to John Coppe in 1391.[60] The present Copt Elm Road was cut in 1865 through its land, and the old house was pulled down about that time. Charlton Lawn stands more or less on its site.

Adjoining Cops Elm was a Cheltenham copyhold and next to that an Ashley copyhold, both held in the seventeenth century by members of the White family. Together they provided the site of **Hetton Lawn** (6.65), built in 1862 by the Reverend Henry George Liddell, grandfather of 'Alice in Wonderland'.[61] Liddell retained what remained of the seventeenth-century messuage (up-graded by William Bolton *c.*1788) and in 1966 this formed a separate house known as **Little Hetton** (6.66): it has since been demolished and only Liddell's 1862 part is left, turned back-to-front so that the main door is now on the south. When Alice stayed here in 1863, her nursery was in the old wing and she knew the drawing-room with its tall windows and very special mirror, with figures of a shepherd, shepherdess, birds, and nests. This and Lewis Carroll's visit to Cheltenham at the same time seem to have begun the story which became *Through the Looking Glass*.

Elborough Cottage (6.67) (Ashley) sometimes paid a Peter's Penny as well as work-silver, suggesting an origin in the early twelfth century. This is a fifteenth-century hall-house with crucks (6.68 and 6.69). A stone chimney was inserted later (6.70), and to support it a buttress had to be built against the outside wall. Though originally thatched,

6.67 Elborough Cottage (on the left) in 1977. The cottages in the foreground replaced Holder's 'Cuddenhill Meese' *c.*1805.

the house is now stone-tiled, and in the early nineteenth century was much prettified in the taste of the time (6.71) though it was not structurally altered.[62] Its history is well documented, considering that there are no Ashley court books for the sixteenth and seventeenth centuries. This was probably the home of Alice Elborough when she made her will in 1542.[63] After that it belonged to the Stubb family – Thomas (1557), John (1564), Richard (1583–1628), Thomas (1628–?) and probably another Richard, a clerk. From the Stubb family it passed before 1666 to Daniel Ellis, a wealthy maltster who died in 1684, and

6.68 The west wall of Elborough Cottage.

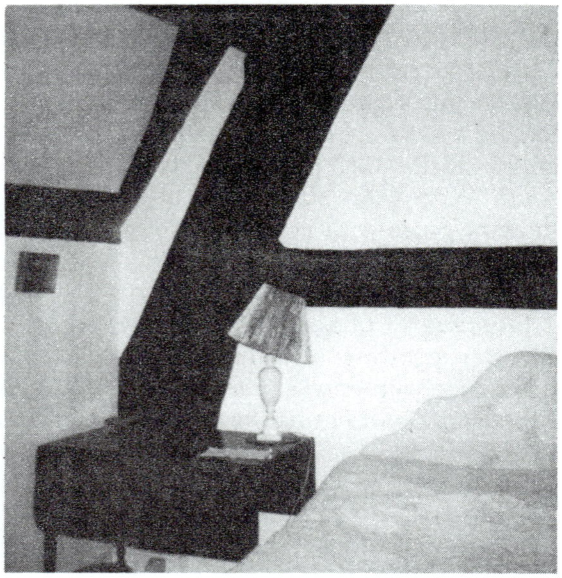
6.69 An exposed cruck in Elborough Cottage.

6.70 This fireplace in Elborough Cottage was inserted in the sixteenth century.

6.71 Lawrence's nineteenth-century 'prettification' of the south side of Elborough Cottage.

6.72 Wraxall House was rebuilt in 1816. It stands on the site of Richard Stew's house which was burnt down c. 1635.

6.73 Hamilton House adjoins Wraxall House. It was built c. 1805–10 on copyhold land which was part of 'Cuddenhill Meese'.

a younger Daniel who in 1697 was in trouble for shooting his neighbour Richard Overbury in the leg with a hand-gun (the gun was confiscated but later returned). David Ellis claimed it as son and heir of Daniel in 1714[64] but he apprenticed his elder son Richard to a Gloucester goldsmith in 1739[65] so in his will he instructed his daughter Mary, wife of William Overbury, to sell. The 1761 purchaser was Daniel Quarington, and in 1774 his daughters sold to Walter Lawrence of Sevenhampton who wanted the land.[66] His daughter Mary Morris and her husband lived here, and the house was improved for them; in 1824 it was put up for sale[67] and was surrendered in 1825 to Richard Pruen and his children.

Brookway Lane used to be known as Stews Lane, and **Wraxall House** (6.72) is on the site of Richard Stew's house, burnt down about 1635.[68] It was Crown demesne in the seventeenth century, which Richard and, after him, John Pates his relative, held by lease, together with land at Battledown.[69] The house was rebuilt twice before the present 'chateau' was built there by Sir Nathaniel Wraxall (1751–1831) in 1816.[70]

Next to Stew's house was a customary tenement (Cheltenham) of the Holder family. The old house was divided in the seventeenth century and later demolished to make way for **Hamilton House** (6.73), **Pear Tree Cottage**, now **Courland** (6.74), and the cottages fronting Cudnall Street (see 6.67) all built in the early nineteenth century. Pear Tree Cottage became the Vicarage in 1838.

A large close west of the lane originally went with the Ashley tenement always called the **Ancient Messuage** (6.75). It was a long, low house which had had its roof raised and another storey added at some time; about 1850 its west wall was rebuilt in brick and **Milford Cottage** built against it. The house may at one time have been a public house and after that was divided into three small cottages. The rooms were very low and had no windows except on the east side, so it was eventually condemned as unfit for habitation.

Tucked away down a drive (once a public road) is Ivy Cottage. This was an Ashley beedle messuage called **Cowell House** (6.76), which Charles Higgs rebuilt in brick in 1808 and then mortgaged to raise money for his improvements at Charlton House. Another Ashley

6.74 Courland (formerly Pear Tree Cottage) was built *c.* 1830 and became the Vicarage in 1838.

6.75 The 'Ancient Messuage' in Cudnall, shortly before it was demolished. Beyond it can be seen part of Raisey House (no. 6, Cudnall Street) in front of which once stood Mansell's beedle messuage.

6.76 Ivy Cottage was rebuilt in 1808 by Charles Higgs from the beedle messuage called Cowell House. Until 1787 a lane ran along the position occupied by the garage in 1979 when this photograph was taken.

6.77 Charlotteville (now called Langton Lodge) was built *c.* 1806.

beedle messuage, **Mansell's**, once stood against the main road in front of no. 6 Cudnall Street. Thomas Billings, a surveyor and builder, bought the garden in 1795 and built a new house on it, then called **Raisey House**, afterwards **Cotswold Lodge**, now no. 6. Two years later, Billings bought the old house as well and pulled it down, leaving a vacant patch in front of his new house. Its coach-house has been converted into an attractive home.

6.78 Charlton House was rebuilt *c*.1810.

Next door was a freehold (Cheltenham) which in the eighteenth century belonged to the Sollis family – Billing's road map of 1798 (privately owned) suggests buildings round a courtyard. That house was rebuilt as **Charlotteville**, now **Langton Lodge** (6.77) about 1806–8.

Charlton House (6.78) (now the headquarters of Spirax-Sarco) is a rebuilding from *c*.1810 of a much older Ashley tenement held by William Combe at the beginning of the seventeenth century and then by Combe's widow Jane who married Samuel Deighton. There is a reference in 1610 to hanging gates across the way against William Combe's barn (to protect Mill Furlong) and in 1627 'att Mr Sam: Deightons in the usual place wheare the poaste standeth'.[71] If Mitchell's map of 1806 is right, the old house was built round three sides of a courtyard, like Forden. By *c*.1696 Charlton House had come into the tenure of Samuel Cooper, passing from him to the Slopers and Higgs (just like Wager Court). Land was added until house and grounds occupied fourteen acres, besides other Higgs land. The present house ought to have iron balconies, which are shown in a sketch by Rowe; and this confirms Mitchell's evidence that the present house was not built as early as Verey thought (*c*.1790); on the other hand, it cannot be later than 1810, when Charles Higgs died leaving an heir, Charles Cooke Higgs, who was a minor and did not come of age until 1818. Meanwhile the house was let; 'John Cooper of Charlton House' was buried in 1817 and his widow carried on her Ladies Seminary (described in such glowing terms in Griffiths' *Cheltenham Guide* of 1818) until about 1825, when Charlton House was let to a Birmingham business man, Frind Cregoe. In fact, this house was never occupied by its owner during Charles Cooke Higgs's lifetime.

In 1882, shortly before his death, Higgs placed restrictions on the future use of Charlton House. The house was to be used 'as a private residence only, and not as a school for boys, a work house, or a lunatic asylum'. What would he have said to its use to house prisoners of war in 1914–18? In 1919 it was bought by the Reverend A. H. Rhodes, Vicar of Holy Apostles, and this Higgs would have approved, for that church was built by him. Rhodes sold in 1934, and then building on the grounds began with Charlton Drive.[72] The building firm was A. C. Billings and Sons Ltd, probably descendants of Thomas Billings of 1795. During the 1939–45 war, Charlton House was used as a headquarters for American Forces.

6.79 Langton House was built by Charles Cooke Higgs *c.* 1826.

Originally there were no houses on the north side of Cudnall Street. One of the first to be built was **Bank Cottage**. The front looks like a brick cottage of the late eighteenth century, but there is timber-framing at the back. Mitchell's map of 1806 marks this, an adjoining house, and one some distance down the street as within the same inclosure, and has written against them 'Mr Rogers'. As with the house against which Mitchell writes 'Lady Mills', Rogers was not the owner but the occupier; the owner was Charles Higgs who had inherited this as part of his uncle Samuel Higgs's property in 1804. We know that Charles Higgs (who had already improved the modest farm he inherited from his father) wanted to make the best of his new possession and found all the houses needed updating.

He seems to have built **Charlton Lodge** on land going with Bank Cottage about 1806; it was a well-built medium-sized house, approached from the street by steps which led to a front door on the east side. There were two good reception rooms, a basement kitchen and offices, and (probably) three bedrooms – this basic shape shows up on plans of the house because the original walls are so much thicker than later ones, and because of detail over the windows. Charles Higgs is thought to have lived here himself while he rebuilt Cowell House in 1807–8 and Charlton House in 1809-10; and when his son Charles Cooke Higgs came of age in 1818 he too lived here until he built **Langton House** (Charlton Park Junior School) about 1826 (6.79). After that he added to Charlton Lodge, first giving it an extra room on the ground floor and an extra bedroom, then an addition at the front so that there was a street-level entrance through a Doric porch into a small hall with a staircase to the real ground floor above. A long verandah was added to the whole west front and carried round to the new road frontage; new servants' quarters were erected on the east side. There is nothing to date any of this except perhaps the Doric porch (Langton House also has one), but it would be more likely the work of a younger than an older man. The outline of the house on the plan when it was sold in 1892 shows it in this state. Subsequently another addition was made at the back; the Victorian conservatory on top of the Doric porch could have been put there by the next owner, Mrs Jane Dorothea Curtis.

On the corner of Greenway Lane and Ryeworth Road are two houses, now **Roadlands** and **Ashley Firs**, built by Richard Freeman in 1798, on two field strips running along

6.80 Whitefriars' School has previously been called Woodlands, Oaklands and Ashley Manor. It was added to in 1837–9. *Above left*: The south front; *above right*: Even the window frames are curved; *below left*: A Gothic window to the dining room. A Gothic chimney piece was also purchased in 1839; *below right*: The summerhouse by the entrance, part of a gazebo.

Ryeworth Road, the first Cheltenham and the second Ashley copyhold. So every transfer of ownership of the second house has meant two surrenders, with an added complication of a freehold conveyance when a piece of freehold was added to the garden. The bay windows of Roadlands were added by Lady Mills, the occupier under a lease of 1807,[73] and the building at the back of Ashley Firs was added when it became a girls' school in 1818.[74]

The house which is now **Whitefriars' School** (6.80) had three earlier names – first it was **Woodlands**, then **Oaklands**, then (without any justification) **Ashley Manor**. After the new London Road was cut at Cudnall in 1825 there was a scheme to make a private road and

Top Left: 6.81 Ryeworth Farm is now called Little Manor.
Top Right: 6.82 Ham House (now demolished).
Bottom Left: 6.83 Ham Court, the west end of Thomas Packer's house built *c.* 1580. The roof was raised *c.* 1724.
Bottom Right: 6.84 The south front of Ham Court built *c.* 1724.

bridge beginning roughly where the present Whitefriars drive starts; this would enable development to take place on the fields beyond the stream. However, the building slump of the late 1820s checked this, and in 1832 Alexander Ogilby bought some land on the further slope as a site for a new mansion. He seems to have built a plain Cheltenham Regency-type house which still forms the back part of the present building – this he called Woodlands. He built a lodge north of the stream where his drive left the projected road.

In 1837 Nathaniel Hartland, who came of a Quaker banking family, bought Woodlands and changed the name to Oaklands. He built on the classic front with a big stone bow window; and then round the corner a Gothic bay to match a Gothic chimney piece in the room inside, and a little later a Gothic oriel. There is some lovely interior plasterwork.[75] The Hartlands added to the estate, and when there was no longer any question of a private road

6.85 A seventeenth-century barn (*left*) and farm buildings at Ham Court.

to any other house, built a second Gothic lodge on the main road. Both lodges have been demolished. This house remained in the possession of the Hartland family until the death of Lady Agnes Dixon-Hartland on 4 November 1955; and after standing empty for two years it was bought by the Carmelite Friars for a school.

The site of **Ryeworth Farm** (6.81) (now **Little Manor**) in Greenway Lane may well be that of the pre-Conquest 'farmstead in the rye inclosure', while the rye inclosure became medieval Ryeworth field. This is the tenement held in 1617 by Robert Holder and his mother, when they paid 10 pence work-silver and a Peter's Penny, evidence of a twelfth-century past. The present house could be seventeenth-century, though so much altered that its timber-framed structure is practically undateable.

Ham

Ham House (6.82) formerly stood back from the road as it turns towards this hamlet. It was built by Richard Haines (of Grove House) on the land of two Cheltenham copyholds about 1800, and from 1819 to *c.*1886 it was let as a boys' school or 'Academy for Young Gentlemen'. It has been demolished to make way for modern development.[76] By the sixteenth century (if not before) Ham was regarded as a sub-manor of Cheltenham, and as such it was sold by Robert Goodrich and his son Richard to Thomas Packer in 1574 for £400.

Ham Court (6.83–6.85) (which may have been the fourteenth-century home of the Cheltenham family[77]) must have been very old-fashioned by then; and about 1580 it was rebuilt as a narrow timber-framed building of two storeys, with close studding and diamond infill at the west end; we do not know what the old south front was like. From Thomas the property went to the eldest son Arthur and then to the second son Alexander, the man who really built up the Ham Court estate – his purchases included Northfield.[78] When he died in 1638, he tried to prevent his estate being squandered. He cut his son out altogether in favour of his grandson, another Alexander, and gave his daughter Margaret all his lands and leasehold for a term of 21 years, subject only to payment of £50 a year to

6.86 Wadley's at Ham.

6.87 Old Ham Farm.

6.88 Ivy Cottage, Ham.

6.89 Another of Powell's 1824 sketches. The glimpse of Leckhampton Hill and the end of another house by the elm tree on the left suggest that this is a house called Noglins at Up End, next to Brunswick Villa. It was divided into cottages and was not demolished until after 1881. If this is Noglins, the distant house is Brierton which was rebuilt *c.* 1860–70.

her brother. It must have been Margaret and her husband Bradley who supplied horses, hay and straw to Prince Rupert's troops during the Civil War, if the story has any basis in fact.

The inventory taken on the death of Alexander the second in 1685 shows that he owned a clock, £20-worth of books and a case of knives, three unusual items to find in a Charlton inventory; but his household stuff was very ordinary. In 1724 the estate was sold to trustees for the Dodwell family as an investment; they modernised the house by putting on the brick south front and raising the roof another storey. Later, when Ham Court was used as a farm, a grain hoist door was cut right through the fine timberwork, which for a long time was concealed by plaster. Other houses in Ham were part of the Packer estate and many are old, some very old, but their history is difficult to trace. The stone tiles from Wadleys (6.86) were taken off in the 1920s to be reused on the Court!

Glenfall is a house whose origin goes back to *c*.1770; the simple farmhouse then erected became a *cottage orné* (as drawn for Griffiths)[79] when Charles Higgs rebuilt it in brick between 1799 and 1808. In 1818 it was sold to Edward Iggulden for £2700 and he landscaped the grounds. Later a carriage drive and lodge were added by the Molyneux family and the house enlarged. But it was not extremely large when it was bought by Arthur Mitchell (of Mitchell & Butlers) in the 1920s. The drawing room, dining room and library were extended, and a large ballroom with sprung floor added. The architect was Sidney Barnsley who designed panelling and bookcases; the furniture included much by Peter Waals (some now in Cheltenham museum). This was the only Charlton house to be affected by the Arts and Crafts movement. It was sold in 1965, the top storey removed and after other uses it is now the home of the Community of St Peter the Apostle; the ballroom has become a very beautiful chapel.[80]

7

In the House: Inventories, 1660–1750

Until the legal reforms of the nineteenth century, all wills had to be proved in the diocesan bishop's court or the Prerogative Court of Canterbury, and a fee was charged for the service. It was commonly felt that the fees charged were too high; therefore, to obviate any abuse, it was made mandatory in 1529 that, as soon as possible after a death, an inventory should be made of all the deceased's moveables and that the charges for probate should be *pro rata*, with the heirs of those owning less than £5-worth of goods paying nothing. Thus, every will should be accompanied by an inventory; but since the inventory was not useful once the will was proved it has often disappeared. However some ninety which relate to Charlton Kings survive in Gloucestershire Record Office dating in the main from the middle of the seventeenth century to the middle of the eighteenth century. Moveables cover all household goods and furniture which are not part of the structure or 'staple to the house'. All farm animals and crops, whether reaped or growing, and all 'implements of husbandry' and tools of a trade, outstanding debts owing to the deceased and all bonds, mortgages and leases are included in the category.

Because of their nature, probate inventories give a vivid picture of what the homes of ordinary people were like and of living conditions generally. They show the gradual introduction of luxuries like looking glasses and clocks, which were more common at the end of the period than at the beginning, and they ought to show any general change in wealth or poverty. In fact, in Charlton Kings they show no significant change during the hundred years covered, but the period is comparatively short and the number of inventories small. There are other limitations. Then as now, valuations for probate were low. The valuation was not made by professionals but by two or three trusted neighbours called Appraisers whose ideas of worth, apart from farm animals and produce, may not have been wholly reliable. For example, Margaret Rich in her will dated 16 December 1681 mentions a Spanish mahogany table left to her nephew as an article of special value. The appraisers of her goods on 1 September 1692 dismiss it as 'an old table'.[1] Apart from these limitations, inventories deal only with moveables. They do not take into consideration houses or land and can therefore be misleading as to the actual financial standing of a family. Margaret Rich's house, New Court, was one of the best furnished in Charlton Kings and her moveables were valued at £103 6s 10d, which is high since she owned no animals or farm produce. But she had been compelled for lack of ready money to take out a mortgage which became forfeit on her death and frustrated her will. On the other hand, Henry Cleevely who died in 1733 left moveables valued at £9 16s 0d.[2] He and his wife Susannah lived in a house with three rooms and a buttery and possessed little more than bare necessities; their one concession to comfort was a warming pan. Yet other sources show that they had set up their son in his own business (he was probably a builder) and arranged marriages for their two daughters who, of course, had to have dowries provided for them. Moreover, after her husband's death Susannah sold the house and its 1½-acre close for £100. It is clear, then, that by themselves inventories are not a safe guide to a person's financial position.

In Charlton Kings, the inventories of yeomen carry the highest value because cattle, sheep and farm crops were the chief sources of wealth. Craftsmen – and there were not a great many – had less unless they practised husbandry as well. The gentry, again a small group, also drew their real wealth from the same source. There are very few inventories for women, because only a spinster or a widow could own property. All a wife's goods passed to her husband at marriage. Indeed, in one inventory, that of Thomas Buckel Junior of Ham in 1688, it is stated specifically that his wife's wearing apparel is valued with his own.[3] Quite often the widow continued to practise husbandry.

There was no particular formula for drawing up an inventory and the appraisers followed their own inclinations. Some clearly put down items as they saw them or thought of them. Others classified them – 'in brass', 'in linen', and so on. But in just under half the Charlton Kings inventories they made the survey room by room, naming the rooms and listing what was in each. This gives some idea of the size and nature of a dwelling. Naturally, this varied: four houses had only two rooms, a living room and a chamber; eight had three rooms; others had hall, kitchen and two chambers; and in six cases the house had hall, kitchen, parlour and three chambers above them. The largest house had nine living rooms. In addition there were service rooms.

The most usual living rooms were the hall, the kitchen, the parlour, and various chambers (that is, bedrooms). Offices included the brew house, which doubled as a bake house in some cases, the day house or dairy, the cheese room, the buttery and cellars. There are several garrets mentioned and one cockloft. Outside were barns, stables and odd buildings; no pig sties are mentioned but most people had at least one pig. However, things are not always what they seem. Elizabeth Ashmead used her cheese loft as a bedroom. Several people used the parlour or a chamber as a storeroom. Moreover, it was not uncommon for a man to sleep in his hall – after all, there was a fire there and other chambers frequently had no fires. One group of testators were obviously old people living with relations (sometimes in a sort of 'granny flat'), keeping only a few treasured possessions in one room, though several of those owned farm stock. By 1660 nearly all houses had a kitchen. Where there was no kitchen people kept up the old practice of cooking in the hall or main room, 'the fire room' it is called in one case. It might be the only room with a fire. Even when there was a kitchen, some families seem to have preferred to cook in the hall; at least, that is where they kept most of their cooking utensils. Mr Daniel Ellis[4] who lived in Elborough Cottage, had a very well equipped kitchen. It contained:

	£	s	d
One table board and form	00	02	06
1 jack, one iron crane with five iron hooks thereon, one cast iron fire back, two per of andirons, one per of iron tongs, three spittes, one per of pott hooks, one iron fender, one trevett, one iron dripping pan and ladle, one gridiron, one skimmer, one flesh fork, two toasters, two lock steels with five irons belonging thereto, and one per of bellows	001	06	02
32 peices of pewter of severall sorts weighing 90 L at 8d per L	003	00	00

	£	s	d
Two dozen of spoons	000	01	06
4 brass kettles, two brass potts, two brass skilletts, one brass pan, one warming pan, all weighing 82L at 10d per lib	003	08	04
One per of small brass scales with an iron Beam	000	01	06
One tinn dripping pan, two tinn flower boxes	000	01	01
One birding gunn	000	05	00
Six shelves	000	02	06
One frying pan and one iron peel	000	02	06

The first group of objects are all connected with the fireplace, for all cooking was done over an open fire. The fuel for the fire was wood, and the secret of good cooking was to have plenty of hot glowing ash but no smoke or flame. The logs were held by the andirons (sometimes called 'dogs'). The jack was a clockwork device for turning a spit which held the meat before the fire to roast it as it was suspended over the dripping pan. To keep it moist it had to be basted with the fat and juices from the pan, using the ladle as a basting spoon. The crane with its hooks was used to suspend pots at the correct height above the fire, for most food was boiled. The flesh fork was a cooking fork. A trivet was a stand to support a pan in front of the fire, and the skimmer was used to remove the scum which forms on top of a boiling pot; all old cookery books advise frequent skimming. The toaster may have been something like a Dutch oven used for cooking small pieces of meat or bacon before a fire.

The kettles in the next section were pots to hang over the fire; in this sense the term is still used in 'fish kettle'. Only one man in Charlton Kings had a tea kettle and he was also the only person to have a teapot; but he was probably French. The pots and pans are cooking utensils, probably to stand in the hot ashes. A skillet had a long handle. The iron peel was for removing bread from a big baker's oven. Peels do not appear frequently in Charlton Kings inventories, though bread troughs for making bread are common enough (Daniel Ellis did not happen to keep his in his kitchen). This suggests that most people did not have the deep bread ovens which needed a peel; they had the ordinary little ovens built into the wall from which the bread can be taken by hand. The warming pan was kept in the kitchen because that was where there were hot coals to fill it.

In other kitchens, other types of cooking utensils are mentioned, such as cauldrons, furnaces (a term used for a vessel for heating water, not the fire under it) and posnets (small round-bottomed pans with a handle and three little legs; these were placed directly on the hot embers). Occasionally there is a saucepan, which is just what it says: a pan for making sauce, just as the saucers which also appear are small dishes for serving sauce or condiments such as mustard or pepper. Salt, on the other hand, was placed in a 'salt' of pewter, glass or even silver. No one in Charlton Kings had a really valuable salt cellar. In the kitchen salt was kept in a salt box, but only one inventory, that of Judith Probert, actually mentioned one; probably in other inventories such things were included in 'other small things of no value'. Another article in some kitchens was the pestle and mortar.

Some kitchens did not have a jack or spit, but many families did not have roast meat often. In point of fact, there are more spits and jacks mentioned in Charlton Kings inventories than might have been expected, indicating that the community at the time was not badly off.

Most pots made to be placed on or near the fire were made of brass, copper or gun-metal, for hollow-cast iron pots were uncommon until after 1709 when the process of making them was perfected, and pewter will not stand the necessary heat.

The hall, which was common to most houses, had been the centre of family life, where almost any activity might be carried on; but the inventories show that it was often sparsely furnished. There was usually a table which consisted of a movable top, the table board, and a stand or trestles to support it; a bench or form or two, perhaps a settle, a chair and some stools. There might be a cupboard and a chest and some shelves. Some cupboards were 'court' cupboards, that is, low cupboards with flat tops on which the family plate, if any, could be displayed. These were often covered by a cupboard cloth, for which green was a popular colour.

There were different types of chair. Joint chairs were the most common. These were made of wood which was jointed, not nailed, together. But there were also 'leather chairs', 'sag bottom chairs' (that is, chairs with a rush seat), 'twiggen chairs' and 'wicker chairs' (that is, made of basket-work) and, rarely, chairs with needlework seats. But twiggen and worked chairs belong rather to the parlour or chamber than to the hall. Sometimes the hardness of wooden seats was eased by cushions, and chests could be used as extra seating. The fact that in the seventeenth century many halls had only two chairs suggests that in some families children still stood for meals while the parents sat. Later, chairs became more common in the hall and sometimes there was an oval table as well as the board. An oval table was gate-legged so that it need take up very little space when not in use. By their very nature, most inventories deal with the belongings of elderly people. Their families were out in the world and it is tempting to picture the old couple drawing up the little oval table to the fire and keeping warm, for halls could be draughty.

Most families had at least one table cloth, but may not have used it every day. Meals were served on pewter plates and dishes or else wooden platters and trenchers. There is almost no earthen table-ware mentioned and archaeological evidence bears this out. There are a few mentions of china. Margaret Rich had a little, and so had Jacob Portret, the gentleman who had a tea kettle, but they were exceptional. Cutlery consisted only of spoons. The use of table forks had not yet reached Charlton Kings. In the seventeenth century, even in the best equipped houses, knives are rarely mentioned and then in the kitchen – only one or two houses had cases of knives. Each person used his or her own knife. Spoons were normally of pewter, though some people owned a few silver ones, but silver items do not seem to have been in everyday use. Mr Thomas Cartwright yeoman, for instance, had four silver spoons and he also had a tankard and a silver bowl.[5] The mention of the tankard is interesting because, unless drinking vessels were silver, they are rarely mentioned. Items of wood or horn were of so little value that they came under some general heading like 'other items not named'. Because food, if not eaten with a spoon, was eaten with the fingers, table napkins were important and appear in most inventories, once under the delightful name of 'hand wipes'. Charlton people seem to have been well provided in this respect.

The parlour, where it occurs, would have been a sitting room, and some were quite richly furnished. The little parlour at New Court had gilt hangings of Spanish leather. Jacob Portret, the gentleman who had the tea kettle, had two parlours. 'In the Great Parlour' there were 'one scrutoir (secretaire), one tea table and china ware, two pair of curtains, chairs, cushions, pictures and other odd things', while in the Little Parlour there were 'one corner cupboard, one table, two chairs and cushions, pictures and china ware'. The china and tea table are, of course, unique; and the old gentleman had his easy chair (the only one mentioned anywhere) and his books in French in the kitchen, where it was warm. Neither parlour seems to have had a fire: there is no furniture for a grate.[6] Other inventories mention oval tables and little tables in parlours, but some parlours seem to have been used as junk rooms, and some as extra bedrooms; and almost any room might be used for sleeping, particularly where there was a large family in a small house.

Turning to bedchambers proper, in the inventories the term 'bed' means what would now be called the mattress. The best of these were stuffed with feathers and the rest with flock. There is no mention of 'straw beds' which occur in some places, and there is only one 'chaff' bed, another indication that on the whole the community was not poor. There are a number of types of bedstead mentioned. The best were 'tester' beds, roofed four poster beds fitted with valances and curtains, often red or green, which were the popular colours, though grey and blue and white are mentioned. These bed curtains were not just for show. They cut out draughts and gave the occupant some privacy in an age when houses were built without passages and the only way to get around the house was through the rooms, as can still be seen in some older houses. Moreover, people rarely slept alone. Any number might occupy the same room, and frequently slept in the same bed. Children often slept head to foot, packed like sardines in a tin. Even a lady like Margaret Rich liked her maid to sleep in her room.

Another type of bed was the 'half-headed' bed which had brackets and bars from the head post and on these the curtains were suspended. There were also 'ordinary beds', a wooden frame to support the mattress, and 'truckle beds' which were only a few inches high and could be pushed under the big bedstead when not in use. However, it is noticeable that there were often more 'beds' than bedsteads, so presumably some people slept on the floor. Some bedsteads had a solid board or laths to support the mattress, but many had bed-cords and bed mats. The cords were strips of leather, webbing or string stretched over the bed-frame and woven into latticework, and then covered by the bed mat. There is nothing to indicate of what bed-mats were made from, but examples elsewhere were of plaited rush or straw.

Beds were furnished with bolsters of feather or flock and frequently with pillows of the same materials; some had bolsters only. Bed-clothes were commonly blankets, rugs and coverlets. Often sheets were used. These might be of linen, holland or flax (all forms of linen); cheaper ones were of hemp, which must have been horribly harsh. Pillows were fitted with pillowcases called 'pillow-beres' (often spelt 'bears' which gives rather a nice picture).

Charlton Kings was remarkably rich in linen. There is no house inventory so poor that it does not list some. Table cloths, napkins, pillow cases, cupboard cloths and towels were common, much more so than in the inventories of some other places. There was a field called Flaxley and several people had wheels for spinning flax, as opposed to wool, so it may have been grown locally. Two interesting items are 'worked bearing sheets' or cloths. These were embroidered sheets in which a baby was wrapped at its christening.

A bed-chamber usually contained chests for blankets and other items, and might also have a hanging press where clothes could be hung. Also there were chests or boxes of drawers. In most cases, no details of clothes belonging to the deceased were given; the normal phrase used to cover them is 'in purse and wearing apparell' but there is an exception. John Gale left 'two coats, three wastecoats, three pr of bretches, two hatts, four pair of gloves' valued at £2 10s 0d; and two pairs of shoes not valued separately.[7] No body linen is listed anywhere. The only form of adornment mentioned are rings, usually of gold, which were worn by men and women. Jacob Portret had a silver watch and chain, but that is not exactly an ornament, and there is mention of one other silver watch.

Boxes and coffers appeared frequently in bed-chambers. There were usually chairs and sometimes a carpet. A close stool was a convenience but not universal. Better-off families had a looking glass – these became more widespread as time went on – and other small luxuries. A comb box and two powder boxes appeared in the inventory of Margaret Rich but her possessions were altogether exceptional. The niceties of dressing were not confined to ladies. Lynett Pates had in his 'parler chamber' (parlour chamber or best bedroom) a large looking glass, a dressing box, four comb-powder boxes, one comb and brush.[8]

Not all bedrooms had fire places, particularly in the smaller houses, but where they did, the usual andirons, pokers and other fire irons appeared. Wood was the usual fuel in Charlton Kings and was a valuable asset, always carefully listed in inventories and often left in wills. It was not easy to come by, for there was little woodland left in the parish, and much must have been hedge brushings and loppings from hedgerow trees which do not renew themselves quickly. Probably there was some coppicing.

Lighting was by candle, probably home-made of tallow in the poorer households, and every household had candle-sticks, most often of pewter but not uncommonly of brass and very occasionally of silver. Judith Probert had a candle-box in which to keep her candles, for they tend to dry out if exposed to the air. Only in her inventory is a candle-box mentioned, but in others they may have been listed as 'other boxes'.

Perishable food stuffs were not included in inventories for obvious reasons; but bacon and cheese were frequently mentioned. In some houses there were large quantities of cheese, far more than a normal household would use, and this was clearly intended for market. Flour or grain for flour is mentioned, also garden peas and french beans. These must have been dried or salted, for they occur in inventories taken when such crops were out of season.

Apart from the living rooms, there were service rooms such as dairies, called day-houses, brew houses, butteries and cellars, though not all houses had all of them. There were also cheese lofts or cheese rooms for storing cheeses, which could have served other purposes at the same time. A day-house might have milk pans (the one article frequently made of earthenware), cheese vats, buckets, pails and cheese presses (nearly always called 'cheese rings'), cowls (a wooden vessel or tub for water, especially one with two ears), and so on. Cheese appears to have been made in the majority of households, but there were few churns, which suggests that butter was not. The brewhouse held all things necessary for the brewing commonly done at home; besides the necessary vessels, maltmills are mentioned, and barrels of different sizes. These might be stored in the cellar. Since the brewhouse was used for brewing once or twice a year only, it could also be used for other purposes, and often the 'powdering trough' (a tub for salting meat) and the kneading trough were kept there: it saved room in the domestic quarters.

Thus the picture of life in the village, as given in the inventories, is of a community well-equipped with the necessities of life, but with only a few of its luxuries, and with no marked rise or fall in standards during the period covered. The inventories by their nature do not deal with the poorer people but other sources suggest that though help was needed in emergencies, sickness, death or fitting out a son or daughter for apprenticeship or service, there was not much real poverty.

8

Places of Worship

St Mary's Church

The Medieval Church[1]

St Mary's started as a chapel of ease to Cheltenham parish church, the Mother Church of the district. The consecration of this chapel *c.*1190 is described in the *Cartulary of Cirencester Abbey* (a house of Augustinian Canons to which the rectory of Cheltenham belonged by gift of Henry I). It was performed by Bishop William of Hereford in the presence and at the request of Abbot Richard, so presumably this event took place during one of the frequent vacancies in the see of Worcester about this period.[2] The site was almost certainly given by Walter of Ashley, whose grant of £10-worth of the manor of Cheltenham had recently been confirmed by Henry II. Walter's share included a strip from Hollow Lane (Horsefair Street) down Church Street to the Hearne Brook; and the site for the chapel and its burial ground north of the church was part of this arable.[3] To give Charlton a chapel would enhance Walter's local prestige and would be convenient for him or his heirs should a manor house be built on the site he had reserved at East End.[4] While the king was sole lord of Cheltenham and its hundred, and the development of Charlton was restricted to a few farmsteads, there had been no reason for any chapel here; but the twelfth century saw an extension of cultivation and for the first time there was a local lord to give a site and enough people to maintain a church, for the nave is always the responsibility of the congregation. St Mary's had right of burial from the start because the land was available and a new burial ground did not in any way curtail the fees due to the Canons.

The original church consisted of a nave without aisles; short transepts; a chancel the same size as the present one and, presumably, a small bell tower on the crossing. We assume a central tower because if it had not been part of the original layout, a new tower built in the fourteenth or fifteenth century would have been added in the then fashionable position at the west end, which would have been a great deal easier. As in most ancient churches, the nave floor was down two or three steps, so that the doors could swing clear of the 'strawings' which covered it, the only mitigation of winter's cold. The nave was 14 feet shorter than it is now and the late twelfth-century west door (which survived until 1877) is shown in Rowe's sketch of the church and on the architect's drawings. The windows shown in old prints were of two lights, with plate tracery heads – one scrap survives, built into the north transept wall (8.2). There appears to have been a north door into the churchyard, later converted to a window, and a priest's door to the chancel.

The old chancel roof was a good deal lower than the present roof, as marks on the arch demonstrate. When the chancel was rebuilt in 1878 an old piscina was found concealed

8.1 St Mary's Church.

8.2 The last surviving example of the old window heads.

8.3 The original piscina.

8.4 The tub-shaped font may have been recut.

8.5 The alms chest made from a solid tree trunk; *left*: closed; and *right*: open.

8.6 The mass dial.

8.7 The chantry piscina.

under the plaster (8.3); and the architect John Middleton agreed to retain it 'in a suitable position' but not in its original place.[5]

Our font is tub-shaped, with the bowl cut into an octagon and decorated with curvilinear tracery (8.4). It may (like a not dissimilar font at Wells) be the twelfth-century plain tub recut in the late fourteenth century. A further relic of the original church may be the offerings chest (now in St David's chapel) (8.5). All churches were ordered to provide one like this to receive contributions towards the third Crusade led by Richard Coeur-de-Lion. It is a solid tree trunk with a lid sliced off and a small cavity hollowed out for the money which was dropped through a slit in the lid. Iron bands and locks protected the contents, and the weight of the chest is such that it would have needed several men to carry it away.

Charlton was to have a service every Sunday and holy day and on three weekdays, the priest serving St Mary's probably alternating with services three days a week at Arle chapel. A mass dial (8.6) (now built into the south wall near the westernmost buttress) marked in hours and half hours indicated the time of service. Because the church of Cheltenham had been given to Cirencester in 1133, neither Cheltenham nor Charlton had its own resident priest; duty was taken by three or four Canons sent over from Cirencester to do a stint in Cheltenham. They lived together and were spoken of as a 'Chapter' during their period of residence.[6] So there was no vicarage and no glebe in Charlton, though the Canons had a tithe barn near the Lyefield by Park Cottages.

The first alterations to St Marys was the adaption of the south transept as a chantry chapel. Its endowment was slender (see page 101), it is not documented on the patent rolls, and it has a four hole piscina to allow rinsings from the chalice to run into the wall (8.7); all these features suggest a date before the end of the thirteenth century. The mark of vaulting on the east, south and west walls of the transept show that there was a chamber above

8.8 Vaulting marks on the transept walls with a fireplace (blocked) above.

8.9 Medieval timbers of the south transept roof.

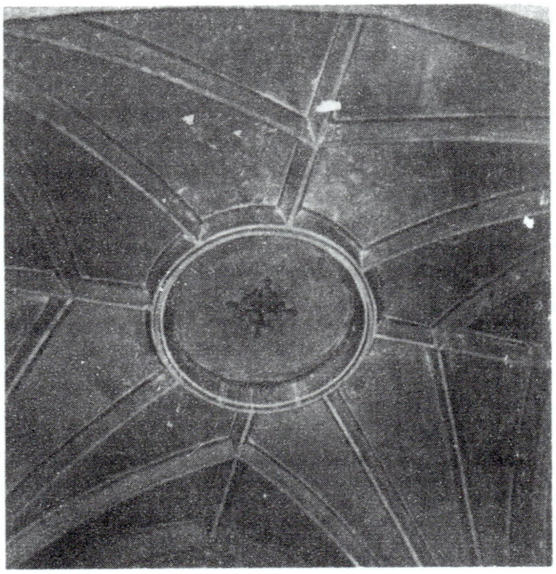

8.10 Vaulting of the tower and bell hole.

where the chantry priest could lodge (8.8); the staircase up must have been between the tower piers and the lost north wall to the chapel. The lower three-quarters of the walls were stone, the upper quarter timber-framing, a not unusual feature of thirteenth- and fourteenth-century building and adopted here to give the extra height needed for the upper chamber. The chantry altar was lit by east and south windows and the room above by a small south window (blocked later). There is a blocked fireplace in the chamber's east wall. The present roof timbers of the south transept are medieval, quarter turned at some time when they had become worn and bent under the weight of the stone tiles (8.9). This chantry was dedicated to Our Lady, as was the main altar.

About a hundred years later, the tower was rebuilt with a very high chancel arch (originally a good four feet higher than it looks now). There are no capitals, the moulding flows up in a continuous curve, a feature found in some Oxfordshire churches of the thirteenth and fourteenth centuries. This moulding, and the ogee openings in the tower, suggest a rebuilding about the time that William Grevill became lord of the manor of Ashley; it would be natural for him to want to impress the parish with his wealth and importance by making a substantial contribution; the parish too was prosperous, thanks to its corn. Parishioners probably wanted a bigger tower so that they could have a ring of bells – quadripartite tierceron vaulting leads up to the bell-opening (8.10) by which the bells could be raised from the floor of the church through the ringing chamber and up to their station in the bell chamber above. As all the old prints emphasise, the tower was absurdly large for the nave and chancel. A will of 1537[7] leaves money for the repair of the bells, showing that St Mary's had had them for a considerable time.[8] So though precise dating of the tower is difficult, the years *c.*1390–1400 seem most likely. The south aisle was added about the same time or somewhat later. This involved piercing the old south wall of the nave for pillars. All we know about them is that they were rather stumpy – later on they had to be enlarged – and this supports a date of *c.*1390–1400 rather than *c.*1490 when slender lofty pillars were the fashion. But the parish may have been doing the job as cheaply as possible; we know from prints that one or two of the old windows were re-used. New windows in 1400 would have been larger and more elaborate.

We know something about the late medieval church from wills. Four lights are mentioned in wills of 1537–1546: the High Altar or Sacrament Light, Our Lady's Light, the Rood Light, and the hearse lights.[9] The Sacrament was reserved, either on or above the high altar, in a 'shrine'. The Lady Light (distinct from the high altar light) was in the chantry. Our rood was probably a crucifix hung in front of the chancel arch from the roof timbers (any trace of its position being destroyed when Middleton did away with the medieval roof). There is no trace of a rood stair or screen on the present tower and if that were built *c.*1390, it would be rather early for one – the fashion for screens became widespread in the mid-fifteenth century (though there are earlier examples). The rood light may have been a hanging or standing light below it; this would not incommode parishioners who would not have gone up to the high altar to communicate more than once or twice a year. Hearse lights were placed round the hearse while a corpse was being waked. It was customary for a burial service to be in three parts: vespers of the dead overnight, *dirige* or dirge at matins very early, requiem mass and committal in the morning. Besides the money left in wills for lights at or after a funeral, there was a half-acre of land given for maintenance of a taper in the church; in 1548 this plot was held by Thomas Dowdeswell at will, subject to payment of 6d a year. It would once have sufficed to buy a paschal candle.

The last chantry priest, Sir William Hall, and probably his predecessors too, had been accustomed to assist the priests-in-charge because the population had grown; there were said to be 300 houseling people (communicants) in Charlton and 600 in Cheltenham. This is not a very clear guide to the adult population because medieval bishops rarely visited their

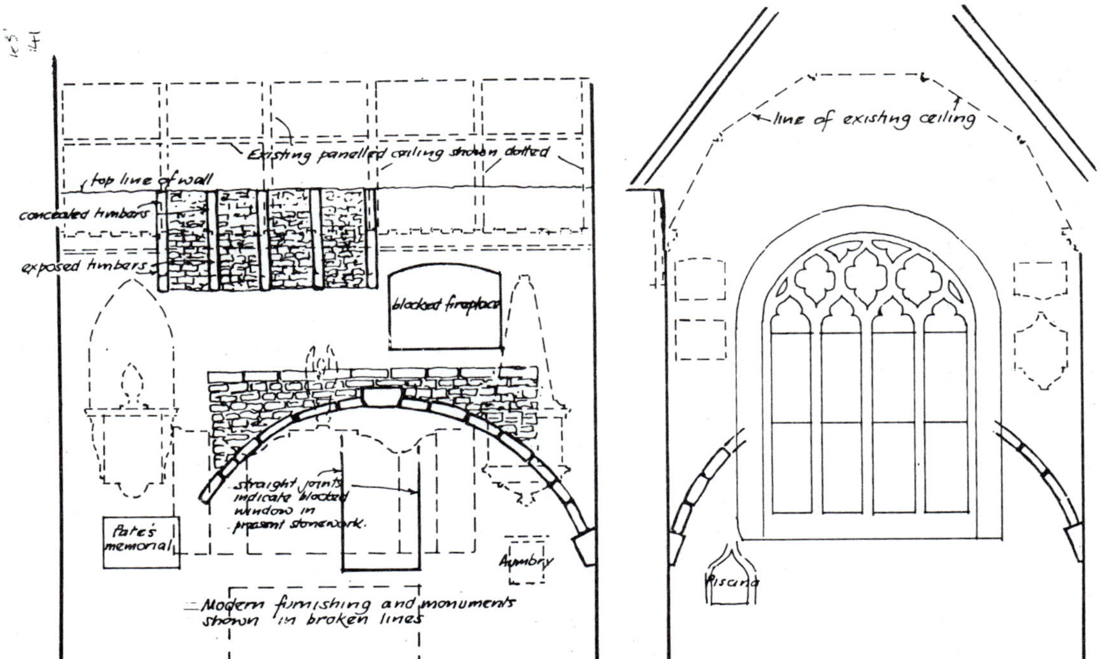

8.11 Diagrammatic elevations of St David's Chapel; *left*: the east wall; *right*: the south wall.

dioceses and children over eight years old may have been allowed to receive Communion without waiting for Confirmation. However, it seems clear that our chantry priest baptised, administered the last rites, and buried parishioners whenever it was inconvenient for a priest from Cheltenham to do it; though references in wills show that a 'curate' (that is, the man with cure of souls) was often present to witness a will, usually made in anticipation of approaching death.[10] Officially all fees for marriages or burials were paid to Cirencester until 1539; after that burial fees were presumably paid to the fermours. But it is possible that Hall received the occasional honorarium which he did not feel obliged to mention in 1548. He became curate himself then and served Charlton until *c.*1553. For him, a stipend of £10 secure was a great advance on 19s 4d, out of which he was having to repay money to the Grevills. As far as qualifications went, he was as well trained as most priests, even if he could not repeat the Commandments in English: he would have learnt them in Latin.[11]

All through the Middle Ages, Gloucestershire had been part of the Diocese of Worcester, and Charlton wills of the early sixteenth century frequently leave small sums to the Mother Church at Worcester. But one of Henry VIII's innovations was the creation of a new diocese of Gloucester and the first bishop was consecrated in September 1541. Henceforward it was the bishop of Gloucester we had to deal with.

The Church in the 16th–17th Centuries[12]

When Cirencester Abbey was dissolved in 1539 all its property, including whatever lodging the Canons had had in Cheltenham, came into the hands of the king. He and his successors granted various leases of the rectory and advowson, only stipulating that the lessees or fermours should find two chaplains and two deacons, paying what stipends they thought fit, and should provide necessaries for Communion, bell-ropes and strawings. These last three items ought to have been bought by the congregation; presumably Cirencester had been in the habit of supplying them. As no definite figures for the stipends were set, the lessees naturally appointed men willing to accept the lowest amount on which a cleric could live, considering that no vicarage was provided. Such clerics would not be graduates of a university and only graduates were allowed to preach; so Cheltenham and Charlton, Sunday after Sunday, had to listen to homilies read from the authorised *Book of Homilies*. The first was issued in 1547, with twelve homilies, the second in 1571 with 21; no doubt the congregation became heartily sick of them. Clerical marriage was permitted under Elizabeth I, but no priest on £10–15 a year without a dwelling could afford a wife and family unless he had private means.

By 1560 St Mary's had lost its shrine, its rood, its lights and any wall paintings it may have had on its plastered walls. (There is no room over the chancel arch for a Doom, but there could have been a Christopher over the north doorway.) The parish was not wealthy enough to have had much stained glass. Instead of any of these, all churches were ordered to provide boards with the Creed and Ten Commandments written up large for the benefit of a more literate congregation. An English Bible and successive prayer books must have been bought, and a new Communion cup. Medieval chalices were small because only the priest communicated in both kinds; now a cup large enough for all Easter communicants was needed and the old chalice was probably handed over to the silversmith as part of the price.

We don't know what parishioners thought about these changes, but they did want properly qualified ministers. In 1609 there were complaints that (in the words of a later petition):

> the said cures of the said church (Cheltenham) and chaple (Charlton) were and had byn

> very insufficiently served, and were and had byn supplyed with ministers and deacons of small learning and not of such sufficiency as by the gracious meaning and intencon of the said late Queen deceased in her Highnes said lettres patent was ment and intended, and that the ocasion thereof grewe by reason of the meane stipends allowed the said ministers and deacons.

The legal position was very complicated. The rectory was worth £600 a year. By 1609 it was held in trust for Mrs Elizabeth Badgehot or Badger and the Higgs brothers, her sons by a previous marriage. Their lease would run out in 1637. James I had already granted the reversion for another term, which did not end until 1652. But in 1612, Sir Baptist Hicks of Campden bought out the last lessees and purchased the rectory outright from the Crown. He could do nothing, however, until the Badger/Higgs interest came to an end, and they were not likely to surrender something that brought in £600 and cost them no more than £30 a year for both parishes! In 1609 the bishop had failed to persuade Mrs Badger to pay her two 'reading curates' more than £10 each and her two lay deacons more than 26s 8d each per annum. Bequests in 1611 and 1612 for buying a decent pulpit cloth or cushion[13] were made in the hope of something better eventually.

John Stubb, Steward of Cheltenham manor and a Charlton parishioner himself, chronicles every step of the hard-fought battle between the parishes and Mrs Badger.[14] Every time some influential person was approached, he was transferred, died or lost his office! A petition of 1621 to the king failed, for James merely passed it to the bishop of Gloucester, the stingy Dr Smythe, notorious as 'one to give very small stipends to his curates'. Endymion Porter was asked to arbitrate because he knew Mrs Badger and was 'a great favourite of the Duke's' (Buckingham) – he ruled that the stipends ought to be £20 for the next five years and then £40 for each minister; but Thomas Packer, representing the parishioners, was persuaded to agree to a reduction to £15 for the time being.

The matter became urgent in 1621 because the minister of Charlton, Mr Wells, departed. The bishop was for some reason left to fill the vacancy. There were three candidates: Mr Winsmore, 'a wandering minister, having wife and children' (Charlton had never had a married priest and shrank from the new experience), Mr Walker, who had preached here and gone down well; and Mr Hugh Williams, who was the bishop's first choice. However Walker was willing to promise to leave if the stipend were increased and meanwhile would accept £15, so the bishop began to favour him. Walker, like the bishop, held up-to-date views of a puritanical nature. The parish had not realised this from his first sermon, but when they did realise it, they turned dead against him. Walker appealed to the bishop, Sir Baptist Hicks, and other influential people. He alleged that the parishioners were trying to deprive him of his livelihood without just cause, and asked for support 'in the better establishing of me heare' and even money for 'the augmentation of the means for better furnishing of my study'. The parish thought this behaviour underhand, and Thomas Packer told him that if all the inhabitants were against him it was his own fault. 'The allowance is intended for a very worthy preacher and good scholar – small hope that you can supply the place', so he had better look for another post by Michaelmas. But Sir Baptist Hicks was sympathetic.

The churchwardens and 85 parishioners then petitioned the bishop to provide 'some sufficient man instead of Mr Walker to officiate the cure' since Walker was 'defective in his place and duety, giving content to none but dayly much dislike to all'. The bishop, though he 'could not justifie him in all respects' thought Walker not dishonest nor lacking in learning (good enough for Charlton) and if he had not agreed to go, would have been glad to let him stay; perhaps £40 might be raised for him as a gift if he left. But neither the Higgs family nor the parishioners were inclined to pay him to leave. So a case was brought and the matter dragged on until June 1624, Walker still at Charlton 'with a full purpose and resolution not to departe or give way to any other person upon any condicion whatsoever'. The bishop, Sir Baptist Hicks and the Higgs family now backed him 'in regard that he contented himself with the olde stipendes'.

But now a new candidate appeared and one with excellent qualifications. Mr Richard Brooke, a Bachelor of Divinity of five years' standing and Senior Fellow of Trinity College, Oxford, was recommended for the post. In 1621 it had been suggested that £55 should be found for the ministers of Cheltenham and Charlton, one at least to be a university graduate, and that after five years this should be raised to £80. If Brooke were appointed then Charlton would have the graduate, but Cheltenham's minister, Mr William Panton, had been there 30 years and surely had a claim. The bishop directed that the £55 should be divided, Panton to have £20 (an improvement on his old stipend) and Brooke £35. Walker tried to put a spoke in Brooke's wheel by writing to Dr Ketle, President of Trinity College, on 5 July 1624:

> Sir, I have for four years space almost compleate, taken much paynes in preaching at Charleton Kings, being heare placed by the Lord Bishop of Gloucester and Sir Baptist Hicks, where I have undergon much persecucon by such amongst us as have withstood all gratious proceedings by my meanes and have set up foolish and prophane vanities, as namely a somerpole on Whitsonday, Churchalls on the Lords daie, dancying in tyme of prayer, a drum ratling about the church in tyme of exercises in the temple, patronising of fornicacon without satisfaccon to the church, putting idlings to the temporall court. And whereas I endevor still to suppresse vice only in my sermons, they are as maliciously bent against me. . . .

The maypole, the Church Ales, and the dancing may have been organised from Old Church House, right against the church! Walker asks Dr Ketle to persuade Mr Brooke not to supplant him, and ends:

> so wishing that John Stubb my neighbour were more wise toward God and less wise to the world, with the remembrance of my duty, I humbly take my leave, leaving you to the protecon of the Highest and resting ever your worships in the Lord to be comended R. Walker.

Stubb must have got a copy of this letter, with its ending, from Ketle himself! Brooke was appointed and licensed on 17 July 1624. On the next Sunday, he appeared at Charlton and ousted Walker. However, the arrangement was that Panton and Brooke should preach on alternate Sundays at Charlton and Cheltenham; and a few weeks later on the Sunday when Brooke was in Cheltenham, Walker entered Charlton church early before Panton and took the service. At Evensong there was a great argument when Brooke came – and Walker took the service again. The following Sunday the church door was kept locked until Brooke arrived, but Walker turned up with some of Mr Higgs's men and tried to push in ahead. He was restrained and John Stubb told him he would 'never more serve in this church unless he could recover it by due course of law'. Walker never intruded again. Soon after this, Panton died and Walker actually asked Sir Baptist Hicks to get him appointed to Cheltenham. But the bishop had already licensed Dr English, to the great annoyance of Hicks who believed that now he had the right to nominate. Stubb assumed that the bishop, who had nominated the last five ministers to Charlton, was the legal patron. This shows how complicated the position was and had been, for both were mistaken. It took another case in Chancery to sort it out; meanwhile the Higgs family refused to pay any stipends at all. The more Stubb and the parishioners 'intreated Sir Baptist, the more violent he was against us'. The court ordered payment of arrears. An interrogatory tells us of the Higgs's reaction.

> Did Toby Packer and Robert Packer gent. two of the plaintiffs then church wardens of Cheltenham and Lodovic Packer, John Packer and Samuel Deighton gent. or any of them come to yor house upon Thursday 3 February last past and show you the said writ of execucon of the said order under seale and read the same unto you and deliver unto you a copy thereof and demand 6–17–6 due unto the said John English for one quarter of a yeere then past by vertue of the said decree and order? Did you thereupon say that they were a company of scabnells or scabnell fellowes or words to the lyke effect? Or what words of disgrace did you then use towards them, [did you] also saye unto the said Lodowicke Packer that he came creeping in unto you lyke a body louse or words to the lyke effect?

However, in the end, the Higgs brothers did pay up. The next step was taken in 1629 when Sir Baptist Hicks, now Viscount Campden, came to an understanding with Jesus College, Oxford. Whenever there was a vacancy at Cheltenham or Charlton, the College was to nominate three men, from whom he or his heirs would pick one. The nominee must be a member of the College, a Master of Arts of at least two years' standing; he was to hold the living for six years only, unless reappointed, and the presentation was to be void if he married or accepted another living. The College was given an endowment of £80 per annum from which a stipend of £40 was to be paid to each minister. This in 1629 seemed an adequate provision even though there were no vicarages and no land on which to build any. The scheme would come into effect in 1637.

Thus for 200 years Charlton was served by men from Jesus College and continued to

8.12 The church wardens' names, Lawrence and Whithorne, can be read on this bell.

8.13 Philip Vaux's tombstone.

8.14 The tomb of Walter Higgs who died in 1698.

have celibate clergy. As graduates they could preach, but would only do so at Morning service: Evening Prayer was said in the afternoon without a sermon.

From 1802 to 1814 the minister was Benjamin Caple Hemming, against whom the churchwardens felt obliged to bring charges in 1811.[15a] In his first six years at Charlton, Hemming had 'omitted to perform divine service in the parish church more than once every Sunday or Lord's Day although it had been the constant and invariable usage of the said Parish from time immemorial to have divine service regularly performed twice every Sunday or Lord's Day, viz. Service and Sermons in the mornings and service without sermons in the afternoons'. He had not catechised the children nor had he taken the special services prescribed by law for 5 November and 29 May each year. All this he had neglected, even though from 1808 the parishioners had been paying him an extra £60 a year for a second sermon. Hemming was corrected and had to pay costs. Presumably he reformed. When the Reverend Robert Williams came here in 1815 the £60 payment was continued, as he recorded in his Parish Book[15b] and he regularly preached at Evensong.

Very soon after the 1629 agreement the parish set about providing pews. In medieval churches people took their own stools or used stone ledges by the walls or knelt at will during service, except when the sacring bell warned everyone to kneel. Now with long sermons, seats were necessary; and *c*.1630–40 St Mary's was equipped and sittings allotted to all existing houses. There were some free seats as well in a west gallery. The date is indicated by considering which houses did and which did not get seats,[16] by bequests *c*.1630 for the reparation of the church, and by the removal of the vaulting in the south transept, for if the Pates memorial is in its original place, as it appears to be, that was done before 1647. St Mary's hung two new (or recast) bells in 1630.

Most Charlton people were royalist in sympathy. A stone to the memory of one Philip Vaux (8.13), slain in a skirmish in 1643/4, records that he died *'pro Rege, Grege, & Lege'* – for the king, the people and the law; and when we got another bell in 1648, we chose the motto 'Fear God, Honour the King'. Walter Higgs's tomb (8.14) records that he 'served His Majestie King/Charles the first A Commission Officer/in his Army', though Higgs survived the war and did not die until 1698. Meanwhile the Commonwealth meant the loss of all

8.15 The Royal Arms in St Mary's Church to celebrate the Restoration of Charles II.

8.16 Graffiti on the porch; some are upside down or sideways.

those customs which in 1624 we had striven to retain. Richard Harrison, a Baptist, was placed here *c.*1650 as 'constant preaching minister' by the Vigilant Committee of the County; he had been a trooper under the Earl of Essex, no graduate, yet he was given the £40 a year provided by Hicks in 1629. When Richard left, he was succeeded by another Baptist, Thomas Harrison, ejected in 1662.

From 1650 to 1660 the parish registers ought to record only births – not baptisms – of children, and in the main this is so, though some eleven parents contrived to get their infants baptised; thus in March 1651 Robert, son of Robert Gale, was 'baptised by Mr Humphrey Randell', then minister of Leckhampton, who was episcopally ordained. But twelve years of Baptist preaching had some effect. After 1660 a few people went on registering the birth, not baptism, of children; and the Baptist church in Charlton Kings probably goes back to the seventeenth century.

For the parish as a whole, the return of Charles II was a welcome event, to be marked by getting a particularly large and fine Royal Arms (8.15) for the church.[17] John Houlder and Samuel Whithorne, the churchwardens, added their names and the date 1660.

8.17 The north side of St Mary's Church showing a boiler house with chimney. (From a print presented to the Society by Bishop Robert Deakin.)

8.18 St Mary's Church, from an illustration in *The Gentleman's Magazine*, 1823.

The Church 1700–1875[18]

Anyone who examines the south porch will be struck by the number of initials cut in the stones, some the right way up, some upside down, some sideways (8.16). One line of text (imperfect) reads 'FROM ALL THAT SIN THAT (US EN)THALLED'. On the church wall is the mark of an older porch roof. It seems that the porch was rebuilt, using the old stone, in 1700, for all initials after that date are the right way up. Perhaps 1700 was also the year in which we had our first church clock. It was bought some time before the first surviving Churchwardens' accounts in 1751; Gale and Goodrich in presenting their two years' account (1752–3) had paid for cleaning the clock on six occasions and for regular winding[19].

The three-decker pulpit removed in the 1860s may have been bought about 1700 too. But the first major alterations to the church came a century later, in 1800. The population of the parish had grown with Cheltenham's, and new houses had been built with no pew or seat in the church. So six parishioners who had no seats applied for a faculty for a gallery, to be appropriated to their use.[20] A south gallery with an external staircase to it was built and the arches raised to improve vision and acoustics. In the same year (according to a later churchwarden, S. H. Gael) the south transept window was enlarged, probably because St Mary's now had an organ and a small mixed choir which sat in the transept. We had one or possibly two stoves to heat the church; a boiler house and chimney are shown built against the north transept in a print of *c.*1820 (before the addition of the north aisle) (8.17).

The congregation was increasing steadily and one extra gallery had not solved the seating problem, which by 1817 was so acute that there was even a proposal to pull down the tower as 'a great inconvenience to the church' and bring tower-space and transepts into the nave.[21] The Vestry passed it – but nothing was done (the bell-ringers saw to that). Then in 1822 John Humphris's plan for a north aisle was accepted. The Lay Impropriator was willing to give up part of the churchyard, which he controlled, in return for ownership of all pews in a new north gallery (gallery seats were preferred to those in the body of the church). The ground floor was kept for 190 free sittings, a stipulation of the Society for Enlarging Churches when making a grant of £300. The whole church was repewed – rather upright pews to meet the requirements of the Society. Those near the west door had higher backs because of draughts. There were two new windows on the north side which were intended to light both the gallery and the body of the church, so they were extra deep; the one that survives has three pleasing heads outside (8.19). At the west end of the nave, two new three-light windows and a central rose window were inserted (8.20). Work on these had been completed by July 1824, when the artist Powell visited Charlton and sketched Old Church House and part of the west end with the rose window. Inside the church, new Royal Arms had been placed over the chancel arch (not quite on centre). Bones dug up when the new aisle was built were reburied under the big yew tree.

Two painted glass windows had been donated to St Mary's, one in 1817 by William Hunt Prinn, the other in 1819 by the minister, the Reverend Robert Williams. Now in 1824–5 the parish paid for a third. This one (and probably the others too) came from Birmingham, from the workshop of the younger Eginton, and cost £111 3s 9d plus 6s 6d carriage.[22] The Egintons, father and sons, produced 'transparencies on glass', rather than true stained glass, and copied dramatic pictures by continental artists. The colours were mainly yellow, light brown and mauve. Examples of such windows are now rare; the 'ornamental glass' is mentioned in the 1865 insurance policy but did not survive the 1877 restoration.

All this work had to be paid for. In 1824 a list was made 'of the owners of Pews in the Body of the Church' and nearly everybody listed paid £6 – a few paid £7 and two were excused: Colonel Prowse (who had succeeded William Hunt Prinn) was allowed two pews free because he had given up 'a large Pew in the south side of the church now made free

8.19 The surviving window in the north aisle from the 1832–4 additions.

8.20 St Mary's Church *c.* 1840 with the three-light windows and the central rose window which was added in 1824. Note also the long building and the workhouse in Church Street and the houses south of the church.

sittings', and Mrs Lovesy had a similar concession. Altogether £371 was raised by this means. Robert Mansell, the churchwarden, was attacked when he maintained that the sittings in the west gallery belonged to the parish, not to any individual; so in 1829 when he gave £50 towards liquidating parish debts, he felt obliged to say that his contribution 'has not been exacted by any vulgar threats or abusive language'. People who had no right to a pew could buy one. George Stevenson of Bafford House purchased pew no. 35 in the south gallery in 1826 for £35; when he left the parish in 1834 he notified the churchwardens that he had sold his pew to General Leighton, who had bought the house. Gael paid £45 for a pew in 1854.[23] Something was done to improve the Sanctuary also. There was probably a new east window; and Alexander Nicholson of East Court gave a silver flagon, 'a rich velvet covering for the Communion table', oak panelling and railing, and 'two Handsome antique chairs'. For these gifts he was warmly thanked in 1828.

An important change occurred in 1800, when the rectory and advowson of both Cheltenham and Charlton were sold by the descendants of Sir Baptist Hicks. Charlton's rectory and right of patronage were bought by John Whithorne who owned Coxhorne House and The Knapp. From him they went in 1816 to his daughter, Elizabeth Lovesy. In 1814 the Commissioners of Queen Anne's Bounty augmented the living from £40 to £64 and St Mary's at long last became totally separated from Cheltenham. But the Lovesys (Elizabeth and her son, Conway Whithorne Lovesy) had complete control over the churchyard and the sale of vaults or common graves; they took all tithes (except those which had been redeemed by landowners), and their only responsibility was repair of the chancel. In 1832 they sold the advowson to Jesus College, thus doing away with the complicated arrangement of 1629. The six-year limitation and the restriction to celibate clergy and members of the College disappeared. For the first time in 1834 Charlton had a Vicar who intended to reside in the parish and almost immediately married a local girl. We don't know how eighteenth-century ministers had managed without a Vicarage – they may have commuted from Oxford. As they were only licensed for a limited period and not inducted, it is very hard to discover so much as their names. But by the early nineteenth century bishops were beginning to frown on non-residents; Williams in 1817 and Watling in 1830 had to ask permission to reside in Cheltenham. Until 1834, ministers had played a negligible part in parish life. It was a shock to St Mary's when the Reverend James Frederick Secretan Gabb asserted himself *vis-à-vis* the parish clerk (who had been making money by selling funeral drapes) and objected to parishioners badger-baiting in the churchyard after Sunday service! Gabb's tomb marks the spot where he seized the badger that Sunday morning and put a stop to the practice once and for all.

Gabb stayed here 41 years and his incumbency was marked by his work for education, both in Charlton Kings and in the town. There were few changes in the church. In 1846 the clock's face was regilded; new stoves were installed in 1856, and about 1859 a new organ was acquired – the parishioners did not pay for it and it seems likely that Gabb did; he had private means and could afford to. Staging for the children's seats was put into the south transept in 1860 and into the north transept in 1864. Lighting was by candles (not lamps) until in 1862 the first gas bill appeared in the churchwardens' accounts, and the pew opener, Mrs Timbrell, received a regular fee for lighting and attending to the gas, a shilling for Sundays when there were two services and sixpence for Thursdays. The gas lighting is mentioned in the 1865 insurance. At some point before 1868, the three-decker pulpit was removed – the resulting row is mentioned in Gabb's obituary[24] and it is said that he would never try to alter the fabric again! As no item in connection with the change occurs in the churchwardens' books, the Vicar probably paid for its replacement. His own views were broadly evangelical and he did not think alterations worth fighting for – one of his curates thought him too easily dissuaded, but his priorities were good schools, not liturgical innovations.

One great change which he did push through was the extension of the churchyard, which formerly terminated where the path goes round the south and east sides of the church. Beyond were houses. To quote Gabb, there were between 3 and 4 thousand inhabitants in the parish and just an acre of churchyard, much of it kept by the Impropriator for brick vaults that he could sell,

> only allowing to the Parishioners as such the right of being buried in one part of the Church Yard. . . The common part of the Church Yard is filled with Graves, so much so, that in making a new Grave there, it frequently happens that the remains of persons previously buried are disinterred. In a few instances, the Impropriator has sold Brick graves in this part also.

The Trustees for the parish charities had pulled down Old Church House intending to give the site for an extension but 'under the Church Building Acts the freehold would on consecration vest in the Impropriator and he intimated his intention to extend thereto the practice of selling Vaults' so 'the Parishioners declined to incur the expense of getting the ground consecrated'. All this comes from a report submitted to the Church Building Commissioners after the passage of new Acts, especially 8 and 9 Vic c.70. The reply still left the ownership question open; so negotiations were started with the Impropriator to find out whether he would accept compensation.

In January 1852 the Vestry was told that Lovesy had agreed to take £200 for his rights; to raise the money, subscribers of 15 or 20 guineas were to have burial places allotted to them in the back or in the front of the existing churchyard, and by the end of February nearly all the money required had been collected. Trustees for the churchyard were appointed and before the end of that year the conveyance had been signed. But the Lovesy family vault was excluded and anyone who had previously bought burial rights had the claim confirmed. Rules were drawn up for the management of the churchyard: 'no coffin unless made of lead or placed within well-cemented stone or brick-work to be deposited less than four feet beneath the surface of the ground'.

Meanwhile a sub-committee set up in 1851 had been looking for extra land. They inspected three sites but the owners refused to sell or asked too much. So the best plan seemed to be to buy up the old cottages adjoining the churchyard. Six were copyhold but

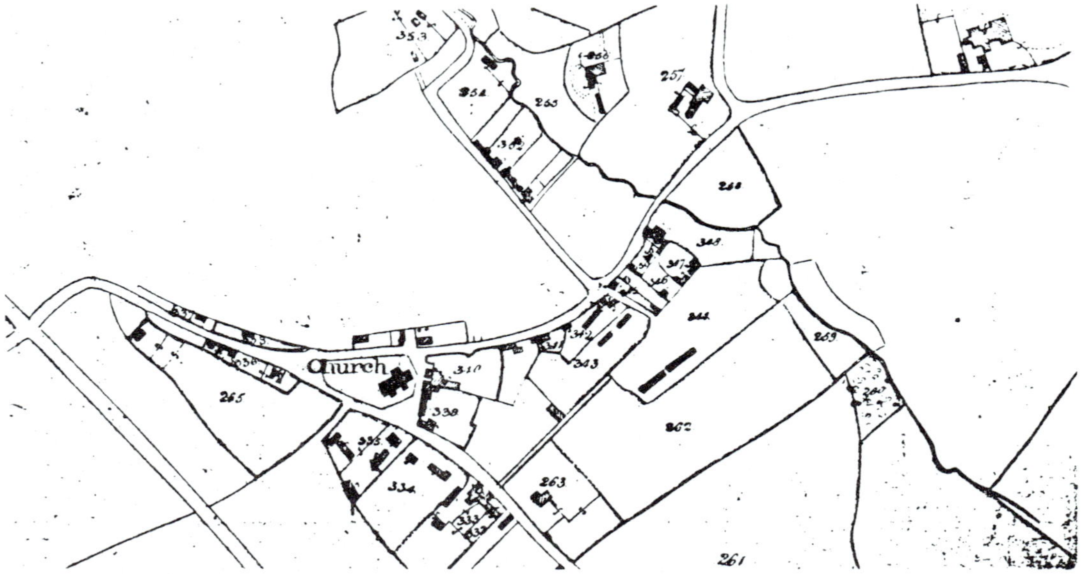

8.21 Tithe map of 1847–8. Note the size of the churchyard and the two houses to the east of the church (TM 340 and 338) which now form part of the churchyard.

the lord of Ashley manor was willing to enfranchise. The parish paid £135 for the first three and £450 for the second three which had land at the back and the right to a pew in church. The last property was freehold, 'an old House called Church Cottage and land adjacent' which the owner would not sell unless 'an eligible investment could be provided for his money'. So S. H. Gael offered to exchange some of his own land near Hewletts Reservoir for Church Cottage; there was to be a money payment as well, and the former owner could keep the building materials. The final purchase price was estimated at £447 10s 0d and £45 for a pew in church. The total cost of the houses was £1032 10s 0d plus expenses and interest charges on money borrowed. In addition, the Old Church House trustees were offered and accepted £19 19s 0d for their empty site. The only problem was the right of way between the two parts of the churchyard; that right was extinguished and New Street substituted. Cutting the road left a triangle of land to the east, on part of which a Vestry Hall was built. This was needed, for since 1850 it had been illegal to hold Vestry Meetings in the church. Finally, the whole churchyard was surrounded by a wall, the lower part stone with iron railings 3 feet 9 inches high between stone piers. The foundations were massive because the whole area is sand, and graves would have to be dug very near the walls. To pay for everything not covered by a rate, eight parishioners lent sums amounting in all to £2000, to be paid off within twenty years by yearly instalments of £100, the order of repayment to be determined by lot.

The Restored Church[25]

The Reverend F. E. Witts had visited Charlton on 22 April 1824, when the alterations were nearly complete, and approved them: 'the whole will be very neat'.[26] 'Neat' was the height of commendation just then; and the parishioners thought they had solved the seating problem in the best possible way. So it came as a shock to them to be told in 1875 (when anyone over 50 remembered the work being done) that galleries in churches were an abomination and must be removed! The new incumbent, Charles Leslie Dundas (1875–83) had come full of zeal to restore a church which he described in a letter to Jesus College as 'very ugly, very uncomfortable, and very badly ventilated'. He and his wife had first seen the church on a wet November day when it seemed extremely gloomy – they did not appreciate any of its architectural features, not even the 1190 west door (not Gothic!).

At a Vestry Meeting held on Easter Tuesday, 18 April 1876, according to the *Parish Magazine* (then in its first year), it was 'unanimously Resolved that the complete restoration of the Church comprising the removal of the Galleries, the extension of the fabric westward by a bay and a half, and the re-seating of the whole floor of the Church, should be carried out as soon as the state of the funds will permit'.[27] In fact, the meeting was very far from being unanimous. Colonel Holmes of Whithorne is said to have jumped on the table and shaken his fist in the Vicar's face! And he was not the only opponent. Gael (speaking as churchwarden at a luncheon given after the bishop had reopened the church) admitted this.

> The opposition which had been made was not in a Spirit of hostility but from a feeling of reverence for old associations connected with their parish Church, which were almost of a sacred character; and also with regard to burial rights. However, the one would in time, no doubt, diminish, and the other had been settled by compromise.[28]

No doubt there was room for change but it need not have been nearly so drastic; blame for this must be shared by Dundas and his architect, John Middleton. A faculty for the work was obtained in January 1877 and removal of the galleries began directly after Easter.

Services continued in the upper portion of the church which was boarded off and seated with chairs. When the children's gallery in the south transept was removed, the piscina there came to light.

The next step was to lift the flooring in the nave, which meant the removal of all the gravestones listed by Bigland. This

> disclosed a state of affairs in connection with the vaults beneath which amply accounted for the unpleasant state of atmosphere which has been for some time notorious in Charlton Church. It was indeed high time that these vaults should be filled in with sand and covered with concrete.[29]

Burials had not taken place inside the church for over twenty years and, according to William James Turner who died in January 1924 aged 80, the real trouble was that the church had got buggy – something quite unmentionable! The sand and concrete raised the level of the floor to that of the ground outside – for the first time there were no steps down into the nave, and some two feet six inches was taken off the height of the chancel arch. The floor under the tower was raised correspondingly. All the gravestones from inside the church were destroyed. Some of those displaced by adding 14 feet at the west end were relocated, others were not. Bones disturbed were re-interred at the south-west corner of the extended churchyard and a willow was planted to mark the spot; it has gone but the place is still indicated by a slight bump. It is understandable that many Charlton people were distressed by this wholesale obliteration of memorials to their forebears.

Nor did they share Middleton's objection to anything not 'Gothick'. They could not prevent his destroying the old west doorway, but they did dig in their heels about the 1824 rose window and in the end he agreed to move it, along with two attendant gargoyles. In the first proposals for restoration it was not intended to alter the two old windows by the south porch, but once work started Middleton got permission to substitute one large window on each side. He also persuaded the parish to let him remove the old nave roof (which he admitted was sound), telling them that an entire new roof would cost no more than an extra 14 feet! This was a loss, historically, but it gave him the chance to substitute a dark oak boarded ceiling. All plaster was removed from the walls. Middleton's new pillars are alternately round and octagonal, and though the effect is restless (as if he couldn't make up his mind which he wanted) the proportions are pleasing. The contractor for the work was Jones of Gloucester.

Lighting was by gas. Ten ornamental brass standards, each with three burners and squat pink glass shades, were installed. Their position can still be traced by the big round holes bored through the ledges of the new pews. The pews were pitchpine and a good deal more comfortable than the previous ones, though they were intended to have 'rug seating' bought from Cavendish House by occupiers.

Dundas dealt tactfully with the opposition and his enthusiasm was infectious. The irate Colonel was asked to be Treasurer of the Restoration Fund and his wife worked a kneeling mat for the Communion rail. Other ladies trained boys for the new choir – for the first time St Mary's was to have a boys' choir and they were to wear cassocks and surplices. Gifts poured in, but noticeably from new residents rather than old Charlton people, and from women rather then men. Mrs Clayton Daubeny of The Grange and her daughters gave the lectern. As the *Parish Magazine* noted:

> It is a handsome work, executed in polished brass and the design is that of a reversible stand supported by four twisted columns (two of them terminating in branched

candlesticks) with a pedestal resting upon four lions. Upon the base Mrs Daubeny has had inscribed very suitable texts.

The church Bible was rebound in two portions to suit the new lectern; and when experience showed that the lectern was too low to be comfortable for the reader, Mrs Daubeny added an oak stand. Mr Bush, a carpenter from Puddingbag Lane (Hambrook Street), designed and made the Litany desk. 'A few friends in Charlton' presented the 'very handsome Brass Altar Desk'. Miss McLeod worked two altar kneeling mats (for servers). Miss Rensch gave a white altar cloth for festivals and Mrs Hunt two new altar books with markers. The Misses Willimott gave the hymnboard. The brass font ewer was bought for £4 6s 0d out of offerings at the Children's Services. The two parish guilds of St Peter and St Mary gave the silver-mounted Cruet.

'Miss Caroline Curry has presented a handsome stone Pulpit [8.22]. It was designed by Mr Middleton in keeping with the architecture of the Tower and carved by Martyn and Emms, and is a striking feature of the Church, to which it is a most welcome and valuable addition.' At first it had no rail. Miss Curry (her elder sister) presented three brass alms basins, and Mrs Winter gave offertory bags.

The restored church was reopened by the bishop on 25 April 1878. Its appearance must have been a surprise to anyone who had not been in touch with the Restoration Committee and not realised the extent of the alterations. The choir vested in the New Street hall (in surplices and cassocks provided by a gift from ladies of the parish), they processed to church singing 'Onward Christian Soldiers' and 'Lift the Strain of High Thanksgiving'; they sang 'The Church's One Foundation' as a retrocessional after the service. The church was decorated with flowers by Miss Abercrombie and Mr Wood of the Cambrian Nurseries. Dundas remarks in the *Magazine* that 'Taking down galleries has increased to a high degree the acoustic properties of the building'; and with plain glass in all the windows the church was certainly much lighter than before. Altogether when 300 parishioners met at a tea in the school-room that afternoon, the general opinion was favourable.

In June 1878 the *Parish Magazine* announced the next step: rebuilding the chancel.

8.22 The pulpit for the restored St Mary's Church, carved by Martyn and Emms.

> It is with great pleasure that we announce that an offer to restore the Chancel . . . has been made by F. Dixon-Hartland Esq in combination with other members of this Family, as a Memorial to the late Mrs Hartland who was so long resident at The Oaklands. . . The Lay Impropriator C. W. Lovesy Esq has kindly given his 'full consent' to our acceptance of the offer.

There was no attempt to enlarge the chancel, but the roof was raised and there were windows in the new north and south walls (instead of a blocked doorway); a new piscina (as well as the ancient one) and oak panelled sedilia were provided. All monuments were removed and repositioned in the nave. The same contractor was employed for this work.

The chancel was dedicated on 7 November 1878 (8.23). Miss Sarah Curry had given 'an exceedingly beautiful Cross for the super Altar . . . worked in brass according to a very handsome design and . . . ornamented with crystals'. It really is a fine piece of workmanship and reflects every gleam of light with dramatic effect. Frederick Dixon-Hartland gave 'two handsome gas standards for the Chancel and a brass altar rail' – this rail, which appears in old photographs of the church, was rather graceful but it was tiresome to clean, and so was replaced in 1956 by an oak rail given by Mrs Littlewood. Mrs Holmes worked a cushion for the sedilia. The third Curry sister, Miss Sarah, gave 'a very handsome linen cloth and napkins fringed with Macramé lace', to replace a cloth dated 1836. Many of the gifts of 1877–8 are still in use over 100 years later.

8.23 The choir and chancel of St Mary's Church decorated for Easter 1879. Note the absence of a pulpit stair and chancel gates and the gas standards in the choir decorated with wreaths.

From his coming here in 1875, Dundas had been working to raise the level of worship and to have more frequent Communions. In 1877 there were 60 Communion services (that is, every Sunday and eight holy days). In January 1878 Dundas could report 'a large increase in congregation particularly among the poorer classes whose presence is heartily welcome'; and on Easter day 1879, in spite of 'unseasonable snow', there were 148 communicants, against 89 the previous year. That autumn there was a week-long parish mission, with special addresses to domestic servants, children, aged persons, invalids, men only, women only, young men, and young women; and many smaller gatherings at places of work – farms, sawmills, yards, laundries – and at private houses.

> On several evenings the clergy and choir (wearing cassocks and carrying lighted tapers) went out into the street singing hymns, and addresses on the Comfortable Words were given at various points – this attempt to 'go out into the highways and hedges and compel them to come in, that My House may be filled' was most successful, crowds of working men thronging into the church, especially on Tuesday evening – a sight never to be forgotten.

By the end of that year, a notice had to be issued: 'As there is now often very little room to spare on Sunday evenings, Children cannot be admitted unless they sit with their parents'; and the Vicar could report 104 celebrations of Holy Communion with 1817 communicants, 'an increase of nearly 50%'. In 1882 there were 208 Easter communicants. All this was not achieved without some cries of 'popish', but Dundas defended his practices as 'the plain teaching of the Church of England'.[30]

In 1880, 'two excellent stained glass windows' were given by William Barwick Cregoe Colmore of Moorend Park in memory of his father, Colmore Frind Cregoe-Colmore, his first wife, Mary (née Owen), and his second wife, Margaret (née Eden). These are the windows at the west end of north and south aisles, and are by Clayton and Bell (Verey); they show Mary Magdalene at the feet of Christ and the women at the Sepulchre. The following year one of the side windows in the chancel was filled with glass given by his brother officers in memory of Lt.-Col. W. H. Newport 'who fell at the Sortie of Deh Khojah on the 16th August 1880 during the Siege of Candahar'. Dundas records it in the *Magazine* without enthusiasm – the design, circles with symbols of the evangelists, was not much to his taste.

The chancel was 'completed' in 1883 by a stained glass window at the east end given by Sir Brook-Kay Bt. in memory of his mother Margaret (which explains why, in addition to St Elizabeth and the Virgin, we have the figure of St Margaret of Antioch with her dragon). 'It need hardly be said that the improvement which it effects in the general appearance of the chancel is very great.' At the same time, as there was no reredos, Miss Caroline Curry gave hangings for the east wall on either side of the altar. 'The Pomegranates and other Embroidery upon them are beautifully worked, as might be expected from their having been executed at East Grinstead', wrote Dundas.

All seemed to be going smoothly. But Dundas foresaw trouble over the National Schools and was hoping for a better living,[31] so in March 1883 he announced his resignation. A presentation was made to him at which he said 'the restored church was to him the dearest place on earth, every stone of which had been laid on, he might say, with sword in hand. . .'. Perhaps this metaphor was only too apt, for once his forceful personality was removed, all the weak points and unresolved problems became apparent.

The Restoration Fund had been exhausted by 1880 and much still remained to be finished. The side aisles had been concreted but not tiled, the south transept was not yet pewed as intended, the organ was giving trouble, the clock was wearing out, Middleton's doors let in draughts, and the north transept (which had not been touched) was reported to be in such a bad state that the chimney and roof might collapse. The vestry was far too small for a choir of 30 boys and men plus clergy. The plaster of the new chancel was of inferior quality, which does not say much for Messrs Jones of Gloucester. The *Magazine* lost money. Worse still, there was a crisis over maintaining the National Schools in School Road. These and the Master's house had been erected in 1872 through Gabb's efforts and it seemed disgraceful to allow Voluntary Schools to be put under a School Board. But the great Agricultural Depression of the 1880s had struck Charlton and there simply was not the money in the parish; in one way or another, everybody was affected. Many who had worked on farms were unemployed, they and their families being supported by wives who took in washing from Cheltenham. A group of ladies raised money with a jumble sale and started cooking penny dinners for the school children. One extra problem, though a temporary one, faced the new Vicar. There was an influx of navvies building the new Dowdeswell Reservoir and provision had to be made for their welfare, in co-operation with their own Missioner.

The new Vicar, Thomas Moore (1883–6) could afford to accept St Mary's because he already had a pension for nearly twenty years' work in India; he wanted to come because he had a brother at All Saints and he thought the Cheltenham climate suited 'Old Indians'. In his letter of application[32] he remarked that he already knew 'some of the more affluent' and that he was 'pretty well known as a good preacher and speaker' in this neighbourhood – he had, in fact, spoken once at Charlton Kings. What he did not say in the letter was that for five years he had been at Minsterley, a rough lead-mining area in Shropshire, and had been crippled by exposure in a snowstorm so that it was impossible for him to walk far to visit. He had not realised the extent or nature of the parish; and he was used to the pace of life in India – he had nothing like Dundas's enthusiasm and optimism. He did make a final appeal to the parish over the schools but by the end of October 1883 they had to be closed until a School Board could be elected. No collection had been taken that year for the Additional Curates' Fund, so the parish lost its £15 grant and our curate was transferred to Holy Apostles.

Moore calculated that the aisles could be tiled for £25, but actually it cost £8 10 0d more than that, and the money for tiling came in very slowly. Rebuilding the north transept was achieved through a timely legacy from Miss Willimott, but as the transept was lengthened to accommodate a small vestry for the choir boys (a sort of wooden box) her £200 was not sufficient. Moore would have liked to 'restore' the south transept and remove the 1800 window but fortunately there was no money for this. There was still not enough seating; Middleton had calculated that the restored church would seat 500 but that figure included seats in the transepts. One solution was to have a Children's Service every Sunday instead of once a month. Vicar and churchwardens agreed that as soon as the bell had stopped ringing empty seats should be free to all comers, but this led to a lot more trouble.

Moore did find a new curate after nine months; and at Easter 1885 when the Vicar was ill, St Mary's had to depend on the curate and on help from neighbouring clergy – even so, Moore was very reluctant to resign. However, 'through the kindness of local gentry and the exertions of Mr Clarke', the churchwarden, debts amounting to £90 were paid and we entered 'the year 1886 nearly clear of debt', a state St Mary's had not achieved for years.

W. J. Mayne (1886–92) came promising the bishop he would maintain the *status quo* – the parish needed time to settle down. His years here were marked by the purchase of a new tower clock for Queen Victoria's Jubilee, and the cleaning of the long-suffering organ: 'an examination of the pipes and other internal fittings has shown them to have been reduced to a desperate condition through wear and want of cleaning and has proved that the work of reparation and purification has not been begun a day too soon'. Money for the organ came in readily and the cracked sanctuary plaster was replaced with white cement at the expense of Mr J. Holder. The Vicar suggested that an iron safe for the records, 'some of them decidedly old', might be paid for by subscription but nothing was done.

Thomas Hodson (1892–1906), a quiet, kind, despondent man who was not strong, worried incessantly over the spiritual state of his people. He had spent his boyhood in Russia and could not understand Charlton's neglect of the Eucharist – he introduced High Church practices for which some were not ready, and he could be provoked into hasty speech which he afterwards regretted. He did not see why Charlton people should object to gifts from a person living outside the parish! In December 1892 an anonymous friend (H. T. Carrington) gave St Mary's a processional crucifix and in the next year Mrs Hodson presented another banner; processions now became quite frequent and it is said that Bush (donor of the Litany desk in 1877) made a point of coming to church whenever there was to be a procession in order to shout 'Idolatory! Idolatory!'. In July 1893 two new bells were bought and two old ones recast, so that St Mary's now had eight.[33] The Gabb memorial window was dedicated in 1894, a new banner was given, and a 'regular worshipper' who lived outside the parish paid for new choir stalls to replace those in use which had always been considered temporary. Now the Vicar began to think of turning the south transept into a chapel and having a light screen between nave and choir, proposals which inevitably caused trouble. One practical alteration of 1898–9 was the enlargement of the clergy vestry and the provision of a separate vestry for the choir, clearing the north transept of 'the unsightly box'.

Until now, Easter Vestry Meetings had been described as 'harmonious'. Those of 1899 and 1900 were so noisy and acrimonious as to achieve mention in *The Times*! They had been reported verbatim in the *Cheltenham Free Press* on 8 April 1899 and 21 April 1900.

Carrington (who had presented the cross and the choir stalls) now wanted to give an elaborate screen designed by Henry Prothero (Middleton's successor) which, put across our narrow arch, would have had almost the effect of an ikonostasis. Anyone interested may study the plan,[34] which started with four feet of solid wooden panelling, then four feet filled in with vertical bars at three to a yard, then three feet of dense tracery and finally two feet and six inches of canopy. A very awkward adjustment of the tracery was needed to fit it into the space available, and the design involved new pulpit steps. In 1899 the proposal was to fix this screen between nave and choir; in 1900 to place it between choir and south transept so that the parish could judge what the effect would be. Carrington thought this could be done without going to the expense of a faculty. Many objected to both schemes. There were those who disliked the design as too heavy, saying it would make the church darker; those who thought it would cut choir and clergy off from the congregation; those who said that if St Mary's needed a screen we should pay for it ourselves; and those who condemned it as popish. It was a first step towards a chapel in the south transept, where the Vicar could have 'an altar and candles which he would crawl behind the screen to worship'! Grievances totally irrelevant to the matter in hand were raked up; and Hodson was provoked into making several very unfortunate remarks – the Vicar's supporters were as noisy as his opponents. In the end the screen was totally rejected. Yet the same donor was permitted to give St Mary's a reredos less than one year later! But the sanctuary had never belonged to the parish and the pink marble arches and white alabaster figures were to be carved by a Charlton man, W. H. Fry. His work deserves more attention than it generally gets; within the conventional Gothic niches, the representations of the Annunciation, Ascension, and Deposition, flanked by evangelists, are treated very simply in an un-Victorian manner (8.24). The silver choir cross was given in 1901, by Arthur Winkley.

8.24 The reredos carved in 1901 by W. H. Fry.

In 1902 and 1903 Sir Frederick and Lady Dixon-Hartland gave oak screens to go across the north and south transept entrances; these too were carved by Fry. The 1877 pulpit had had no rail to the steps; one had been given in 1896, but this was now replaced by one of intricate ironwork given by W. Price. The improvements of 1901–3 were completed by the sale of the old organ and purchase of a new one. The old one which dated from *c.*1859 was sold for £80 to Churwell Mission church near Leeds, where it was still in use in 1986. The new organ cost the huge sum of £793 and was by W. Hill of London. It is still remembered with regret for its lovely tone, but its pipes and pumping handle nearly filled the north transept. And now the time was ripe for the introduction of a daily Eucharist which has been maintained ever since.

Objectors in 1899 had complained that the church was getting darker; this was an unfortunate result of new windows, the 'Armour of God' window given in memory of Colonel Holmes and his family in 1895, the 'Raising of Jairus' daughter' window given in memory of Edith Vassar-Smith in 1896, and about the same time the Daubeny window, 'As in Adam all die. . .'. Design-wise, the best window in the church is that given by Lady Norman in memory of her husband General Norman who died in December 1899, but as this is in the south transept it can only be seen at close range; it would be better at the end of a long vista. The last two windows in the nave were filled in 1911 and 1914 and completed the 'dim religious light' desired by Middleton and his contemporaries.

In 1906 came Edgar Neale (1906–37), a Vicar whose most obvious characteristic was his enjoyment of everything. Neale was not afraid to speak out when he thought something was wrong, but equally he was warm in praise when things went well. Though a strong Anglo-Catholic himself, he was to make no changes until he had been here seven years, but at once, under his direction, the choir began to improve out of all recognition.

In 1908 the Dixon-Hartlands offered to give chancel gates and wanted to place a memorial in the church. The churchwarden, Major Dudgeon, still hoped for a big wooden screen; Hartland insisted that this was not what he had offered to give. Meanwhile, 'a lady parishioner' was 'very anxious to erect alabaster and marble panels in front of the ends of the oak stalls'! While this correspondence was going on, the memorial 'The Angel of the Resurrection' by Wade arrived in Charlton. Hartland wrote:

> I am very glad to hear the statue has safely arrived and that you think it beautiful. It will be a great ornament to your church, and if you treat it in the same manner as one by the same sculptor in a church in the Midlands, it should bring you in some revenue . . . I suggest that you do not allow it to be shown to strangers except at 6d a head to church funds but of course that is as you like.

The Angel was put into an alcove formed by the tower arch and what had been the vestry door – a new door was made further east. She is not to everyone's taste but as a rather better-than-average example of early twentieth-century sculpture, she will find her place given time. The final design for chancel gates was by Lady Hartland herself and was executed by Messrs Hart, Pearce and Co.; the order was given by her immediately after her husband's death.

The new Vicar's interests are seen in a suggestion in May 1909 that the organ bellows might be blown electrically, taking power from the tram cables. But as the nearest point was 240 yards away and the supply would be liable to interruption each time a fault occurred on the tramway (which wasn't rare) the Borough Electrician advised against it. So the church had to wait for an electric blower until Neale had been here 21 years.

The chapel in the south transept was made possible in 1911, when Miss Hay furnished it in memory of Louisa S. Harris; the reredos carved by Alfred George Washbourne Hailing was superimposed on the original table in 1938. A screen between the chapel and choir had been given in memory of Elizabeth Maude Bullock who died in 1923.

The present head on the churchyard cross was given by Miss Gabb in 1913; it was said that if anyone else had offered it the parish would have refused, and to placate some, the old sundial head was placed on a new pillar near the north entrance to the churchyard.

Most churches, chapels and organisations such as Friendly Societies in the nineteenth century had their banners to carry in procession; and St Mary's had had banners since 1875. Four new ones were given in 1910: the choir banner by Major Shewell, the Guild of St Mary by its members, the Guild of St George by the Vicar, and the Guild of the Holy Name by the curate, 'Bumps' Gardner.

Members of the congregation had worked new frontals from time to time; there were new green and violet ones in 1908, and the pomegranate one, still in use, was finished after more than two years' work in 1913. On Easter Day 1914 the servers appeared for the first time in scarlet cassocks and lace cottas. But Neale did nothing about vestments for himself until two sets were offered and accepted in 1915, the gift of Mrs Percy Shewell-Creek, Miss Hallam and others. He said of this: 'I never make changes, I hope, in a hurry. I have preferred first of all to teach the Catholic doctrine of the Sacrament of the Altar as faithfully as I know how and to waive for a time the question of proper "ornaments" of the celebrant.' Even then, he used the vestments for Choral Eucharist and processions, but the surplice for all plain celebrations.

In 1914–15 the brass gas standards were replaced by three-light inverted incandescent pendants suspended from the arches; then in 1922, when electricity came to the village, electric light was installed in memory of William Henry Bagnall of Bafford House.

Meanwhile in 1917 the vestry had been enlarged at the expense of Mrs Percy Shewell-Creek. The rood, designed by George Ryland, was erected in 1920 as a War Memorial, and in 1924 an aumbrey in the chancel (now in the chapel) was given in memory of Tom Fry and Walter Fry – the latter had been verger and sexton for 21 years. In 1938 a baptistry was created by the removal of two short pews at the southwest corner and the font was brought from its old place at the west door. This was done as a memorial to Neale and his 31 years as Vicar. An elaborate font cover previously given by the Reverend Nigel Nash and his wife was discarded. Middleton's draughty doors had been partially cured *c.*1886 by the erection of an inner porch at the west door – it was in pitchpine with purple bubble glass. This was replaced about 1940 by the present oak door given in memory of Georgina Helen Heber-Cooke who died in 1932.

There are stories innumerable about Neale, his total commitment and his joy, his love of music and missions, pageantry and processions, above all his love for St Mary's ('a young cathedral'), his choir (the best on earth, even when they misbehaved and made him lose his temper), his people. Some of these stories have been collected[35] but they will only convey a faint impression of the man to those who did not know him.

The next Vicar, Michael Hollis (1937–42) spent little time here – he was a Chaplain to the forces from 1940 to 1942. He left to become Bishop of Madras (1942–7) and then Bishop in Madras and first Moderator of the United Church of South India (1947–54). At St Mary's he was succeeded by Walter Wardle (1942–7), afterwards Archdeacon of Gloucester; Robert Deakin (1947-73), later Bishop of Tewkesbury until his death in 1985; David Yerburgh (1973–85), and Graham Bryant (1985 to date).

Vicarages and the Living

The first Vicarage was Pear Tree Cottage (now Courland) in Brookway Lane, acquired as a parsonage in 1838. It was a recent building but had been squeezed in between other houses; the whole site was only an eighth of an acre (890 square yards) so there was almost no garden, and to quote the report on it by Frederick Waller, the Diocesan Architect, in 1875:

> the House was originally intended for the residence of the Vicar of the Parish but it has not been so used for many years. It is in every way undesirable as such, it is upon a very small piece of ground and overlooked on all sides and with very bad approaches.

There were two moderate-sized sitting rooms, a small entrance hall, staircase and WC, 'this latter in all ways most objectionable', kitchen and offices, four bedrooms, a cheese room and store room upstairs; a very small stable and coach house 'closely attached'; 'adapting it to the requirements of a Clergyman of the present day . . . would seem to me an almost impossible task', wrote Waller. Gabb had lived at Balcarras since *c.*1858 and had let Pear Tree Cottage; but for the last two years had not been able to find a tenant.[36] At that time, Holy Apostles had been built but was not yet separated from St Mary's. When that happened, Pear Tree Cottage would be outside St Mary's parish. Dundas in 1875 was living for the time being at Moorend House.

So the first Vicarage was sold for £544 8s 7d and Dundas was without any official residence. He was forced to buy Hearne Villa in Church Street, and of this house he wrote in 1882 to the Principal of Jesus College:

> I am at present residing in a small house which I was compelled to purchase myself, but

which is not at all suited for the purpose and is moreover altogether too small for my family – I have now lived in this cottage of my own for seven years.

Moore rented a house; all we know about it is that when he left his successor reported: 'the house occupied by the late incumbent is now without an adequate supply of water, it having failed during his tenancy, and there is no prospect of this want being remedied'. For a time Mayne had to live outside the parish in Bellevue House, London Road. 'This however I hope is only temporary, as I have taken two small houses which will I hope serve as a makeshift (although somewhat inconvenient).' These two houses were nos 1 and 2 Lyefield Villas in Copt Elm Road, which still show inside that they were once linked.

A Vicarage Appeal had been launched in 1882; and by 1889, with a grant, the parish had the money to buy The Grange in Horsefair Street for £2240 plus costs. About 2½ acres of its land had already been sold to Edwin Attwood, but still another 2½ acres went with the house, and there was a coach-house and stabling. Hodson, with private means and a large family, found this exactly suited to his needs. But Neale in 1906 had nothing to live on except his stipend and to him The Grange was a dreadful liability, even though it was let to Mrs Heberden for about £60 a year. Dilapidations, for which he was responsible, swallowed up more than his Easter Offering every fifth year. Neale lived in a very modest way in Cirencester Road and when Mrs Heberden died, the parish was glad to sell its white elephant for a mere £1474. It was pulled down in 1933. So when Hollis came in 1937 he had nowhere to live, and for a time he occupied one of the small bungalows opposite Charlton Park drive. Then The Wold was bought and was the Vicarage from 1938 to 1965. Finally a comparatively new house in Church Street was acquired and enlarged.

If providing a suitable Vicarage had been a problem, increasing the stipend was even more difficult. In 1814, when Charlton finally became independent of Cheltenham, the stipend was raised from £40 to £64 a year. An attempt to raise it again was made in 1885 but was frustrated because the Ecclesiastical Committee for Endowments would not make a grant unless the patronage were transferred to the bishop and Jesus College demanded £300 for it; besides, our population was 3950, and to qualify for a grant it needed to be 4000! However, in 1886 the College agreed to transfer the patronage to the bishop as a free gift, provided £100 were raised to increase the endowment and this sum the Vicar W. J. Mayne was willing to pay himself so that we should be eligible for a grant from other church societies; he hoped the Endowments Committee would then help towards the new Vicarage and in fact £500 was applied towards this end.[37] The actual transfer of the advowson was not achieved until June 1888.[38] Hodson launched an Augmentation Appeal in 1899. He explained the incumbent's income as £65 2s 4d (including grants), about £40 in fees and about £50 in Easter Offerings. As he pointed out, offerings were variable and burial fees likely to diminish as the churchyard became full.[39] But this fund had to compete with concurrent appeals for the organ and for mission rooms, as well as the usual missionary efforts (to which St Mary's then contributed roughly double what it spent on church expenses). To the parish, the Augmentation Fund seemed less urgent. Still, about £500 was collected, which would bring in around £30 a year. In 1908 the Ecclesiastical Commissioners refused to help because with fees and Easter Offerings the Vicar was getting just over £200! Hodson had bought up the tithes in the hope that they could be acquired to help the living, but a chance to buy them from his trustees after his death in 1915 was missed.[40] But then several welcome gifts came along. Mr and Mrs Bagnall gave £100 in 1916 to mark their Golden Wedding; Ralph Walker left £100 to the Vicar which was used to increase the stipend; and Mrs Jane Holmes's bequest of an annuity of £50 brought the total to nearly £200 in hard cash. In 1924 the Ecclesiastical Commissioners added £21 a year, and the £200 mark was topped. After Neale's death in 1937, the parish raised £1300 in his memory, £1135 to increase the living and the rest for the baptistry.[41] It seems a pity this could not have been done in his lifetime to have given him a little comfort (but he was so generous that most of the extra would have been given away).

The Vestry Hall or Parish Centre[42]

Until 1850, when an Act was passed 'to prevent the holding of Vestry or other meetings in Churches', all parish meetings were held in the nave of the church as the only public building available. Smaller meetings took place in the church vestry and so meetings of influential parishioners representing all the ratepayers became known as Vestry Meetings. If these were no longer to be held in church, another building had to be provided and the Act permitted churchwardens and overseers of parishes with a population exceeding 2000 to purchase land and to build. In Charlton Kings there was a suitable plot of land available, part of the land bought in 1854 to extend the churchyard and make a new road. The Poor Law Board approved the conveyance of a triangular piece on the east side of the new road (New Street) to the churchwardens and overseers at a cost of £80 and gave permission for £600 to be raised for erection of a hall, and this was built by early in 1857. It was intended to be used as a Reading Association and Working Men's Club when not required for Meetings. When a Board of Health took over the government of the parish in 1862 it met in the Vestry Hall. Improvements were discussed and better heating put in, but major schemes for enlargement and alteration came to nothing.

The Local Government Act of 1894 divided the civil from the ecclesiastical function of the parish, and because the Vestry Hall stood in the name of the Overseers of the Poor, as well as of the Churchwardens, ownership now vested in the Board of Guardians. This left the old parish and the new Urban District Council homeless. The UDC decided not to purchase the old Hall, but to build a new one on London Road; and St Mary's could not afford to buy but had to make do with a corrugated iron hut erected in 1902 on land leased for the purpose from Cooper's Charity (this parish room is now the Nursery School). So the Hall was only used for occasional meetings. Parish parties were held in the St Clairford Hall above the Working Men's Club. By the early 1920s, the old Vestry Hall was nearly derelict. However, the need for a proper parish hall was felt and General R. G. Burton pressed for the acquisition and extension of the old Vestry Hall because it was so close to the church. So in June 1926 the Ministry of Health authorised the sale by the Board of Guardians for £275, and this whole sum was given by Lady Dixon-Hartland. It was decided to extend the hall by one bay and add a kitchen and cloakrooms; Billings the builder's tender of £1098 was accepted, and Lady Dixon-Hartland gave another £265 towards the cost. It was formally opened by her on 20 April 1927 as St Mary's Hall (8.25).

In 1983 a further scheme for improvement was drawn up by the Parochial Church Council and after a public meeting the plan was adopted and the full cost raised. The hall was re-opened as a Parish Centre by the Bishop of Tewkesbury, Robert Deakin, on 30 March 1985.[43]

Holy Apostles Church

The idea of building a new church and dividing the ancient parish was mooted early in the 1860s, and in 1862 Charles Cooke Higgs donated a piece of his land for the site and £1000. The triangular plot between the London and Cirencester Roads would provide a commanding position for a splendid Gothick church, a landmark when seen from a distance and lavish within. Higgs thought that subscriptions would come in readily since the area was being developed with houses 'of the better sort'; he may have been influenced by the convenience of a church next door to his own residence, Langton House. However, the scheme did not meet with much response. House-building was proceeding more slowly than expected (few of the Battledown plots were taken up at first). Many people would have preferred a site in Ryeworth or Ham and had been asking for a church to serve those more isolated areas. Higgs's site would be no nearer than the old parish church. Others feared that if a new parish were created they would lose their burial rights in the churchyard at St Mary's; the new church was to have no burial ground, and there was as yet no public cemetery. Many assumed that Higgs was giving a new church as reparation for the evil doings of his ancestress Mrs Badger! So little money came in and eventually Higgs paid the whole £7000 himself. John Middleton's plan for the church is dated 1865 and countersigned by Higgs alone. The foundation stone was laid in March 1866.

Holy Apostles was to be the nineteenth century's ideal of a church and Higgs spared no expense even though he found himself bearing the whole cost. To quote Verey:

> the interior has a nave with five-bay arcades with pointed arches, deeply cut foliated capitals, Apostles in roundels in the spandrels . . . and a very lofty steep-pitched roof. The chancel arch has Middleton's usual band of two different coloured stones on short polished granite shafts supported by flying angels. In the chancel two-bay arcades, a five-sided apse with diapered walls, a stone and marble reredos, richly cusped windows, and a painted roof.

8.25 The Vestry Hall (now the Parish Centre) was reopened in 1927 as St Mary's Hall. *Back row*: Messrs Freegard (churchwarden), Gurney Catherine, Peacy, Hamlett (undertaker), Fry (churchwarden), Villar (architect), McLaren, Billings (builder); *front row*: Miss Bullock, Mrs Freegard, Gen. R. G. Burton, Lady Dixon-Hartland, Revd Edgar Neale (Vicar), Miss Smith and Mrs Fry.

8.26 Holy Apostles Church in 1871 before the school had been built.

Bands of contrasting stone can be obtrusive in a church but here the soft blue and cream tones are in keeping with the theme of Nature expressed in the flowers, leaves, fruit, birds and beasts carved on the capitals and corbels of the nave and in the diaper work of the apse. One unusual feature is an emphasis on Reformation history; heads of leaders of the Reformation, here and on the continent, act as supports for the head-moulds on the windows of north and south aisles. Throughout the church the quality of the carving by Boulton and Sons is outstanding. The acoustics are excellent and the building is sympathetic to music. The outside is less happy; the rusticated stone favoured by Middleton for all his building work now seems clumsy. The tower and spire he designed were never built. Altogether, Holy Apostles is a more satisfactory church inside than out (8.27), but that (if there has to be a more and less) is as it should be.[44]

The new church was not finished until 1871; it was opened by the Bishop of Gloucester on 5 June 1871 but was not consecrated for another fourteen years. During that time it was still subject to St Mary's and had no full time clergy. Services were taken by the Reverend Frederick Gowson Potter and his successor F. H. Nevill, who combined this with conducting a boys' school at Ham House; they were assisted by Albert Charles Higgs, a relative of the founder. After Dundas came to St Mary's in 1875, the curate-in-charge at Holy Apostles had no easy time between Higgs (who assumed he owned the church) and Dundas (determined as Vicar to have the last word). But Higgs died in 1884 and on 2 June 1885 the new church was consecrated and the new parish became totally independent. The parochial division ran along the Chelt, then up Copt Elm Road, part of Greenway Lane, Ashley Road and Oakley Road, leaving Ryeworth and Ham in the old parish, as much cut off as ever.

8.27 The interior of Holy Apostles church in 1966, before it was damaged by fire.

While Holy Apostles was attached to St Mary's, some information about its affairs can be found in the *Parish Magazine* of the mother church. So in the June issue of 1885, the Vicar, Thomas Moore, wrote:

> On Tuesday the 2nd of June, Holy Apostles Church erected as a free gift to Charlton Kings by the munificence of the late Mr Higgs will be consecrated for divine service by the Lord Bishop of the Diocese. This beautiful Church contains 650 sittings of which 250 are declared to be free for ever. We would much prefer all seats were free, as 250 seats is but a scant allowance for the 1,500 poor who inhabit the district assigned, but the Clergy must eat if they are to preach and to eat they must have an income, and the income at Holy Apostles, also secured by the generosity of Mr. Higgs, will only pay for the rent of the Vicarage.

At £240 per annum the living was quite a good one in terms of the day. It has remained a Trustee Church and not short of money for maintenance, though the bulk of the pews were still let in 1910, when seats at the back were marked 'These seats are reserved for the Poor of the Parish'. The advowson (after the first presentation) was vested in the bishop. Incumbents have been E. J. Bower (1885–9), F. H. T. Curtis (1890-7), D. Harrison (1897–1903), H. A. Corke (1904–19), A. H. Rhodes (1919–38), R. H. Northcott (1939–44), C. Peers (1944–66), P. S. M. Walton (1966–81) and Malcolm Duthie (1981 to date).

Holy Apostles has always been a 'middle of the road' church and since 1875 has provided for those who did not care for the High Churchmanship of St Mary's. However, some of the original arrangements at Holy Apostles were found wanting: there was no proper choir vestry and the font was at the top of the church. The only early *Parish Magazine* to survive, that for 1891, reports the decision of the Vestry Meeting to apply for a faculty to move organ and font, and this had been done by September.

> *The Baptistry* The Font now stands at the West end of the Church, protected from accident by brass standards and crimson cord. The Drawing for the completion of the Baptistry by Mr Higgs the Architect, may be seen at the entrance of the Church.

The re-erection of the organ had begun. Meanwhile in August the Vicar was appealing for 'Memorial Windows, in memory of loved relatives' and

> two handsome Metal Screens (one in the place of the old curtains) – to screen the Choir Vestry, as it is unseemly that the robing of our large Choir should be done in sight of a part of the Congregation.

Such a screen was erected in 1893; and a splendid vestry was built at the west end of the church in 1934.

In 1970 the chancel and organ were struck by lightning and the resulting fire destroyed the chancel roof, but thanks to the strength of Middleton's ceiling, the fire did not get through into the sanctuary. This provided an opportunity for some rearrangement. The chancel has been screened off with a glass screen and has become a Lady Chapel with 40 seats. In the nave there is a new oak Communion Table, choir stalls, and semicircular oak communion rail (these can all be removed when the church is used for concerts). Above them is a hanging cross made of unpolished aluminium alloy. The font has been moved to the north side and the organ to the south side. The church was reopened after the fire in June 1972.

The first Vicarage was at Langton House, and the ground between church and house is marked on one plan as a site for a Vicarage. Instead, part was used in 1924 to build a parish hall to replace the one in Rosehill Street which had served since 1906 (the old Coltham Fields school room). Various houses including Charlton House have served as Vicarages.

The Baptist Church

During the Commonwealth period, a Baptist named Harrison, trooper to the Earl of Essex, was placed at Charlton Kings by the Vigilant Committee of the County. He was, presumably, the Richard Harrison 'constant preaching minister' mentioned in 1650 who was receiving the £40 per annum stipend arranged by Sir Baptist Hicks in 1629. From Charlton he moved to Netherton near Fairford and Maiseyhampton, and his place here was filled by Thomas Harrison, ejected in 1662, who seems to be the man found preaching in London in the 1670s as an Anabaptist.[45]

These men left their mark on Charlton and after the Restoration there were four families who refused to have their infants baptised. The children of William Randle, William Welch, Francis Crumpe and Richard Daves were entered in the register as 'born' simply, down to 1671/2; and this suggests that the Dissenting Meeting in the home of William Welch, registered at Quarter Sessions in 1690, was a Baptist meeting. There were 16 Anabaptist families here in 1735 and 1743.[46]

After that, private houses were licensed from time to time, including Lawrence Dyer's in 1810 and John Bridgeman the shoemaker's in 1828 and 1834; Bridgeman may very well have been a Baptist for the family later insisted on burial without rites. But when Lieutenant John Burgh Rochfort came to settle in Charlton Kings in 1865 and started preaching in a house in Moreton Terrace, the congregation he collected did not call themselves anything more specific than Christian. Rochfort was then living at Bafford Cottage (now Bafford Grange), and as numbers increased meetings were transferred to the

8.28 The interior of the Baptist Church (before it was rearranged at the time of its Centenary in 1975).

garden or Coach House at Bafford. After that they took over the Old Chapel of the Free Methodist Church, spoken of in Church minutes as 'Charlton Kings Chapel', possibly in Ryeworth. It was in that chapel that on 27 December 1871 the congregation of 25 was formally constituted as a Church of Christ, with a trust deed embodying seven articles of doctrine. Membership was to involve an open profession of repentance and of faith in Christ, evidence of a holy life, and unfeigned consent to Articles 3 and 6 – the doctrines of Atonement and the Trinity. By 1875 the church was sufficiently established to buy land for their own chapel; and on 25 June 1875 William Henry Hall of Barns Hay and his mortgagee conveyed to five trustees for £245 'all that messuage or tenement, baker's shop, yard, garden, buildings, and erections thereon – now or late in the occupation of Charles Wheeler baker, John Belcher, and Henry Baylis, on the south side of the highway or street called Church Street'. The trustees were John Burgh Rochfort of Charlton Kings Esq, Charles Wilson, John Lance of Cheltenham draper (founder of Lance's shop), Henry Beard of Cheltenham grocer, and William Cleevely of Charlton Kings builder. On the site of the three old cottages (shown in the print of 1824 on page 53) the trustees were to erect a chapel or meeting house, vestry room, school rooms and offices, as a place of public worship. A committee was appointed to get plans and estimates for the school room, class room and vestry.

Money to buy the site was raised by a mortgage to the Building Society; and money to build the chapel had been collected by 17 April 1876, when the Church and Deacon's

Minute book[47] records 'heartfelt thanks to God for his great goodness in sending "the silver and the gold" to pay for the building of the Chapel', while at the same time expressing 'a hope that the money borrowed for the purchase of the site may be repaid at no very distant date'. All the building was done by William Cleevely (8.28). The chapel cost £488 17s 10d (including the architect's fee) and the School Rooms £85. The chapel was lighted by gas from the start, though the original fittings were replaced in 1882 as 'too heavy and out of character with the building'. Instead, 'four new six-jetted circular fittings' were installed. In the same year, the trustees purchased for £40 an adjoining plot owned by Mrs Buckle (the land at the back of the shop which is now a hairdresser's). This enabled the school room to be extended to 20 feet in length and a new class room 18 feet by 14 feet to be built. The work was done by Cleevely, and the whole, plus repainting the chapel, cost about £150. Nothing is said in the minutes about heating; but in 1891 a proposal to heat the building 'by Hot Water on the Low Pressure System' was adopted; and in 1900 the pipes from the well under the chapel were renewed.

William Cleevely had been responsible for all the building; he was one of the five trustees of 1875 and one of the four Elders chosen in 1876. But in 1879 he and his wife found themselves obliged to resign their membership of the church over Article 7 (not originally compulsory): the eternal punishment of the wicked. A Sunday School teacher, Mr Merrit, had been removed from the list for teaching that the future punishment of the damned would not be eternal; and this caused Cleevely to express 'his sorrow that the question had been brought forward, as, if it came to the point, he himself did not accept "the everlasting punishment of the wicked" '. He and his wife Emma and Mr Telling left over this; and the Cleevely family transferred their allegiance to Cambray.

Until 1887 the Chapel had not been attached to any denomination; but now the question of its being registered for solemnisation of marriages arose. Rochfort as Pastor:

8.29 John Burgh Rochfort who started the Christian group which became the Baptist Church in Charlton Kings.

> stated that the Chapel could not be licensed for the celebration of Marriages until duly registered and that the Registration fee was 2s 6d. He said that he thought there would be a decided advantage in having it done and also in joining some regular Denomination; he himself would prefer the Baptist Denomination and he believed that a great many more of the Members would also. The change, he explained, would not affect those at present members of the Church, whose position would be unchanged, but new members joining would have to be baptised before becoming Church members; other Christians and those who belonged to other Churches would still be admitted to the Lord's Table.

A special meeting was held on 23 May 1883 and the changes were agreed. Henceforward, the Elders were to be called Deacons in accordance with Baptist practice.

The first Baptistry was in the school room. When the duties of the Chapel Keeper were set out in November 1888 these included lighting fires, turning off gas, cleaning windows and getting the rooms ready for meetings; and

> on the occasion of a Baptizing Service it will be the Chapel Keeper's duty to prepare the Rooms and see that the baptistry is properly filled. The sum of 1s to be allowed by the Church for this and 1s for clearing up afterwards and drying the dresses and 6d for each female dress got up [washed and ironed]. The Rooms (School and Class) to be washed out once every month from 1st Oct–1st April and once every three months from 1st April to 1st October.

The salary for the ordinary duties was £6 a year.

8.30 The Reverend Garnet Powell and members of the Baptist Church at the time of their 75th Anniversary.

In 1888 another problem arose. Rochfort on account of ill health wanted to resign the position of Pastor. The Pastor of Cambray agreed to undertake some of the duty, provided it did not interfere with existing arrangements, and was to receive £12 a year. But the Church at Cambray accepted no responsibility for Charlton Kings and claimed no control; in practice, this and later arrangements for a shared ministry had limited success. Oversight of the church at Charlton rested principally on Mr A. W. Ryland until his death in 1932; the organ installed in 1934 was a memorial to him. Since 1938 the church has had permanent full-time Ministers without any significant break. A list is given in the *Centenary Handbook* – H. W. Cladburn (1905–7), F. Wyan (1918–21), W. R. Wilson (1926–35), H. Lloyd (1938–46), Garnet Powell (1947–57), C. O. Price (1957–63), R. J. Webber (1965–74) and Basil Hill (1976 to date). A Manse was bought in 1955, and a new one built in Grange Walk in 1975.

A new Church Constitution was approved in December 1966 and came into effect on 1 January 1967. Under it, the Church still remains open to all Christians who wish to share Communion. There has, in fact, been only one occasion on which a group from another church was barred. This was in 1880 when it was resolved

> that a social tea meeting be held the first convenient opportunity . . . for Church Members and all professing Christians who sit down with us to the Lord's Table as well as other professing Christians in Charlton *excepting* members of the Primitive Methodist Chapel at Ryeworth.

8.31 The Mothers' Union at Bafford House in 1898. This branch was formed in 1892.

The reason for this exclusion is not known, although it is possible that the Primitive Methodists had been responsible for this congregation leaving Ryeworth in 1875. Tea Meetings were always held on Mondays (the day on which the dirty laundry was collected and put to soak, before the labour of the week began for most of the women), and the amount of food bought is stated on some occasions. Thus on 25 October 1880, when 30 were expected, they provided 15lbs of cake (7lbs currant, 8lbs seed), a quartern loaf, 8 Brunswick loaves at 3d, 1½lbs of butter, ¾lb of tea, 5lbs of sugar, ¼lb of coffee, and ½ gallon of milk. They must have liked their tea sweet. Such social gatherings helped to hold the church together.

A scheme for refurbishing the church and replacing pews by chairs was adopted in 1963 when a new pulpit was given in memory of W. H. Ryland (son of A. W. Ryland). Then to celebrate the centenary in 1975, a more radical rearrangement was decided on and at the same time the old school room was replaced by the Carey Hall and another meeting room. The architect for this was Colin Bolt.

Methodism in Charlton Kings

There have been a number of attempts to introduce Methodism to Charlton but for one reason or another none have lasted very long except the Primitive Methodist chapel in Ryeworth which had a life span of 81 years.

House Meetings

A Circuit plan of 1822 (referred to in Bancroft Judge's *The Origin and Progress of Methodism in Cheltenham* of 1912) indicates that there was a 'preaching place' in Charlton Kings; this may have been in the house of Oliver Watts, licensed as a place of worship in that year. Another house, John James's, was licensed in 1836 and may also have been for Methodists.

Church Piece Chapel

In 1828 a group of Cheltenham men bought land in Church Piece, on the corner of Horsefair Street and Grange Walk. The site measured 22ft x 74ft. To raise the money to build they had to arrange a mortgage and in 1836 the mortgagee foreclosed. The *Cheltenham Chronicle* for 22 December 1836, in speaking of the sale of the building for a parish school, calls this 'Charlton Chapel (now occupied by the Wesleyan Methodists)'; but it seems more likely that it was an offshoot of Rowland Hill's Cheltenham Chapel built in 1808–9. Nothing is known about its activities during the nine years of its existence.

Cudnall Chapel

A new start was made immediately by ten Cheltenham tradesmen who acquired a plot 24ft x 52ft on the north side of Cudnall Street. It was surrendered to them at Ashley Manor court on 14 May 1838, together with 'the chapel now erecting by the parties to whom the surrender is made'.[48] The building was 'enlarged' in 1846; perhaps the galleries were added then. We know that the chapel had galleries, for the Sunday School had to be held in the gallery while the church was being repainted in 1861; and this explains how they could accommodate so many in such a small area. In the 1851 census this Chapel is described as Wesleyan Methodist, erected 1838, 92 free sittings, 82 other sittings, afternoon congregation that day 17, evening 65, afternoon Sunday School 36 only, though on the books were 27 males and 58 females. Of these, 18 boys attended day school and 3 used to do so; 36 girls attended school and 9 used to do so. The return was signed by William Henry Cornforth, Minister, of 22 Great Norwood Street. The Sunday School was, apparently, the most flourishing part of the church, and its records are the only ones to survive.[49] In May 1845, there were 49 scholars on the school register, but some were forced to leave on account of poverty. The register notes: 'James Purbrick does not attend for he is a poor boy – no clothes'. Four girls, Margaret and Rhoda Ann Dicks, and Elizabeth and Matilda Pates, could not attend after 29 June, 'no shoes'. This is a side of Charlton life about which one hears little; and the economic theories of the day seem to have barred any attempt to help such children. In August 1848 David Margretts 'left on Political Grounds'. In spite of difficulties, the Sunday School grew. The teachers' minute book describes a joint anniversary service and treat:

> The children assembled and walked down to Wesley Chapel, St George's Street. After a suitable address from the Rev. B. B. Waddy, at 1 oclock all the different schools walked down to the Folly Field. After enjoying themselves together, the Cake and tea was distributed at 4 oclock; between 5 and 6 oclock our own school left for home and were conducted by the teachers to Charlton turnpike [at the Beaufort Arms]. Teachers returned to Wesley Chapel School for evening. . . . May every school prosper more abundantly.

On 1 March 1863 the Cudnall children joined with those of St Mary's in a joint treat to celebrate the wedding of the Prince of Wales. They all met at the Vestry Hall 'received Wedding Favours and walked in procession to the Revd Gabb Clergyman, round to the London Road, up to the Infant School, all uniting together and an abundance of tea and cake supplyed by Contribution through the Church Wardens' – in other words, they marched from the Vestry Hall, down Brookway Lane to the Vicarage at Pear Tree Cottage, along Cudnall and London Road, down Spring Bottom, and up to the old Infant School in Mill Lane adjoining Yew Tree Cottages.

Children received prizes for feats of memorising: the whole of Psalm 119 or three chapters of Isaiah. But it was not all learning by heart. It was found necessary to say that no new children would be admitted to Sunday School during the month before a treat! On 6 August 1865 there is an entry: 'Spent a happy 20 minutes with these children. Signed Robert Ceraig Converted Conjurer by the Lord's Grace'. There were then 76 scholars on the register; how many attended weekly we cannot tell, since the numbers are totalled for each month – the highest recorded was 71 in July 1866. Naturally the numbers fell off during bad weather and during periods of sickness.

One problem was to find teachers. There were two local women who were very faithful and others who came reasonably regularly from Cheltenham, but one had to be drawn from as far away as Winchcombe. Adults in the congregation were influenced, according to Bancroft Judge, by the Wesleyan Reform trouble, and a feeling that Circuit interfered too much. Whatever the cause, the Chapel came to an end suddenly in April 1867. Thomas Palmer entered in the Sunday School book: 'Gave an address the last Sunday and very pleased with the school attendance and very much regret it has to be given up for I think a good work is being done for the Lord.' The chapel was sold in 1867 to the Reverend Henry George Liddell of Hetton Lawn, and by 1869 had become a private house.[50]

Wesleyan Reform Chapel

Adult members had been drifting away from the Cudnall Street chapel for some years before its closure and a rival Wesleyan Reform or Free Methodist chapel had been started in Ryeworth. But by the end of 1865, this 'Charlton Chapel' was available for Rochfort's congregation; in an account of the origin of the Baptist church written by him in 1905, he speaks of worshipping there for ten years before the move to Church Street. Ryeworth was sold in 1875 to the Primitive Methodists (though directories as late as 1879 continued to speak of a Reform Chapel there). No records survive.

Primitive Methodist Chapel, Ryeworth

This cause lasted 81 years. Sale of the property was sanctioned on 6 June 1956, which confirms 1875 as the date when the chapel began to function. An anonymous letter to Jesus College, Oxford, referring to Gabb's resignation as Vicar in the autumn of 1875, complains that 'Dissent latterly but especially during the last few months has been spreading like a flood over the Parish – a new Chapel was opened last Spring [Ryeworth] and another large one is now being built in the heart of the village [Church Street]'. Unfortunately no Primitive Methodist records survive for the period before 1932 when union with the Wesleyan Church took place. Later records are scanty too.[51]

A newspaper cutting describes the final service.

> The little Methodist Chapel at Ryeworth has, virtually, closed after serving the needs of the Methodists of Charlton Kings for the past 81 years. The few last remaining regular members of the congregation were joined by friends from other churches in the Cheltenham Methodist Circuit.

The reasons for closure are given as decline in congregation caused by removals, deaths, and the fact that the greater part of the development of Charlton Kings had been on the other side of the London Road; it was thought better to concentrate efforts on such places as Bishop's Cleeve which badly needed a church.

> Mr Quine and others in the Methodist movement have the satisfaction of knowing that the needs of the few who are being deprived of their church will be met by friends of the Baptist Church in Charlton Kings.

A nice resolution to the resentments of 81 years before. The conditions for sale of the building insisted that 'the premises shall not be used for the manufacture, distribution, sale or supply of intoxicating liquors nor for any purpose in connection with the organisation or practice of gambling in any of its forms nor as a public Dance Hall'; all inscriptions, decorations or ornaments relating to use of the building as a place of worship were to be removed. But it was difficult to find a purchaser because the local authority would not allow vans to park in the narrow road. By 1962 the asking price had dropped from £1000 to £400, and at this figure it was sold for use as a warehouse.

Meetings at the Charlton Brewery

Between 1905 and 1910 a group from Bethesda held meetings at the former Charlton Brewery (previously the Prinn Arms) in Cirencester Road. Again, the initiative came from outside Charlton, and it did not lead to a permanent Wesleyan church. A Circuit Commission on Reorganisation looked for a Charlton site in 1935–8 without success.

Sacred Hearts Church

In 1939 La Sainte Union sisters opened a school at Charlton Park. Benedictine fathers from St Gregory's in Cheltenham said Mass in the small chapel there which began to be used by the Roman Catholic population of Charlton Kings. It was soon overcrowded on Sundays

8.32 Sacred Hearts Roman Catholic Church.

especially with the coming of evacuees, so Mass was transferred to the school hall and later to the old stable block.

Then in 1946 it was announced that a new Roman Catholic parish was to be formed in Charlton Kings – the parish of the Sacred Hearts of Jesus and Mary. Fr John O'Donnell was appointed as the first parish priest and was at first accommodated by local people. A building fund was set up and in 1954 the presbytery was built on land generously donated by the nuns' congregation. In 1955 the construction of a church to seat 250 people got under way and the foundation stone was laid on 11 February 1956 by the Right Reverend Joseph Rudderham, Bishop of Clifton. The church was built in a simple modern style, with a hint of late perpendicular in the big west window.

On 30 June 1957 Bishop Rudderham officially blessed and opened the church. By then the parish priest was Fr McDonnell ('Father Mac') who faced a debt of £26,000. This was cleared and in 1982 the Silver Jubilee of the church was celebrated and the church solemnly dedicated by the Right Reverend Mervyn Alexander, Bishop of Clifton. The first baptism in the parish took place on 29 February 1948, but not in the church.

Parish priests of Sacred Hearts Church have been Frs John O'Donnell (1948–Jan. 1953); Patrick Ryan (Jan.–Sept. 1953); Edward McDonnell (1953–78: before his retirement he was made a Canon but despite this was still known locally as 'Father Mac'; he retired to Nazareth House and died in February 1980); Gerald Rodgers (1978–9); Patrick O'Donovan (1979–Jan. 1987); Anthony Trafford (1987 to date).

Other Roman Catholic Orders represented in the parish are the Carmelite Friars at Whitefriars School; Missionaries of St Francis de Sales at Courtfield until *c.*1983; the Poor Sisters of Nazareth who moved from Bath Road to their new premises on the site of Springfield in 1968.

Charlton Kings Brotherhood and Sisterhood

The Brotherhood in Charlton Kings was started in 1910 for fellowship, Bible study, and mutual encouragement in the Christian life, part of a nationwide interdenominational movement which grew out of the 'Pleasant Sunday Afternoons' of the nineteenth century. The Sisterhood here followed in 1920. In 1932 the members were able to build their own hall on the corner of Lyefield Road East and School Road on an empty site which had been a drying ground for a laundry. Foundations and walls up to the damp course were put in by Albert Cleevely and Son builders, and the rest of the work was done by the members themselves. There were six foundation stones laid on 3 July 1932. The first by Edward J. Burrows FRCS proclaims: 'A token of supreme faith in the brotherhood of man'. Other stones were laid by the Reverend R. H. W. Bouth MA, JP; Alderman P. P. Taylor JP; A. W. Martyn Esq CC; C. M. Morton Esq; and Councillor F. J. Peacey JP. The names illustrate the wide spectrum of support for the movement and how membership cut across denominational boundaries. Now (1986) the future of the movement and the hall is in doubt.

9

Law and Order

The medieval tithing system was intended to promote order in the community because under it everyone was responsible for his neighbours' acts, and the tithing man in charge of the area could be fined if he did not report unlawful activities. As a rule, the tithing man was content to say 'all well' at the half-yearly great courts. This was an office in which every tenant had to serve in rotation, but women and the infirm might do duty by deputy. John Holder in 1635 was acting as deputy for Margaret Holder,[1] Joan Gardiner widow was ordered to find a suitable substitute in 1692,[2] and in 1694 John Gale was likewise to find a suitable person in his place.[3] The parish constable was also appointed in rotation every year. The office was unpopular, for failure to perform its duties might result in a fine. In 1610 John Whithorne, the constable of Charlton, was said to have concealed a certain affray and drawing of blood made by Thomas Warden on one William, servant of Richard Pate gentleman – Whithorne ought to have been fined 3s 4d, but for some reason the sum was excused.[4] In 1627 the constables of both Cheltenham and Charlton were fined half a crown apiece for allowing 'vagabonds and sturdy beggers' to walk through the town unpunished.[5] Vagrants were feared and punished accordingly.

Brawls were not uncommon in Charlton Kings and parish constables were expected to report them. Thus on 8 April 1585 John Blicke reported an affray by Thomas Gotheridge (of Ham) on John King (of Cudnall) and Thomas as aggressor was fined 4d.[6] A more serious fight occurred in March 1598. Reginald Machyn made an affray on Ralph Free, servant of William Ridgedale; Ralph retaliated and both men drew blood. Each was fined 18d.[7] More serious still, Robert Hawthorne (living at the fine timber-framed house in Spring Bottom called Hawthorne's and also tenant of a third of Northfield farm with its sheepwalk) drew blood on Richard Gooderich (of Ham) and was fined 3s 4d.[8] Women were not above fighting. Margaret, wife of Philip Crosley, drew blood on John Griffin's wife against the king's peace in 1613 – it cost Philip 12d.[9] And in 1634 when Margaret Rudgedall and Mabel Diggason swore at each other and then had a good stand-up fight, mutually drawing blood, Mabel alone was fined; apparently the court blamed her for the whole regrettable incident.[10] When Daniel Ellis was presented in 1697 for shooting Richard Overbury in the leg with a hand gun, his gun was taken away from him but later returned.[11]

To be found walking abroad during the hours of darkness was enough to get a man suspected of evil intent. James Page in 1627 was said to be a common *noctivagus*.[12] He might be a poacher, like Walter Cherrington, wont 'to shoote att' and follow partridges '*cum tormento*' (with a snare), or Richard Stevens who 'commonly takes partridges *cum retibus suis*' (with snares or nets); both were fined 5 shillings.[13] William Wills the younger and Thomas Horne were presented in 1693 for keeping greyhounds to destroy game.[14]

In Charlton, however, most of those who poached were taking fish. On 12 January

1628/9, eleven men were accused of having fished the previous March in the river leading from Dowdeswell to the mill of Walter Martin (Charlton Mill in Spring Bottom); perhaps this was a first offence, for they were fined 6d each. But John Dickeson, John Whithorne, Richard Ballinger and Philip Crosley junior who fished in the common stream in Charlton in 1630 were fined half-a-crown apiece[15] and John Jones alias Friday of Charlton shoemaker, said to be a common fisher in the stream there to the great destruction of the fish was fined 3s 4d in 1635.[16] Even bathing in the stream was reprehensible: in 1693 John Grevile gentleman, Samuel Kent and Thomas Tucker were presented 'for destroying the fishing within the said mannour . . . by laveing in the Brooke',[17] though they were not actually fined for it.

Charlton had very little woodland and fuel for firing was scarce. Hence the accusations against Thomas Freame, William Weare and John Gooderich in 1609 that they were common hedge breakers to the hurt of their neighbours[18] and a similar complaint in 1631 about Roger Robart, living in a tenement of Walter Whithorne.[19] John Bayliss in 1627 had cut and carried off wood and timber out of the hedges and bounds of Richard Pates, Thomas Horwood and others, but he seems to have been only a boy (he is described as son of Henry Baylies of Charlton) so he was fined no more than 4d.[20]

We don't know what induced William Whithorne in 1630 to dig 'anglice morter' (clay) in the highway in Gryndels Foord Lane to the harm of wayfarers – this was a muddy bridle road between Moorend and Leckhampton (due to be closed in 1784).[21] And why did Alice Cherrington widow lay herself open to be presented in court for 'incroaching upon the lord's waste and spoyling the highway' in 1694 – and where did she do it?[22]

Many games, such as bowls, quoits, stawball and trap, were unlawful and those who played them were presented in court. The trap was 'a shoe-shaped wooden device with pivoted bar that sends a ball from its heel into the air on being struck at the other end with a bat'; 25 Charlton men were said by the constable and tithing man to have played stawball and trap or quoits in 1609.[23] Cheltenham had a bowling green, if Charlton did not, and the names of those fined for playing suggest that some Charlton men were there. Even William Panton, minister of Cheltenham, was among those fined![24]

Constable and churchwardens jointly were responsible for supervising strangers who might be received in the parish as tenants or inmates. They might become chargeable to the parish under the 1601 Poor Law Act! In 1613 the court ordered that anyone receiving under-tenants or inmates must give notice to the constable and churchwardens so that security could be given. Thomas Johnson, born outside Charlton, was said to have lived here five months without doing this, so he was fined 10 shillings.[25] William Dickenson had received John Reignolds as tenant in a Charlton cottage; they were fined 40 shillings and 10 shillings respectively, though Reignolds was a Charlton name and John may well have been kin to people living in the parish.[26] Mary Trinder widow took a lodger, William Mills labourer, and both were fined.[27] The law against inmates could even apply to sons-in-law, according to an order of 1625.[28] These are only a few instances out of many and, considering wage rates of the seventeenth century, the fines were severe.

This system of law enforcement worked fairly well in the seventeenth century because public opinion was usually behind it; the fines would not have been enough to deter if there had not been the fear of getting into one's neighbour's black books. Exposure to ridicule in the stocks was the ultimate sanction; Charlton stocks were renewed in 1763 by Anthony Mustoe who was paid 17 shillings for timber and work. Where public opinion condoned the offence, the courts could do little. So people who built cottages without four acres of land, against the Elizabethan Act, merely paid a yearly fine; and those who kept playing-cards in their houses were not deterred by being fined 1 shilling periodically.

In the eighteenth century, fighting and poaching and receiving incomers without giving security to the parish for them still happened, but now they were the concern of the Justices of the Peace, not of the Hundred court. The tithing man's role in supervising his neighbours faded out but the parish constable's correspondingly increased. When neighbours were no longer obliged to present misdeeds, minor matters went unreported. In the *Gloucester Journal* of 23 January 1769, John Whithorne complained of two cases of arson at The Knapp; during the night of 27 August 1768 his barn, stable and stock of corn were destroyed by fire, and on 19 January 1769 a large pile of firewood by the house was burnt, so that 'there are the greatest reasons to believe the same were, by some evil-minded Person or Persons unknown, maliciously set on Fire'. But there is nothing to suggest that his reward of £50 was ever claimed.

Dodington Hunt and his son William Hunt Prinn stocked Charlton Park with deer, which invited a new type of trespasser. In September 1810 two cases were brought; William Piff of Cheltenham yeoman helped to steal a fallow deer, and William Taylor, a Cheltenham butcher, killed one – the complainant against both was Prinn's gamekeeper Thomas Ballinger.[29]

How effective the parish constable was in checking and detecting crime is a matter of dispute; where evidence survives, it seems that his local knowledge could be invaluable. He might on the other hand turn a blind eye. We know very little about crime in Charlton in this period, but no doubt it ran an average course. Certainly Charlton was one of the parishes which saw no need for a county police force in 1840. The first police station was in Church Street, where the slope now goes up to the public library. It was in a new house, one of a pair William Bain had built on the site of Cleevely's old Ashley manor tenement; a small cell added at the side for locking up drunks was enough to convert it. The police station gave the name Bobby's Alley to the adjoining footpath up to Grange Walk. In 1858 the building still belonged to Bain – it is listed in the rate book no. 311 as police station (g.e.r. £7 10s 0d).

We know the names of a few of the policemen who worked here in the early days: 'Sergeant' George Rodgers (daughter baptised May 1844), Thomas Tanner 'policeman' (son baptised June 1851), Cresant Jeffs 'policeman' (daughter baptised March 1852), John Midwinter 'police officer' (daughter baptised August 1854). Towards the end of the 1850s came Alfred Keen, but he married without permission and found himself obliged to transfer to the Wiltshire police (not returning to Charlton until about 1865).[30] In 1858 the police station was occupied by Samuel Fowler.

The police station was still in Church Street in 1873 but by 1879 had moved to Horsefair Street, to a pair of houses back from the road opposite the War Memorial. The former cell is still at the back and there was at one time a way there from Chestnut Walk (Gladstone Road). This is marked as the police station on the first large scale OS map of 1884, but shortly after that the station moved back to Church Street, to the house formerly called Milverton, now The Roses, which was in a better position to control The Merry Fellow and the men who congregated at Attwood's Corner. Again, a cell was added at the back. Finally when Copt Elm Road was at last built up, the police station moved to a pair of houses there, one used as a dwelling and one as a station; and it remained there until Charlton lost its own resident police altogether.

There are many stories about Charlton's police sergeants. Frank Neather and A. E. Palmer have recalled Sergeant Day, 'Dapper Day', and his methods with the young. 'I've had many a cut with his cane across my backside for scrumping and he'd say "Now go home and tell your father I gave you that cut and he'll give you another one!".'[31] Scrumping apples was an accepted practice with the young; and going along the hedges to knock out the birds' nests (not to take the eggs) – this was perhaps a relic of days when boys got paid for killing sparrows.[32] Connie Herbert (née Chapman) tells of the tricks boys would play on Sergeant Day, tying a length of black cotton to his knocker and across to a tree in the road, so that when he came out, his off-duty bowler hat would be knocked off![33] Still, though there was a good deal of mischief, there wasn't much malicious damage and very little real crime.

Day was followed by Sergeant John Hughes in 1919, and (as his son recalls)[34] he and his two constables patrolled the whole parish (all the ancient parish of Charlton except a small area from Holy Apostles church to Hales Road which had been taken into Cheltenham) *on foot*. On the rare occasions when an arrest had to be made, the man arrested had to be taken into Cheltenham to the Central Police Station on foot or by public tram. There is a story of a man arrested for poaching; he was being walked down the Cirencester Road when all of a sudden he broke free, swung himself over the stone wall of Charlton Park and got clean away and for a week he hid in a tree (one of the pollard oaks on the Beeches) where he was fed by his wife, before he was recaptured!

10

Ale Sellers, Beerhouses and Public Houses

Anyone in the seventeenth century could set up an alehouse but he was responsible for the good behaviour of customers and he had to keep the Assize of Ale and sell in standard measures. The constable kept an eye on his activities. But it was often easier to pay a fine in court than to buy properly authenticated mugs or jugs. The constable William Whithorne in 1614 informed the court that Richard Stephens was selling ale in illegal measures; six years later, Richard Stephens was still keeping a common alehouse and still breaking the Assize. Another persistent offender was William Crump who in 1611 and 1612 gave short measure, kept cards in his house, and allowed his customers to play illicit games!

An ale seller was expected to see that people did not get drunk in his house. John Machin in 1627 admitted a certain John Gellfe of Charlton to his house in time of divine service and let him remain there until he was very drunk. Jane Parker, wife of John Parker, received John Dole of Charlton and others and let them all drink themselves drunk – we know, incidentally, that John Dole was Mr Grevill's man. Alehouse haunters and common tipplers were dealt with firmly by the court and might even receive corporal punishment.

It is unfortunate that the alehouse recognisances (which alehouse keepers should have entered into to ensure good behaviour) have been lost. So apart from those who erred, we do not know who kept alehouses or where until after that method of 'licensing' was abolished in 1828. The relaxation of the law led to an outbreak of new but usually short-lived alehouses, beerhouses and public houses. Information about them comes mainly from directories and from deeds, but some (not by any means those that survived longest) have left a trace on local memory. We still talk of the Fox footpath, though the Fox only lasted for some 15–20 years as a beerhouse and the building was pulled down before 1939. This list follows the roads, starting on the London Road at the parish boundary. Names marked * are still active (BH = Beerhouse; PH = Public house).

London Road

***The White Swan** stood on the London Road where it ran down to Dowdeswell Mill and so on along the Chelt. When the reservoir was constructed, the White Swan was moved to the new road and became **The Reservoir** (PH). Mr Bee, son of the landlord 'Buzzer' or 'Busy' Bee, says that for a long time the old sign with a swan on it still hung there.

The Beehive (BH) was built on land called Mansells Middle Field (TM 149). It seems to have started when there was a brickyard across the road and continued as a beerhouse until

1919, when the big bow window was added to what had been a plain brick front. For years after that, the name Beehive could still be read on the wall.

The Fox and Goose (BH) started *c.*1830 when William Flatcher converted two Ashley copyhold cottages into a beerhouse managed and later owned by Thomas Western;[1] it had ceased to be anything except cottages by the 1850s,[2] and they were demolished before 1939.

Mazeppa (BH), listed in Hunt's *Directory* 1844, was kept by John Mountjoy. This was the house later known as Noah's Ark or The Ark, which from 1901–*c.*1914 became a mission room, and from 1939–45 was a factory.[3] It was demolished shortly after 1945.

Plough (BH), listed in Hunt's *Directory* 1844, was kept by John Trotman. The Plough must have been somewhere at the end of East End Road, for one Census area ran from The Anchor (*q.v.*) to the Plough and covered Church Street and East End. So it was there as a landmark in 1851. Can it have been at The Hitchings?

Cotswold Inn. From 1815 the Nelmes family were buying property at East End and by 1848 William Nelmes (the younger) had a cottage and rod of garden here (TM 356). The tithe apportionment does not say that this was a public house, but it had become one by around 1860. It was demolished *c.*1960.[4]

***Duke of York** (PH) was built in 1848 on land which had gone with Over House.[5] It is listed in the tithe apportionment as owned by Thomas Jackson and occupied by William Taylor (TM 241); Mary Taylor as occupier, and Isaac Smallcombe as owner are listed in Harper's *Directory* of 1857 and the Rate Book of 1858.

New Inn, also built on Over House land, *c.*1849 (not there on tithe map, see TM 242). It is listed in Harper's *Directory* of 1857 with John Greening as owner. In 1860 this property was conveyed to Benjamin Wood and in 1862 he sold it again for £500; shortly after that it ceased to be an inn. In 1882 the name was changed to Lindon Lawn and a new kitchen was added; it has since been extended again and is now two dwellings.

Conway House, now called The Close, was built to be a public house but had ceased to operate as such before 1848 (TM 250). It may have been a private house by 1844, for it is not listed in Hunt's *Directory*.

Bell (BH) at Mill Cottage, opposite Bridge House, was listed in Hunt's *Directory*, 1844 as kept by Edwin Chapman.

***London Inn** (PH) was built after the new London Road was cut in 1825–6, perhaps about 1834, by Sampson Marshall (whose son was baptised in April 1835, the father being described as innkeeper). In 1840, when another plot of building land was sold, the purchaser was given the right to lay pipes 'under the road adjoining to a messuage or premises belonging to Sampson Marshall called London Inn. . . for the purpose of carrying water from' an existing well; 'if there is not enough water from the well aforementioned or from either of the wells now used by Sampson Marshall and for the use of the London Inn', the purchaser might sink two wells under the private road![6] So the London Inn was operating under that name before 1840, though Hunt's *Directory* of 1844 omits it. By 1857, Harper's *Directory* gives the innkeeper as William Melvin who in 1844 had been at the Prinn's Arms. After 1868, the London Inn became the venue for Ashley manor courts which were held there until the 1920s.

***Beaufort Arms** (PH) may have been built by 1806, when Mitchell shows a house near this site. About that time the toll gate was transferred here from Gallows Oak, and there was a toll house on the triangular patch of ground to the front. The inn and adjoining houses are built on a slant from the road because of a stream, now culverted, which runs down from the Slad and once crossed the London Road here. The Beaufort Arms is listed in Hunt's *Directory* of 1844 with George Mann as innkeeper, and in Harper's *Directory* of 1857 with James Clifford.

Hales Road (corner with Park Street)

***Russell Arms**, listed as an Inn, was kept by Stephen Nash in 1857. (If the name was intended as a compliment to Sir William Russell of Charlton Park, the arms now displayed are wrong!)

Park Street

***Crown Inn**, listed in Harper's *Directory* 1857, was kept by A. Hambling. There were also two beer retailers in this street, W. Smith and W. Young.

Rosehill Street

Black Horse (BH) listed in Harper's Directory 1857, was kept by William Cox.

Cudnall Street

Merry Fellow (BH) was listed in Hunt's *Directory* 1844 and 1848 and in Harper's *Directory* 1857 as being kept by Samuel Hogg – perhaps in the 'Ancient Messuage'. About 1858, Hogg transferred to a new house, two cottages put together, on the corner of Mill Lane and Church Street (entrance in Mill Lane, now School Road) and took the name with him.

Church Street

Blue Boys (BH), listed in Hunt's *Directory* 1844 as being kept by John Best. This may have been at St Mary's Cottage, strategically placed opposite the churchyard gate in Church Street. A house is marked on Mitchell's 1806 map. If so, it has long been divided into two dwellings; part (now an electrician's) was for many years the premises of Hamlett the undertaker. The other doorway seems the older.

Charlton Cottage (BH) David Denley, listed in Hunt's *Directory* 1844, may have been at Forge Cottage, which is shown in a print of *c.*1840 as a small cottage with a gable attic window and what may be meant for a sign over the door. In 1672 the Crumps held the nearby forge, so it seems possible that the William Crump of 1611 and 1612 who ran an alehouse and gave short measure operated here. Church Street was often called Charlton Street at that period, which would account for the name of the cottage.

Prince of Wales, built as a dwellinghouse by William Henry Hall, and then turned into The Prince of Wales, was listed in 1857 with Robert Hewinson as innkeeper. Later William Dyer transferred here from a house nearby. In 1875 this was turned into the British Workman (club) and is now The Vine coffee shop.[7]

***The Merry Fellow** had transferred from Cudnall Street to its present location by the time the 1858 Rate Book was compiled. No. 253 is a beerhouse and cottage, owned and occupied by Samuel Hogg, (g.e.r. £15 and £2 10s 0d). By the end of the century, the Merry Fellow was selling Stroud Ales and was famous for its 'fighting beer'.[8] Under 'Doc' Attwood it used to open very early in the morning to serve hot drinks to men going to work, according to the late Frank Neather.

'Near Church Street' in 1844 and 1848 was a beer seller, William Smith; he appears as W. Smith beer retailer and grocer in Harper's 1857 *Directory*. A year later, the 1858 Rate Book lists a beerhouse 'Near Crabend' owned by John Finch and occupied by William Dyer. This must be the house now called Hilltop, which shortly afterwards became part of Attwood's grocer's shop and post office. William Dyer moved from here to the Prince of Wales just round the corner. William Smith had moved to The Royal.

Church Piece

The Six Bells (BH) is listed in Hunt's *Directory* 1844 as run by Thomas Mitchell – perhaps, therefore, it is the one later known as **The Carpenter's Arms**, run by Mr George Mitchell's grandfather, Stratford Mitchell, and if so, the only old house left standing on Church Piece.
The Welsh Harp (BH) was listed in Hunt's *Directory* 1844 and again in 1848, with John Moulder as the innkeeper.
The Jolly Admiral; the house was built between 1852 and 1857 by John Packer of Leckhampton. It was sold to George Hodge, a Cheltenham brewer, in 1862; before the next reference in 1884 it had become **The Endeavour**, with W. R. Burroughs as licensee; by 1888 this was Frederick Burroughs. This public house closed in 1908 and the building was divided into three Endeavour Cottages. When Church Piece was cleared to make the site for the library, the stone cellars of The Endeavour were laid open to view.[9] The cellar walls were of dressed stone and well built.

Horsefair Street

In 1843 Richard Ashmead was renting a small garden near the Pound from the Charlton Park estate;[10] and in Hunt's *Directory* of 1844 he is given as occupier of **The Anchor** (BH) 'near the Church'. The tithe apportionment of 1848 shows Richard Ashmead as living in Horsefair Street at Pound Cottage (TM 337), and lists him as baker, too. So his was the public house which has survived in local folklore as the place where you could buy beer by the pound. A census district in 1851 started at the Anchor. But by 1858, the Rate Book does not suggest a public house here.
The King's Head (PH) On the opposite side of the road, on the site of the house called Rosebank and the adjoining properties, there stood in 1832 'a messuage or dwellinghouse, out offices, malthouse, brewhouse, coach house, gig house, stable and lofts, kiln and cellar or store-room' with land measuring 342 feet next the road, 330 feet at the back, 62 feet deep at the east end but tailing off to 10 feet at the west. With the house went a seat in the south gallery of the church. This property was conveyed by Robert Gore to Elizabeth and Ann Carr spinsters on 1 December 1832. After Ann's death, Elizabeth contracted to sell it to Thomas Jackson for £495 (but reserved the pew for her own use); and Jackson, before the conveyance was signed on 13 April 1849, had already begun to pull down most of what stood on the site and to build other houses there. (Information from title deeds for 34 Horsefair Street.) It sounds as though the buildings Jackson demolished were very old and had ceased to be used as an inn sometime before; The Anchor had replaced them. The registers of electors support this view; in 1832–3 Jonathan Franklyn claimed as occupier of The King's Head; and in 1842 and 1852 Richard Ashmead as owner and occupier of the Anchor Inn.
***The Royal** (PH) was built in 1830, as its façade proclaims. It replaced, probably, Old Church House on the other side of the road, which was demolished in 1827–8. It was built on Cheltenham copyhold land by William Hamlett, but soon passed into the possession of James Agg Gardner, and so has remained attached to the Cheltenham Brewery. In 1844 the occupier was William Bird and in 1847 Edwin Chapman (who had moved here from the Bell).[11] By 1858, the Royal was run by William Smith, the man who in the 1840s had been a beer retailer 'near Church Street'. The Cheltenham ale sold here was always known as

singing beer', to distinguish it from the 'fighting beer' sold at the Merry Fellow. Around the turn of the century, when Tom Gosney was the landlord, the Royal was often called The Monkey House because Tom kept a monkey on a pole in the garden as an attraction to customers – that garden which, sadly, has become mostly car-park.[12] Built at the same time as the Royal, and part of the premises, was a cottage (in the 1920s, Sim's bakery) which used to have pretty Gothick windows, now removed.

Cirencester Road

Prinns Arms (PH) (wrongly given as Prince's Arms in 1832) was rented by Samuel Carter in 1832 which allowed him to claim a vote. No vote was claimed in respect of it in 1842 and by 1844 it was run by William Melvin (who moved from here to the London Inn). Prinn's Arms ceased to be a public house soon after 1844 but, as Brunswick Villa, by 1857 belonged to Charles and William Turk, lessees of the malthouse in Moorend Street (New Court Road), and was the place where they started the Charlton Brewery. In 1880 the brewery was managed by Henry Clarke and only ceased *c.*1895. It is said that all the brewing equipment was left in the cellars and simply sealed with concrete. In the 1920s part of the building was Midwinter's garage, and since then has been used as a shop.

***New Inn**, now called **Little Owl**, replaced the Prinn's Arms as a public house for Up End. It is listed in Harper's *Directory* for 1857 as run by William Bate. This inn seems to have been built on the site of a messuage held in the sixteenth and seventeenth centuries by the family known as Alexander alias Mansell.

Ham

There was a malthouse at Ham Court in 1848 (TM 137) in the occupation of John Burrows; and in 1857 Ham had no less than five beerhouses run by Ann Burrows, John Dowdeswell, William Fry, Edward Williams and Thomas Window. One was the Red Lion.

Pub Tokens

Twopenny and penny tokens for the 'Royal Hotel, Charlton Kings' have been found in the parish;[13] and now a threepenny token for the 'New Inn, G. M. Eaketts' (landlord *c.*1920–30) has been discovered. These tokens are made in brass. They were given as change, and of course could only be redeemed by buying more beer! Some lead tokens with the initials 'WM' were found in a garden in Water Lane. These could be pub tokens too; but as they were found near Charlton Mill, they might be seventeenth-century tokens issued in connection with corn ground while Walter Martin was miller, *c.*1612–25.[14] The theory that they were used while this was a fulling mill can be discarded.

11

Looking After Our Poor

The enquiry into Chantry endowments in 1548 showed that Charlton Kings had a chantry supported by rents from a messuage (the Old Church House) with a two-acre close, closes called Ulsone (2 acres) and Stroode (1 acre), a feeding in Whitefurlong in Stroode field (1 acre), two acres in Goldfynche field, another feeding at Freeman's Brook near Goldfynch (2 acres), a feeding in Swymplow (1 acre) and Ballse Grove (½ acre) in the field called Stannotford. These were all leased to Thomas Hewghes by indenture and brought in 19s 4d.

A group of public-spirited Charlton men bought up these endowments and by 1617 were holding Old Church House and 11½ acres of land from the king by fealty. This was the start of the parish property intended to be used for the relief of the poor. By 1617, the same men with some others had bought a second freehold messuage with land in the common fields, and had divided this 'long rainge of building' with its half-acre garden into nine dwellings – the 1617 tenants are listed in Norden's survey. These were poor and infirm people who needed homes.

In 1700 a full list of the parish lands was set down in a Vestry book.[1] This shows that over the years, the parish had acquired more property either by gift or by purchase. Charlton then owned:

(1) Two closes of meadow at East End called Barland and Hudcroft.

(2) Two closes of meadow or pasture called Goldfinch and White Furlong: these included most of the Chantry land; the rest of (1) and (2) had been bought from Giles Grevill gentleman deceased.

(3) At the south end of Blind Lane 'there is a small tenement now inhabited by one Samuell Kent, which place in Ancient Times has been knowne by the name of Jocketts, and is now a parish house'. This was the messuage 'formerly of John Yoket' (or Joket) mentioned in a deed of 1403.[2] By 1700 it had land of Mr John Cox to the east and of Richard Clarke to the west, which means that the 1403 house site was on Clarke's land and Borrowhulle's in 1403 was west of that, where the tithe map shows a cottage with 1¾ acres of garden ground (TM 264). So the 'laundry' cottages in Croft Road now occupy the site of Jocket's.

(4) In the Lower Field of Charlton (but in Naunton tithing) were two ridges (1 acre), one shooting north and south of Gongfurlong and the other in Long Greenall (both by Greenhills Road). (3) and (4) were leased to John Batten, Kent being his sub-tenant.

(5) A house or tenement with a small backside standing on the east side near the church 'haveing the house and land of Jane Dowdswell on the South and East side

of the house and backside, and the house of Mr Anthony Webb on the north side thereof, formerly inhabited by one Richard Mason a Butcher deceast, but now is Void'. Webb's house was the one with a big porch (TM 340)[3] and the parish house part of TM 338. It seems to have been thrown into the adjoining tenement very soon after this list was made – Webb's house survived until the churchyard extension of 1855.[4]

(6) 'Alsoe there is a long rainge of building on the North side of the street called Churchend Street now inhabited by diverse poore people, at the east end of wch said house there [is] a garden about quarter of an Acre more or lesse wch Garden is now in possession of one Jno Cleevly', with Frigmary or Trigmerry Lane at the east end. (In fact, the whole site was half an acre of which Cleevely rented only a part.[5]) The land ran right down the north side of Church Street from Walls Close.

(7) Two lands (½ acre) near Pillford Wall, one small land or pick in Pillway Mead Corner, one land in Short Greenhall, let to Samuel Whithorne. (These were mostly in Naunton tithing.)

(8) A land in Stoney Furlong, a butt in White-Breach-Corner, a land in Cully-Ford-Field shooting across the highway; a barn, backside and orchard in More-end, with More-end Street on the east. These were let to Whithorne. (The barn, originally a messuage, and orchard were almost next door to his Moorend House.)

(9) Lands in Westall, Naunton and Sandford tithing, let to Thomas Jeffs.

(10) A rent of 10s a year given by the will of Walter Mansell and payable out of his free lands called Swimploe, Goldfinch and Freeman's Brook. (These were probably Chantry lands – the trustees must have given Mansell a long lease of them, in return for which he left this money in his will. If so, the land came back to the parish eventually.)

(11) £10 'given by one Grace Denton of Cirencester, formerly when a child kept by this parish, to buy two poore women two shifts yearly, put into the hands of Thomas Batten the churchwarden'. (According to the *Further Report of the Charity Commissioners 1819–1837* this money was afterwards invested, rather unwisely, in buying land at Moreton Valence.)

Some of the land listed in 1700 had been bought as recently as 1694. The Charity Commissioners were shown the indenture dated 11 May 1694, and the money for the purchase was raised by a parish rate in 1696 (the first rate of which we have a record). It did not bring in quite enough – there is a note in the Vestry book of £3 repaid to Samuel Cooper 'when the poores grounds were bought and the money fell short to pay for them, Paid by Direction of a Vestry, to compleat the purchase'. The Grevills were disposing of all their property by degrees between 1694 and 1701 so they were willing to sell to the parish.

Rents were used to assist the sick and poor, pay for funerals, apprentice children, and keep the houses in repair. Wood from the parish land was cut and sold periodically.[6] So the poor ought to have been well provided with dwellings and over £8 a year in rents as the lands were let in 1700. Had the trustees acted responsibly and granted short leases, these rents could have been raised from time to time to an economic level. However, they chose to save themselves trouble by granting very long leases, tantamount to sale, in return for very moderate rents, the actual value of which was bound to diminish with time.[7] Apart from that, rents were very often in arrears.

In 1714, the three trustees demised to John Prinn of Forden House (Charlton Park) their house or barn (see (8) above) between lands of William Tanty to the north and Thomas Green to the south, the adjoining orchard, garden and close, the Common Pleck in

Charlton Field (see (4)), besides five ridges of arable in Naunton field (see (7)). He was to hold these for a term of 10,000 years and pay £3 a year rent, out of which he might deduct any tax and the church and poor rates. In 1720, the trustees reaffirmed this and included all their land in Lower Field and Naunton, the rent being raised to £5 10s a year. They also let Prinn have the cottage called Jockets (see (3)) which he then gave to Whithorne in an exchange – by 1775, when the sub-tenant was Daniel Humphris, the old house had been allowed to fall down. The Prinns were so sure that these demises were for ever that they incorporated the parish lands into their inclosures and finally into their park, and by 1800 the 1720 lease was lost.

Samuel Cooper, the lawyer who advanced the money to buy land for the poor in 1696, was obviously worried about these long leases. When he set up his own charity under his will dated 11 October 1729, proved 1743, he laid down that no lease of his charity lands was to be for more than seven years. He left a freehold close of pasture called Cuttham Butts (purchased from John Wright), and two copyhold closes called Battledown (purchased from Thomas Smith) in trust for teaching six poor children, the surplus to provide 40 shillings-worth of fuel for aged and disabled poor men and women of Charlton Kings not receiving any parochial collection or pension, and 10 shillings apiece for their clothing. Recipients were to be nominated by the trustees with the churchwardens and 'the graver and wiser of the parishioners'. In 1775 seven new trustees were appointed to hold both the old parish lands and those of Cooper's Charity, and henceforward the two were indistinguishable. There was one new parcel: an acre of land called Howard's Acre in Moreton Mead in the Parish of Moreton Valence, bought with Grace Denton's money. By 1775 the parish must also have owned the three parish cottages (11.1) in Spring Bottom (said a hundred years later to have been ours from time immemorial) – this omission was presumably an oversight when the deed was drafted.

The rent from the Moreton Valence meadow was difficult to collect – a pencil note against the entry says none had been paid for many years before the inclosure award of 25 October 1823 reallotted the Charlton land and awarded the parish only two roods and 39 perches, including the site of a private carriage road.

In 1803 William Hunt Prinn succeeded to Charlton Park. He appears to have had scruples about the parish lands which his father, grandfather, and great-grandfather had been happy to incorporate into their estates. In 1815, after his fellow trustees had served him with formal notice to quit, he began to take legal opinion about the validity of the leases of 1714 and 1720.[8] After reciting the terms of those leases, the case continues:

> As it is imagined that some of these lands lie in the very centre of Mr Prinn's Park and Pleasure Grounds, it is an object of very great importance to Mr Prinn to support these leases if they can possibly be supported . . . in case the leases cannot be supported, Mr Prinn is desirous if practicable of effecting an Exchange with the Trustees upon the following plan, to which there is no doubt they would consent if justified in so doing – To ascertain the comparative value of Land at the time of the Demise and now, and Mr Prinn to give in exchange an Estate of such a Rental as will be equivalent to the increased value of the rent reserved . . . .

Prinn himself was a trustee: ought he to resign before an exchange? the answer given was that, on an application to Chancery, the leases would certainly be set aside and the Court allow an exchange, but Prinn must of course resign. So in 1819, the parish gave up all claim to the original lands and received instead Upper Hill Ground (6a.3r.4p.) with a coppice, Tinker's Oven (6a.1r.17p.) with a coppice, and Hyett's Hill (3a.2r.0p.) without the

11.1 The last of the parish cottages in Spring Bottom (1984).

11.2 The iron hut erected 1902 as the Parish Room is on the site of the Workhouse.

coppice.[9] All these can be found on the 1811 map of the Charlton Park estate and were near Dowdeswell Wood. They were tithe free because Prinn had redeemed all his tithe in 1810.[10]

Up to this time, Charlton Kings had had no workhouse but in anticipation of the need for one the Charity Trustees in 1817 exchanged a plot at the east end of their front strip in Church Street for a plot at the west end of the next strip which belonged to James Cleevely.[11] No conveyance was signed until ten years after the workhouse had been erected in 1826! (11.2) It lay back a little from the street; according to Alfred William Keen (1860–1953) it stood much where the nursery school is now, its yard and garden being on the east, behind the almshouses.

Both the 1819 Trustees were dead by 1824 and Charles Cooke Higgs, their legal representative, had done nothing about replacing them. He was a conscientious but dictatorial man, desiring the good of the parish so long as people did what he thought right! The parish became afraid that the charity lands might be lost through neglect. An inscription in the churchyard reads 'SACRED / To the Memory of Giles Ashmead who died Feby 5th [183]0 in the 84th Year of his Age / He was a honest Char[acter] and Industrious man and his dying request to his Son and Daughter was / Never to forsake the Poor nor give up the Cause of / the Charities until the / Poor had got their Rites . . .'. At a meeting of parishioners on 3 October 1832, Higgs was directed to appoint additional Trustees, and this he duly did, but not until 4 April 1834.[12]

It is worth looking at the 1834 list of parish properties and comparing it with the list of 1700. Charlton Kings parish as such owned nothing – the Spring Bottom cottages were still left out – but the Trustees held:

(1) A toft or parcel of land on the south side of the church, on which 'the house called The Church House formerly stood'. This fine timber-framed house had been pulled down in 1826–7 in the hope that the site could be added to the overcrowded churchyard, but the scheme ran into legal snags.[13]

(2) 'All that tenement divided into several habitations and occupied as Alms Houses by

11.3 Laburnam Cottage.

11.4 The 1826 almshouses.

divers poor people, with the buildings and ground thereto belonging, having the street called Charlton Street or Crab Way south. . .'. This was the old long range of 1700 still standing.

(3) 'All those cottages with the shops, buildings and ground occupied by John Humphris and John Peacey and their undertenants'. This was a yard which the Trustees had leased in 1820 for a smithy, but (without the Trustees' knowledge) John Humphris and his wife had transferred the business on 1 May 1832 to Edwin Humphris, perhaps a nephew. The story in the Humphris family is that the stone cottage called Laburnam

Cottage (11.3) was built here by Edwin when he was getting married – he left his wedding breadfast to rush back and put the roof on, so that he and his bride could spend their wedding night there! This fixes the date as 1833. Edwin Humphris married Emma Williams on 31 October, and according to the Rate Book (entry 323), he was still paying rates in 1858 as tenant to the Charity Trustees. The rent was only 2s 6d and for many years this was not collected, so by 1914 the Humphris family believed themselves to own the cottage; however, they had no title deed and the Trustees made good their right.[14]

(4) Five tenements 'occupied as Alms Houses by Thomas Moss, Charles Wheeler, Thomas Bloxsome, William Clapton and Margaret Ashmead with the gardens thereto belonging'. These were the new Almshouses (11.4). The rooms may have been an improvement on those in the old building but they had no amenities till *c.*1918 – occupiers still had to fetch their water from the pump.

(5) 'All that messuage erected and used for the Poor House of the parish . . . with the buildings and yards thereto belonging.'

(6) Closes called Bareland, Hudcroft, Goldfinch, White Furlong, The Bell Acre, the lands in the Breach and Cuttham Butts.

(7) The closes given in exchange by Prinn.

(8) The allotment in Moreton Valence.

The list does not exactly tally with the information grudgingly given to the Charity Commissioners sometime between 1819 and 1837 – Charlton didn't believe in letting outsiders know too much! The Battledown closes, being copyhold, were not included here. 'Lands in the Breach' suggests that Charles Cooke Higgs had already given some of the land which later supported the night school.

Under the new Poor Law Act of 1834, control of the workhouse passed from parish to Guardians, though not until the Charlton property had been valued at £850 and a rent of £32 10s. fixed. There is an inventory of the contents of the Poor House in February 1836, when the Guardians took over.[15] But the new policy was to collect all paupers into one

11.5 Cooper's Court, built on the site of the Church Street almshouses.

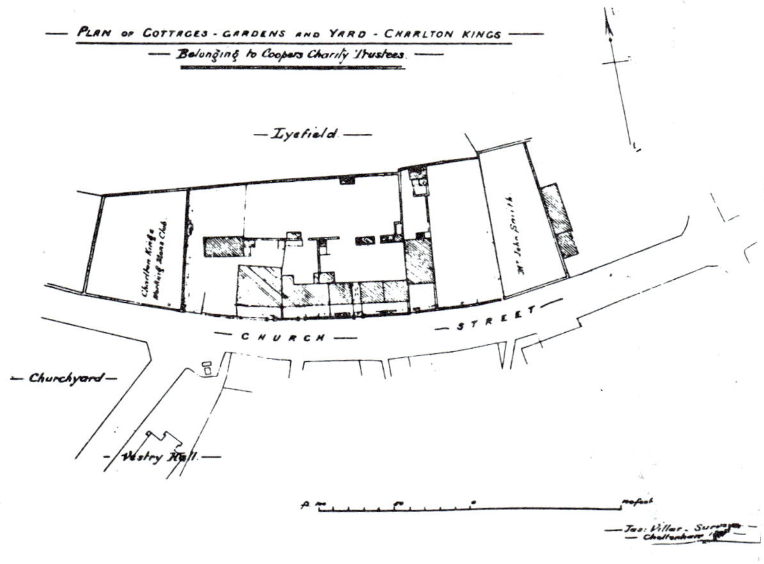

11.6 Plan of cottages, gardens and yard belonging to Cooper's Charity Trustees.

central building, so in 1842 the Cheltenham Guardians gave notice of giving up possession.

New Charity Trustees were appointed in 1850, and the freehold property conveyed to them was the same as in 1834, except that a brick cottage (lately occupied by Peacey, then by Rowley) had been built at the east end of the new almshouses. This was Woodbine Cottage. The Poor House and the long buildings were still standing – they probably went in 1854, reducing the number of almshouse places just when the population was growing. The site of Old Church House was thrown into the churchyard in 1855.

In 1856 the trustees had money from the sale of timber and gravel from Barlands and other Charity lands to invest. For £65 they bought a plot next door to Woodbine Cottage, part of the land they had sold to Cleevely in 1817. It measured 45ft 5 ins against the Street. Then in 1864 they acquired Hewletts Gate turnpike house for £40; it adjoined their Battledown land. They sold back to John Cleevely Smith the plot east of Woodbine, but now the price was £100! New Trustees appointed in 1880 took over (*inter alia*) the two 'tofts', unused sites, where the Poor House and long building had stood. In 1884, no doubt to their relief, the Trustees were able to sell the Moreton Valence land for £45 19s.

Many people in the parish felt that there was a need for a club, something which would offer more than the 'British Workman' with its very limited accommodation. So the Trustees agreed to sell for this purpose a plot on Church Street, 4337 sq.ft. east of Fanny Margaret Anne Lovesy's property (Wall's Close) and 192 sq.ft. next to it, the site of a shed. For the whole they received £120, and the foundation stone of the Workingmen's Club was laid in May 1888.

By 1891 the Trustees had leased to Charlton Local Board part of what had been Edwin Humphris's yard, his descendants retaining the cottage. On the yard the Board erected a shed for their equipment, the building shown on the 1891 plan. But the Urban District Council substituted the yard and fire station in Horsefair Street. So in 1902 the church was allowed to put up a corrugated iron building to act as Parish Room; this now serves as a nursery school.

During the present century, the Charity Trustees have gradually sold off most of their land. Higgs's land on The Breaches provided the site for the new schools and for the misnamed Glynrosa Road. The cottages and almshouses were pulled down in 1970 and

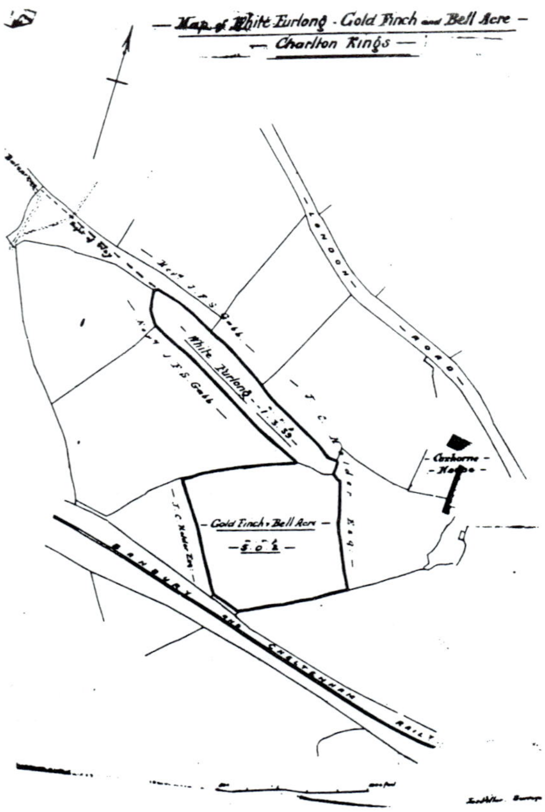

11.7 Charity lands in 1891. The original line of the main road can be clearly seen by White Furlong.

Cooper's Court built in their place (11.5), providing old people with flats far superior to anything that went before. Inhabitants of the long building and the 1826 Almshouses would marvel at the comforts now offered to their successors.

Charlton, in fact, has maintained the ancient tradition of sheltered houses for the elderly and infirm. There are a great many local authority flats and houses, varying from East Court and Greville House, for those needing most help, to Eager House, Little Herberts Close, Gilbert Ward Court, Longleat, Bafford House (to name a few) for the more able. There are also private schemes like Nazareth House, run by the Sisters of Mercy, for terminal cases, and flats at Guardian Court, Park Grange, Lyefield Lawn and so on.

Meanwhile the three old parish houses in Spring Bottom had passed from the parish into the possession of the Local Board of Health and were in such bad condition by 1876, in spite of regular patching, that the Board applied successfully to the Charity Commissioners for permission to rebuild. From the Board, the cottages went to the Urban District Council and then to Cheltenham Borough, which pulled them down as they fell vacant. The last occupant of the remaining house died in 1984. It had no amenities and she had still been fetching her water from the public spring. But she refused to be moved and her beautifully kept garden was always a blaze of colour.

12

Education in Charlton Kings

Cooper's Charity School

Samuel Cooper of Charlton House, in his will proved 18 May 1748, left money for teaching poor children. Six were to be taught for two years and after that their places were to be filled with another six, and books were to be provided for them. We don't know where they met (not, as once suggested, in the stone cottage). Teachers mentioned in Vestry books were Mrs Sallis (1776–92), Mrs Robins (1793–1802) and Mrs Dyer 1803–?. They were paid £4 a year (sometimes in arrears). New books for the Charity School were purchased occasionally and the cost entered in the Vestry Book.[1] After Coltham Fields school in Rosehill Street was built in 1837, this charity money was diverted to its support. It is still available for certain educational purposes.

The National School

A Sunday School was started in 1825 and in 1831 this developed into a weekday school which was held at the Poor House in Church Street which had been built in 1826. The Sunday school continued for boys and girls, but the weekday school was for boys only. In 1837 a more suitable building became available. In 1828 a group of nine Cheltenham men had bought land in Church Piece on the corner of Grange Walk and Horsefair Street and had built a Methodist chapel on it. The site measured 22ft × 74ft. But to raise funds for building, the trustees had had to mortgage and in 1837 the mortgagee foreclosed. A meeting of Charlton parishioners was held in June 1837 to decide on the erection or purchase of a school-house, and the £200 needed to buy the chapel was raised by donations and by grants of £50 from the National Society and £10 from the Treasury. So on 12 August 1837 the chapel was conveyed to the Reverend James Frederic Secretan Gabb (the Vicar), William Bayliss, Samuel Gale and Joseph Cooper Straford, all of Charlton Kings. The building consisted of a room measuring 25ft 7ins × 20ft 3ins, which was reckoned large enough for 84 boys; 63 moved in on 18 September 1837. Another room for girls was ready by February 1838; this was 18ft 9ins × 20ft 6ins. The first trust deed was dated 18 October 1843, when Gabb, Bayliss, Higgs and Straford declared the school 'to be in union with the said incorporated National Society'.

We know a good deal about this school, for its 'Book of Proceedings' from 1831 to 1855 survives.

> The Master is to set a pious and good example, to be regular in observing School Hours, to abstain altogether from Public Houses, gambling etc. and to have a careful regard to

> the Children's conduct out of school. To make and keep the School Books in a correct, neat, and clear order. To collect subscriptions, aided (if necessary) by the Mistress. To receive at the rate of One Penny per week for each Scholar (besides the Sunday pay) *from the Visiter* [sic] to be reckoned according to the ratio of attendance. To receive *from each Child's parents* One Penny per week and One penny additional for writing and arithmetic. [The master was in no danger of being over-paid!] Children must attend *regularly and punctually* [and come] clean-washed, combed, and with clothes well mended.

School hours were from nine to twelve in the morning and from two to five in the afternoon, between Lady Day and Michaelmas, and from half past one to four between Michaelmas and Ladyday; on Sundays the children were expected at nine in the morning and again at two in the afternoon. These were long hours for young children but the trustees were hoping to compensate for the short span of school-days. Most pupils would leave by the time they were ten, and few attended for more than two years altogether.

> A Register is daily kept of all children present and absent, whether with leave or without; also a cash Book of weekly payments. If any child be absent for a whole Week, or the Parents fail to pay weekly on the Day appointed, such Child will be suspended or dismissed [though allowance was made for sickness or accident] . . . and any *reasonable* leave of absence *at the request* of a Parent will be granted. No Child shall be *admitted* into the School, nor *dismissed* from it, except by the acting Visiter [sic]. It is particularly expected, that no Parent will take a Child away without *giving notice* to the Visiter and acknowledging the Benefits received.

At the same time, it was recognised that the parent might have a legitimate grievance.

> If a Parent has found cause for complaint, or is *dissatisfied* with a Child's treatment or progress, it is highly desirable, that the Visiter may be made acquainted with the cause of offence, in order, that if he *think it just*, means may be taken to have the fault amended; or, if not, that he may at least obtain the *benefit* of so much *experience*.

Out-of-school behaviour was a matter for concern.

> Disobedience and Immorality (such as bad words, lying, cheating, stealing, or wilful trespass and mischief) *at all times*, and playing at *football*, or any other noisy and riotous game, *on a Sunday*, will be punished in School; and if persisted in, such Child will be expelled. Parents are desired to instruct their Children to come and go, to and from School, in a quiet and orderly manner – to treat everybody but especially their *betters*, with respect – and in short, as these Rules throughout have no other object in view than the temporal and eternal welfare of *their own* offspring, it is hoped they will have them strictly observed.

All this was probably wishful thinking – Charlton boys have not been notable for their quiet, orderly behaviour or their respect for their betters!

To help the master, twelve monitors were appointed, with a thirteenth as reserve. But masters were the problem – the first three appointed did not stay long enough to make a mark. When the school transferred from the workhouse to the Horsefair Street building in 1837, the master John Bennett was paid a salary of £25 a year in addition to the children's pence. Slates and pen and ink were provided but children had to buy copybooks. When girls were admitted in 1838 they had to pay 2d a week for reading and 4d a week for extras – an odd piece of sexual discrimination! The mistress's salary was £10, made up to £28 a year from the pence and other sources.

On 6 August 1838 an official questionnaire about the school was completed. The building was well-built of brick, dry, airy and well ventilated but 'The school-house sounds very much, probably from it having a flat ceiling'. There was accommodation for 84 boys and 58 girls in two class-rooms; and there was space for coal, wood, and the necessary offices, but no playground. The average number of pupils on the books was 70 boys and 56 girls and the average daily attendance was 55 boys and 25 girls. Both master and mistress claimed to have been trained – they had each had four weeks at Cheltenham National School! No dwellinghouse was provided for them, but coals and candles were found for the school.

The boys were taught reading (from the Bible and Mrs Trimmer's abridgement of it), writing (running hand), arithmetic (as far as practice), geography (using Pinnock's Catechism) and the history of England. The school actually possessed maps of Palestine, England and Gloucestershire. The girls learnt writing, marking and plain sewing. When Mr Perry left the school in 1853 he was given a present in acknowledgement of his services; his salary had been raised to £42 and he had received all pence over £12. The school had a pupil teacher as well, and the Inspector in April 1854 reported improvement. Monitors had been reintroduced, and the only trouble was lack of funds which the Managers earnestly solicited. Enough had been raised by 1855 (with the aid of a small grant) for the school to be furnished with parallel desks which 'much facilitate the preservation of good order and effective teaching'.

12.1 Coltham Fields Infants School: the former schoolroom built in 1837, and the mistress's house.

Now it was time for 'the reconstitution of the Trust as a legal Charity. . . to admit the control and inspection of the Government and the renewal of the Trustees'. The new Trust deed was signed on 30 October 1855; and from 1855 this school was run for boys only.[2]

Mill Lane School

When the Reverend J. F. S. Gabb became Vicar in 1834, there was no school in the parish except the one held in the workhouse. So on 7 July 1835, he and five of the wealthier parishioners acquired a plot of land in Mill Lane (now School Road) and built a school house for the 'education of poor children . . . in their religious, social and moral duties', supported by subscription and managed by Trustees. A new trust deed took effect on 25 January 1850. By this time the school had in practice been limited to girls and infants. After 1855 it seems that the girls from the National School came here.[3]

Rosehill Street Infant School (known as Coltham Fields School)

Rosehill Street was a new development on what had been Coltham Field, and to provide for the needs of the inhabitants, Gabb, on 19 May 1837, bought a plot on the north side of the street with a 42ft frontage. A school had been built by October of that year and a schoolmistress's house was added in 1838 (12.1). It was financed by subscription and by Cooper's Charity; and after 1846 this school and the Mill Lane school had a common Board of Trustees and shared finances. The buildings were Gabb's property until he donated them to the parish in September 1857. This school closed about 1900,[4] and the building was turned into a parish room for Holy Apostles Church in 1906.

The New Schools in Mill Lane

On 11 January 1872, the Reverend J. F. S. Gabb wrote to the Charity Commissioners, explaining a scheme for extending 'popular education on the Voluntary principle' in Charlton. It included the purchase of a new site for the National Boys School adjacent to the Mill Lane School, the building of two new schools there, and sale of the Horsefair Street building. The new National School would be under the same Trusts as the Mill Lane School (the deed of 1850, not that of 1855), so that eventually the two could be amalgamated. (This did not in fact happen until after the formation of a School Board.) The site was part of the garden of the old house called Joyce's, now Charlton Cottage, so only a footpath separated the two schools. A local builder, William Cleevely, built identical schoolrooms and classrooms on either side and a master's house between them, with an archway so that the public right of way was not obstructed (it was used until *c*.1945) (12.2). The schoolroom on the south was for the boys, that on the north for the girls and infants, and both were lit by gas. The new schools were opened on 15 January 1873, a date commemorated for some years afterwards by a school treat.

Holy Apostles School

Holy Apostles Church was completed in 1871 and a photograph of the new church, with very young trees planted round it, shows it without the school. That was added during 1872–3 and opened for boys in September 1873, the girls following in the early part of 1874 (12.3). An undated paper in Gabb's handwriting, which was with other papers of 1874, reports on the Charlton Kings schools, those in Mill Lane having been open for a full year

12.2 The National Schools of 1872 in School Road.

12.3 Holy Apostles School was built in 1872. Higgs's drinking fountain stands nearby.

'whilst the handsome new rooms erected by C. C. Higgs Esqre have been opened for a boys' and a girls' school' accommodating 200. This meant that with 167 boys, 112 girls and 156 infants at Mill Lane and 101 infants at Coltham Fields, there was provision in the parish for a total of 736 children, a hundred more than the Education Department had required. Gabb concluded hopefully that 'unless the population increases very rapidly this will

12.4 Higgs's night school and master's house are now the Scout Headquarters.

probably suffice for some years'. At first the new church was not separated from St Mary's but in 1885 Holy Apostles became an independent parish with its own school. Coltham Infant School fell within the new parish and was unnecessary when there was a better building within walking distance. The separation of the two parishes explains why, when the Lyefield Schools became Board Schools, Holy Apostles remained a Church School, and as such was liked by many parents, even though from 1908 onwards the Education Authority declared the accommodation to be inadequate.[5] It did not move to a new site until 1966 and the new building is still incomplete; it now takes 180 children.

Higgs's Night School

In 1855, the Horsefair Street school committee considered the desirability of starting a night school in the parish. Soon afterwards such a school was started, using the Horsefair Street building. It taught the basics: reading, writing and arithmetic to boys who had missed out on day schooling, and as 'Mr Higgs' school' it too qualified for a grant. Thirty boys were presented for examination in 1871; 25 passed in reading and writing, 23 in arithmetic.[6]

About 1870, Charles Cooke Higgs built a separate schoolroom and master's house for this school on his own land at East End (12.4), though the schools continued to be associated for grant purposes until 1874 and the day school master, Mr Folley, taught in the night school and was paid £20 per half year for doing so. Difficulties arose because Higgs still treated the night school as his own and received the grant himself. His formal Deed of Trust was not signed till 13 November 1880.[7]

The night school was open between the hours of seven and nine each day except Saturday and Sunday; boys under 16 paid 3d a week and those over 16 paid 6d, but punctual and regular attendance earned a bonus of half the fees, and books to the value of the other half at the end of the session. The Trust's income came from nine acres of adjoining land, let out as allotments (the site of the present junior school and Glynrosa Road).

Education became compulsory in 1880 and in the 1890s attendance at night school began to drop. In 1897 the trustees decided to introduce some more advanced subjects, including drawing, shorthand and French, and then numbers rose so dramatically that the hall was no longer big enough. So it was decided to join Cheltenham Grammar School evening classes and move the venue to the boys' school or the town. On 1 August 1905 East End Hall was let as a Church Lads' reading room and club, and from September 1914 it was shared by the Lads' Club and Charlton Kings Scouts. It has continued to be the Scout Headquarters and was sold to the Scouts in 1954.[8] The Trust's funds are still used for educational purposes.

The Board Schools and Council Schools

Again and again in his *Parish Magazine*, the Reverend Leslie Dundas (Gabb's successor) warned parishioners that unless they contributed more generously to the upkeep of the schools, a School Board and School Rate would be foisted upon them. But Charlton was passing through a period of depression and it was very hard to raise money for anything. For a short while in 1883, the schools were actually closed pending the election of a School Board, and a draft deed of transfer was approved on 26 November 1883. Already the buildings erected in 1872 were becoming inadequate. In 1891 a piece of land on the opposite side of the road was purchased and here a new school was built in 1894 for the boys (the present infant's school) (12.5); the old boys' school was used for the girls and the old girls' school for the infants. This arrangement continued until the transfer of all except the infants to East End.

The land behind the 1894 building was a recreation ground managed by the Working Men's Club; since the First World War this has been leased to the Education Authority, first as a playing field and then as the site for extra buildings. This lease runs out in 1988. When

12.5 The 1894 Board School (*left*) with the 1872 schools opposite before the bell-cote was removed. Note the end of Yew Tree Cottage in the distance.

12.6 Mr. J. F. ('Boss') Fry, Headmaster of Charlton School, 1897–1925.

the schools moved, the dual origin of the 1872 schools again became obvious. The infants' school (originally Mill Lane School) was pulled down immediately and the site built upon; the girls' school (representing the National School) was used for a time as an extra parish hall, and has now been converted into dwellings. Money from the sale is available for educational purposes.

Two Headmasters of 'Crab End College'

Charlton has been fortunate in having two notable masters, Mr Folley (who saw the transfer of the school from Horsefair Street to Mill Lane and continued in office until his death in March 1897) and Mr J. F. Fry, 'Boss Fry' (12.6), whose outstanding contribution to education formed the subject of an article in the *Bulletin*.[9] Folley's obituary in the *Parish Magazine* for April 1897 is worth quoting because of its comments on Charlton boys:

> As a Master, he possessed teaching capacities of a high order, as evidenced by the long series of 'excellent' reports obtained from H. M. Inspectors. His power of maintaining discipline was equally great, although whatever may be the case now, there was a time when Charlton boys were not the most amenable to discipline. Indeed it used often to be said that 'No one but Folley could manage the boys of Charlton'. Yet he was so genuine and so just, that he won the affection of the boys generally, and the majority of those who are now the fathers of families in Charlton must look back with gratitude to the influence which he exercised upon them.

12.7 The girls' mandoline band, *c.*1909–10.

Folley was followed briefly by a master totally unable to control the boys; and then came 'Boss Fry' under whom 'law and order became for a while a benevolent dictatorship but the subjects soon found that they could have as much liberty as they could earn. He was a man who believed in what he was doing and he enjoyed doing it', to quote an appreciation by George Ryland who had been taught by him and who taught under him. 'If one definition of education be "learning to live a civilised life in a civilised community", his was an example for all of us to see. He lived in the village, he was part of the village, and what interested pupil or parent was of interest to him', but beside and beyond all that, he introduced his boys to books and papers and to the world outside school in a way not common at that time in any school.

Charlton Kings County Junior School

In 1968 the Junior School moved to new buildings at East End formally opened in February 1969. The infant school is still (1986) in the old buildings on the west side of School Road.

Charlton Kings County Secondary School

In 1958 the secondary school moved in stages to its new buildings at East End erected on land which had been Law's farm. The new school was opened in April 1959 by the then Speaker of the House of Commons, the Rt. Hon. W. S. Morrison; and since then the buildings have been greatly extended and a sports hall was built in 1983. Now the school is ready for a new phase.

Balcarras School

Balcarras School came into operation on 1 September 1986. It is a comprehensive school for 11–16 year olds, and forms part of a complete scheme of reorganisation of secondary

12.8 A girls' school group *c*.1909. The teacher on the left is Miss Emily Statham who died in April 1980 aged 93.

education in Cheltenham. The main change is that the school takes pupils of higher academic ability than before, and the subjects and courses offered for study will therefore be much wider. Boys and girls who before would have been taken by the two Grammar Schools may now opt for Balcarras School, and staff and resources are available for this type of child, so all children of whatever abilities, skills and social backgrounds can find something in the school to suit their needs. Some extension of buildings is going on and pupil numbers will eventually be about 700.

Private Education

Charlton in the early nineteenth century abounded in private schools: the locality was regarded as 'so salubrious'. For boys there was an Academy for Young Gentlemen at Ham which lasted from *c*.1819 to *c*.1886 – it advertised itself as intended mainly for the 'sons of Gentlemen in the Indian Service'. For girls there were several exclusive schools – Miss Arabella Cockburn's 'Academy for Young Ladies' at Charlton Villa (now Ashley Firs) from *c*.1818–49, Mrs Cooper's Seminary at Charlton House, *c*.1810–20, and the 'Select School for Young Ladies', twelve pupils only, at Moorend House. At Castleton House (now Courtfield) Mrs Wells also received a limited number of girls. These small establishments did not last long (both Moorend House and Castleton became private lunatic asylums). Other schools of a similar kind were Mrs Hart's at New Court (1837–42), Mrs Castle's at Anastasia Cottage (1837–46), Miss Gregg's Academy at Charlotteville (no. 2 Cudnall Street; 1837–48), and Mrs Arnott's at Cambrian Villa (*c*.1850–70).[10]

The scope for private schooling was reduced by the establishment of the two Colleges (though they were not open to everyone) and of Pates Grammar School for girls and juniors under the 1902 Act. Yet private schools could still cater for young children and those less academically minded. Miss Roche's 'Collegiate School' at Trefaldwyn and then at Linden Lawn provided a pre-preparatory school for little boys and a 'genteel' education for girls from *c.*1912–30 (when she moved into Cheltenham).[11] For a short time *c.*1960 Mrs Littlewood ran a pre-preparatory school at Ashley Firs; there were five staff (two fully qualified) and 42 pupils in the age range 3–8 years passed through the school.

Sacred Hearts' Convent School for girls was established at Charlton Park in 1939 and Whitefriars School for boys was started at the house known as Ashley Manor (previously Oaklands) in September 1958. In 1987 they are to be united as a co-educational school for the 14–18 age group under the new name of St Edward's.

13
The Clubs

The Reading Association

When the Vestry Hall was first built in 1857, the *Cheltenham Examiner* reported on 22 April:

> Our Charlton neighbours appear determined to make the most of their new hall without delay and at a meeting held on Wednesday evening – Sir William Russell, Bart, in the chair – and attended by the clergy and leading gentlemen of the neighbourhood, a resolution was agreed to for the formation of a Reading Association, and a liberal subscription for the immediate commencement of the concern was at once opened. The Institution is specially intended for the benefit of the working men of the parish; the headquarters of the association will be at the Vestry Hall, which will be supplied with newspapers and books, and be open every evening, in the summer from six to ten, and in the winter from five to ten o'clock.

The issue of 12 May 1857 reported further:

> Charlton Kings Reading Association
>
> The inauguration of this association took place on Wednesday last at the New Vestry Hall of the village, on which occasion a lecture was delivered by the Rev. T. H. Potter, curate of Dowdeswell. The opening was attended by a large number of persons, among whom were included the most influential of the parish residents. Sir W. Russell M.P. presided over the meeting, and congratulated it on the establishment of the Association, expressing a hope also that the young men of the village would avail themselves of its intellectual advantages.

How long this Association functioned we don't know – it seems to have faded out before the next venture in 1876.

The British Workman

Soon after 1858 William Henry Hall let his house and workshop in Church Street as a public house, The Prince of Wales. When the adjoining property was sold in 1875 as a site for a chapel, a group of men, some attached to St Mary's and some to the new chapel, agreed to form an association and buy out the pub. On 5 January 1876 it was conveyed to John Burgh

Rochfort, Henry Jordan coal merchant, Benjamin Wood nurseryman, William Cleevely builder, and Edwin Attwood grocer, all of Charlton Kings, for £300, and became 'The British Workman', an institution 'lately formed in the Parish of Charlton Kings for the purpose of providing accommodation for reading and the profitable employment of leisure time and for supplying Refreshments on Temperance Principles and at fixed prices to the Members and under certain conditions to the Inhabitants in General of the said Parish'. Members were to pay 4 shillings a year and the institution was to be run by a committee of nine chosen by subscribers from members resident in the parish or within five miles of the parish church. The place was 'never to be used for Religious Services or Political Lectures or discussions or for any theatrical entertainments or concerts nor to be used or allowed to be used as a place for the sale of any intoxicating liquers'.

With so many restrictions on its use, The British Workman became simply a place where members could sit in the evening in front of a good fire and read the newspaper, smoke, and perhaps play draughts or dominoes. The idea of supplying coffee or tea probably faded out because times were so hard that men could not pay even a penny a cup; certainly nothing was served after 1900. The newspapers by then were always a day old, passed on by the Working Men's Club.[1] The British Workman came to an end about 1914, and in 1915, the trustees having decided that the trust had failed and was 'incapable of being performed', the property was sold.

Charlton Kings Working Men's Club and Institute

The parish had already been enjoying penny readings and fortnightly winter concerts for some years. On 12 October 1885 a meeting was called 'with a view to inviting the working men of the Parish to discuss freely a plan for establishing a Church of England Working Men's Club for Charlton Kings. . . . the wish of the Clergy in calling the meeting is, that a club should be established with a working committee elected by the men from members of their own body . . .'. If the club were so established, it should receive the proceeds of the current season's concerts. After some opposition by those representing The British Workman and discussion of whether its rules could not be modified to allow discussion and singing, a committee under the secretaryship of Horace Edwards was nominated; and the new institution was established as from January 1886.[2] The objects, according to a brochure of *c.*1904, were 'to afford members the means of social intercourse, mutual helpfulness, mental and moral improvement, rational recreation, and good fellowship. It is non-sectarian and non-political': very important considerations in the late nineteenth century when feelings ran high. Members paid 5 shillings a year and membership was open to men of all classes over 18 years of age. Wives and female friends could be admitted to the reading room on Mondays and Wednesdays.

The Club started in four rooms at Ruby House, Cudnall Street, rented for 4 shillings a week. Then in 1887 the committee bought a piece of land from the Charity Trustees for £120 and advertised for tenders 'for the erection of a plain substantial building. – It was just at this time that the late Captain St Clair Ford came forward with designs for the present handsome structure, and by his own help and that of his family and friends, the additional cost over and above the humbler building contemplated by the Committee was defrayed'.[3] He also raised money by organising bazaars, so that by the end of 1888 the whole £2000 had been paid, except a £350 mortgage. This explains why his name is on the foundation stone, laid 19 May 1888, and why the large upstairs room used for meetings and concerts was named after him. When complete, the Club had a reading room and library, a games room, the St Clairford Hall seating 300 persons, a bar or refreshment room, lavatory and baths, billiard room, rifle range and, at the back, a large recreation ground for members and their families.[4] The Choral and Orchestral Society met here; and there were a number of members' clubs for whist, draughts and chess. All the illustrated papers were available, as well as ordinary daily and local papers, so that, as the brochure remarks 'by joining the above Institute you will get privileges which you would not otherwise be able to obtain' as well as recreation and fellowship. The Club still prospers, though it now offers slightly different facilities and for a nominal subscription.

14

Earning a Living

Down to the late nineteenth century, agriculture was naturally the principal means of earning a living for Charlton men. The majority of men whose children were baptised at St Mary's in the years 1813–57 give their occupation as farmer, dairyman, milkman, hurdle-maker, gardener, labourer. But there were always some alternatives.

When a list of able-bodied men for the militia was drawn up in 1608 it included four tailors, two glovers, four weavers, two carpenters, one joiner and one smith.[1] And in the baptism register for 1813–57 there were still two glovers, Ashmead and Webb, and two stocking weavers, Shepherd and Stephens. As one would expect, there were tailors, shoemakers, butchers, bakers, grocers, four millers, five blacksmiths or farriers, a corn factor, four wheelwrights, a coal seller, an ironmonger, a cooper, a chimney sweep, letter carriers, innkeepers and beer sellers, and various professional men. But there were also some more unexpected trades.

There were still three maltsters: the Turk family at the malthouse in New Court Lane, Williams and Lawrence; a tallow chandler, Matthews; a copper plate printer; a paper stainer, Perry (whose workshop was in London Road near the parish boundary), three white smiths; a coachmaker; a hatter; a fly proprietor (first Dangerfield, then Davis, presumably the predecessors of Cripps in Cudnall Street); three cabinet makers; and men described variously as statuary, sculpterer, carver and marble mason – we know from *The Diary of a Cotswold Parson* (p. 15) that by 1824 the workshop of George Lewis the monumental sculptor was operating in Charlton Kings (also in the London Road, nearly opposite Sandford Mill Road); this workshop continued to function into the twentieth century.

But after farming, building was certainly the chief source of employment. The registers are full of names of carpenters and joiners, bricklayers, stone masons, plumbers and glaziers, plasterers, paperhangers, painters. Charlton clay was being turned into bricks; men described as brickmakers include Ewens, Hawkins, Barns, Hayward, Thackwell, Ford, Hawkins, Dyer, Bastin and Yeend, and this does not give us a complete list for these years. We know also of Shill's brickyard on London Road opposite The Beehive, and the large scale Ordnance Survey map of 1884 marks a number of brickworks or old brickworks. There was one near Sandford Mill Road, one in Greenway Lane, one on Battledown, one in Ryeworth, and one on Cirencester Road (on the site of the modern Gadshill Road) and probably others.

There is a history of Pilford Brickworks in the *Bulletin*.[2] Its difficulties and successes were pretty typical, and among the Pilford records[3] are reports in 1878 and 1885 on other yards then operating near Cheltenham. The first report was by Henry Woods and George Hunt. They saw 'a small yard 1½ miles from Charlton Kings' which had been started 34 years previously by Mr Thackwell, a working brickmaker earning 15 shillings a week, who died in 1875 worth £20,000. (Thackwell's name appears first in the register in 1838.) Only clamp bricks were made here, selling at 30 shillings per thousand from the clamp or 35 shillings when selected, but sand for brickmaking had to be carted three miles and bricks sold in Cheltenham had to pass a toll-bar. However, Thackwell's bricks were in demand, and 42,000 had been made and sold in 1878. This sounds like the Cirencester Road yard. When its clay was worked out, an attempt was made to use clay from Catshay but this was not suitable and the yard closed soon afterwards. It is shown on the 1884 Ordnance Survey 25-inch map but may not have been working. The next yard visited in 1878 was on the north side of Cheltenham, where bricks were sold at the same price as Thackwell's. Then Wood and Hunt looked at 'a yard with steam brick-making machinery, fire-heated drying shed, and patent kiln', where the proprietor's avowed aim was to make a large quantity of brick and undersell his neighbours. Wood thought he 'will be beaten by his expenses and must be very careful that his new patent kiln and machinery do not ruin him', but this prediction was mistaken. When Reginald Astley visited the same brickyard in 1885 he found that a new engine was being installed, the steaming shed held 30,000 bricks, and the Hoffman kiln could make 60,000 bricks a week. This was Battledown. Its pressed bricks sold at 35 shillings per thousand, common bricks at £1 per thousand, square floor tiles at 7s. 7d. per hundred, roofing tiles at 3 shillings per hundred; and the works could even turn out ornamental flower pots and busts of people. It employed about twenty men and boys.

From Battledown, Astley went on to Yeend's. Yeend appears in the register in 1857 so his works had probably been operating for about 30 years and he was feeling the competition. He made mostly common bricks, about 35,000 a week, sold in Cheltenham at £1 per thousand delivered, and was said to employ 'a lot of men and boys'. Yeend told Astley that there were only three yards near Cheltenham now, where before there had been nine. And when Astley went to Ryeworth, he found it shut, only operating in the summer.

The Pilford site was in Upper Pilley, just inside Charlton Kings parish boundary, on land which had belonged to Sir William Russell as part of Southfield farm. Its advantages were access to a public highway, good sand within half a mile of the yard, clean, good and abundant earth, a good water supply, and 'all down hill for barrowing of clay'. It was estimated in 1878 that £300 would be enough to start the brickworks in a modest way. So brickmaking began in 1879. But other brickmakers lowered their prices and by 1885, when Astley made his report, Pilford was not paying its way. It was charging 35 shillings per thousand for pressed bricks, 24 shillings per thousand for common bricks for building and £1 per thousand for less hard bricks for interior walls. Power was supplied by a four-horse-power engine. Part of the trouble came from lack of publicity for the works, part from neglect by the manager who had a great deal of local influence and could not be easily removed, and part from inadequate investment in machinery. In 1886 it was reported that 'The Battledown Co. have built another kiln at a cost of £1000 to make an increased number of bricks'. So competition was severe. However, in 1886 Pilford had an order for 120,000 pressed bricks for Cheltenham Workhouse (10,000 a week) and in 1887 the yard was turning out eleven types of brick and five sizes of pipe. In 1888 it supplied all the bricks for Charlton Kings Workingmen's Club. But when Lady Prinn died in July 1888 and money charged on Southfield had to be raised, it was questioned whether Pilford could continue. In the event, it did continue and was even extended; in 1890 it was 'doing very well'. About 1897/8 it was sold and new machinery installed, but this did not improve the products. Eventually Pilford was bought in 1907 by Messrs Webb Bros Ltd of Battledown and dismantled. The Cheltenham Natural Science Society noted that

> for pottery making some of the Pilford clay is too full of 'irony' fragments which make the earthenware black. . . . Very good-coloured and regular-sized bricks were turned out, and also moulded bricks, tiles, and drainpipes. The common bricks were not very successful (although they were used for the first Ash-Destructor chimney), being commonly supposed to exude salt, and were always more or less damp, and were for that reason not very much used in house-building.[4]

Presumably these were the salty bricks often seen in garden walls round Cheltenham.

That was the end of brickmaking in Charlton Kings. Extraction of sand and gravel had been going on throughout the nineteenth century and continued into the 1930s, the last site being the Grange paddock. The older holes left behind were not filled but have been built on by degrees; hence the Gravel Pit Cottages on London Road (where there was once a small printing press) and the holes left on either side of Sandhurst Road. Later excavations have been levelled, as happened to the Sandy Lane gravel pits now built over; or filled in, as happened to the hole between Cirencester Road and the Laundry; and to the hole at the Grange; both of the latter were used by the Urban District Council as refuse dumps. That has given the community a pleasant open space and a playground; and explains why both sites are unsuitable for building.

Neither brickmaking nor sand and gravel extraction employed a great many men; and when the great agricultural depression struck about 1880, many who had worked on the land were unemployed. Cheltenham's growth had come to a stop, there was little house building and very little alternative employment. But here the development of Cheltenham as an educational centre helped. Charlton wives became the bread-winners, taking in washing from the four Colleges and from private houses. This is why so many Charlton houses have (or had until lately) a large wash-house at the back. Miss Hamlett at Conway Cottage was employing ten to a dozen women; a public drying ground was kept for the convenience of the laundries in Horsefair Street (it is now allotments) – the wet clothes were taken up there in baskets and put out to dry. The Matthews brothers with their dray used to go round collecting the hampers of dirty clothing to be washed and took back the clean clothing at the end of the week to the Colleges; Connie Herbert remembers her father doing the same for the private houses served by Longleat.[5] The Diamond Sanitary Laundry in New Court Road had started in 1879 and employed a lot of girls.

All this kept Charlton from the workhouse, but the result was that husbands depended on wives (which Thomas Moore as Vicar disapproved of!) and old Mr Turner remembered days when a dozen unemployed men would stand all day round Attwood's Corner 'and not two halfpence between them to rub together'. The desperate unemployment of the 1890s is referred to in the *Parish Magazine* for January 1891 and 1892 and again in March 1895.

15

Local Government

Charlton Kings started as part of the manor and hundred of Cheltenham and, when it got its own church, as part of the parish of Cheltenham. The parish here only gained full independence in 1814, though long before that the Vestry had been the controlling body and had run everything in Charlton (except the parish lands which had been handed over to trustees). The population grew in the nineteenth century and in 1862 a Board of Health was set up. That was followed under the Local Government Act of 1894 by an Urban District Council; finally in 1974 Charlton was reunited with Cheltenham as part of the extended Borough. Under the Board of Health, our population in 1881 was 3950. But then the boundary was redrawn, cutting off the area between Hales Road and Holy Apostles Church, so that in 1901 under the Urban District Council it was only 3806. It had grown to 6034 by 1946 and to 10,177 by 1971.

Some Problems of Local Government

The Sewer Story[1]

Under the Public Health Act of 1848, which provided for the election of Local Public Health Boards, and under a Local Government Act of 1858, Charlton Kings acquired a Local Board of Health in 1862. It had power to deal with roads, street lighting, nuisances and sewage; and increasingly its chief concern was the last, for in the mid-nineteenth century our streams were the open sewers of the parish. Geography made it inevitable that Charlton sewerage would get into the Chelt and pollute it, with serious consequences for Cheltenham; on the other hand, the last thing Cheltenham's Improvement Commissioners wanted was to become responsible for the sewers of Charlton Kings! Some houses in the Coltham area were already draining into their sewers and other houses which had cess pits were allowing surface water into the drains, and for none of these houses did the Commissioners receive any rates.

The Cheltenham Commissioners were so unhelpful that Charlton Kings began to consider other possibilities – could the sewage be utilised? On this scheme Mr Williams, Chief Clerk to the Commissioners, wrote privately to his surveyor: 'Charlton people seem to be such fools that one must be more careful of them than though they were rogues!' A plan to turn Sandford Mill into a sewage farm for Charlton was defeated because only part of the mill buildings were in Charlton and because some local residents objected. Williams commented again: 'They seem to be a set of muddling and most unbusinesslike people, but we must get on with them as well as we can and bad as they may be, and trust that sooner or later they will take their own business into their own hands.' The Commissioners, on the contrary, were horrified at the possibility of such a thing; not only was Charlton planning to make the outfall of their sewage into the Chelt but they had obtained the consent of the Secretary of State! Could Cheltenham stop this under the powers of its own Local Government Act? The Local Government Board Office, the Home Office and the local MP were consulted. Eventually Mr Williams sent all the papers to Lord Montagu, head of the Parliamentary Commission on Sewers, declaring;

> We have here spent between twenty and thirty thousand pounds in cleaning and keeping cleansed the Stream called the Chelt which passes through the heart of the Town, and now our neighbours above, namely the Local Board of Charlton, propose to pollute it more or less. It is indeed true they say that they shall, by some disinfecting process, so contrive that their outfall shall take nothing but pure water, but if I rightly read the evidence taken by your Lordship, this is simply impracticable and that the only way of not fouling the stream is by not going into it at all.

Lord Montague's answer was not encouraging: towns higher up a stream could pollute the next town's drinking water with impunity. 'Disinfecting Processes are, every one of them, a total failure.' However, consent for the scheme seems to have been withdrawn.

In 1866, when the matter was raised again, there was a critical report from the Cheltenham surveyor on the state of streams running into the Chelt, particularly the Hearne Brook: 'into this stream a most offensive ditch runs, besides many drains from the populous part of the village through which it flows'. Charlton pointed out that water-courses running into Sandford Mill pond settle there before they reach the Chelt, so 'pollution must be comparatively trifling', and Bafford Brook carried little pollution because it ran through the grounds of Charlton Park and settled in the pond there. Ham Brook was used for drinking purposes, and pollution would be inconsiderable! But again Charlton was told to provide sewers for its own district.

During the next four years, a variety of methods were discussed. If land could be found for collecting tanks and fields where the sewage could be 'utilised' and if a night cart with a suitable 'bed' could be obtained . . . . But landowners were very unwilling to permit this use of their land. In 1870 the Charlton streams had to be cleansed by hand; some of the sewage recovered was used on Mr Burgess's nursery.

In 1870 the Sewage Committee of the two Districts met and discussed union. There were five main points: all connections were to be made under the supervision of the Borough Surveyor; Charlton Kings was to pay £80 annually according to the number of houses connected to the sewers and their rateable value (but who was to rate them?); the sewers were to belong to Cheltenham, and Charlton would pay £20 extra for their use (too much!); this agreement could be ended on 12 months' notice (very unsatisfactory to Charlton); and details were to be agreed by the two Surveyors.

As an alternative, Charlton's Board produced yet another scheme by which the District would gain between £70 and £80-worth of liquid sewage; Ryeworth, Ham, East End and Bafford would be 'irrigated separately', with landowners in the outlying districts being asked to 'utilise' the sewage. That from Cudnall and Church Street was to be conveyed to a pumping station in Spring Bottom; with steam pumps the liquid could be lifted to a large area of arable and pasture land above Ryeworth and Greenway Lane. Sewage from the Coltham area where sewers were not provided by Cheltenham could be served by a second lift to land above Battledown. The Board hoped that as the land was used for dairying there would be a demand for fertiliser. And as the old parish cottages at Spring Bottom already belonged to the Board, there would be no question of having to buy land for a pumping station there. After much correspondence, Charlton got so enthusiastic about the plan that the Local Government Board was asked to sanction raising £3000 on the rates. In reply, the Board sent down Mr Rawlinson to look into the scheme and also to arbitrate between the Charlton Board and the Cheltenham Commissioners for joint sewerage, with the result that the request for £3000 was turned down and the joint scheme received government backing. But although a draft agreement was produced and agreed to, subject to minor alterations, there were still problems: was Charlton to be connected to the Chelt or to the High Street sewer? Ham might have to be drained into a tank, Cheltenham's main sewer would have to be enlarged at an estimated cost of £471, Charlton would have to raise a loan of £4300 on the general rate.

For a year nothing was decided. Then residents who lived near Cheltenham's sewage farm began to object, there was trouble at East End because a waste water pipe was blocked, and there were complaints about cesspits. The Charlton Board had now appointed a Medical Officer of Health; and the Clerk was told to remind Mr Rawlinson of his promised 'Arbitration'. Charlton was worried that the District would have to pay for work in Hales Road and Old Bath Road which would benefit Cheltenham as well (one half of the road being in each), and might also have to compensate Cheltenham when Charlton sewage went into Cheltenham's sewers. After all, the foul watercourse down Hales Road, the culverted stream, would be taken out of the sewer and the amount of sewage which it carried instead would be a good deal less. But of 700 houses it was proposed to connect, 542 had a low rateable value and therefore 'for many years we shall only be sending slop waters from the cottages and a modicum of sewage from the larger houses near the high road' – a very false prediction. Cheltenham insisted that Charlton must construct the sewer from London Road to Hales Road and Coltham Terrace and divert into it all drains and sewers that had previously used the Hales Road watercourse, which might then be connected with the Chelt. And Cheltenham still wanted to have the right to sever the whole connection on six months' notice, a proposal which enraged Charlton.

By September, Mr Rawlinson was ready to set out the Heads of Arrangement under which the two areas were to be considered as one District for sewage purposes. All sewage should be dealt with at Cheltenham at the Commissioners' expense, Cheltenham would complete all sewers in that area necessary for receiving sewage and storm water from Charlton and connect them with the existing tanks, Charlton would complete at its own cost all drains in that area, pay a lump sum of £500 to enable the Commissioners to enlarge the system and £100 annually for use of the outlet sewers and works. Any future dispute was to be settled by the Local Government Board and the cost assessed. The agreement was to remain in force for 30 years from 1 January 1875.

But Charlton was not yet ready to agree. Besides other objections, the Board thought three months far too short a time for an application to raise a loan, get out estimates and tenders, let alone build sewers. Another year passed, but at least the surveyor had had time to draw up detailed plans. In the end, the Local Government Board supported Cheltenham; and finally in 1876 both Districts executed the Agreement. It had taken 14 years!

Tenders and specifications were drawn up and advertised; Charlton accepted a tender by Mr P. Ward. The loan was sanctioned and £500 from the Public Works Loan Committee was sent to the Commissioners so that they could get started on the outfall works. In July the Board discussed the best means of connecting 'Private house drains with the Main Sewers' and at first was in favour of the contractor doing it; later it was suggested that householders would save money 'by connecting their own drains while the main sewers are being laid'. This was a mistake, for people then connected drains without letting the Sewerage Committee know and sometimes used the wrong materials. Mr Higgs, as owner of Charlton Lodge, first complained about the line of the sewer and then wanted to connect his old 'Brick Barrel Drain' with the Cudnall Street sewer; when told he would have to lay down proper pipes in order to make 'an efficient connection' he took no notice and was reported as having connected his existing brick drains with the new glazed pipes. The surveyor pointed out that it was impossible to form good joints between brick and glazed drains, and that the bricks could easily get into the sewers and block them; but the Board was not sure if it had power to compel Higgs to relay them!

The other big problem concerned rights of way for sewers to be laid across private land: not all could be put along existing roads. There were frequent complaints about sewers being laid in the wrong place or where they were not wanted through the Moor End Estate, or about them damaging elm trees at The Hermitage. The sewers were even blamed for a landslip behind the Girls' and Infants' School – according to the surveyor, this was due to the inefficient way in which the embankment forming the school playground had been constructed. In September 1876, the Cheltenham surveyor reported that the new sewers there were completed and ready for the 'reception of the Sewage of the Charlton Kings District'. But not until the following year was the Charlton Kings surveyor able to report their main sewers constructed, £816 9s 10d being due to the contractors who had been obliged to puddle the sewers where they passed through water-bearing strata. Damaged roads had then to be repaired.

But the story of the sewers was not at an end. Already by March 1882 the Charlton Sewerage Committee was suggesting that 'the System of Sewers constructed in 1876–7 were reasonably sufficient for the needs of the District but taking into consideration the increase of Buildings . . . the Committee are now of the opinion that the time has arrived at which it would be justifiable to raise a further loan for the purpose of extending the Sewers'. Charlton was expanding far beyond 700 houses![2]

A Fire Service[3]

From its inception, the Urban District Council was responsible for ash collection and street watering (necessary when the roads got so dusty in summer). The first Urban District Council yard was on London Road between the blacksmith's shop (on the site of the garage) and the triangular orchard on the corner with Cudnall Street (the site of the butcher's and fishmonger's). Then in 1901 the new council offices were built opposite and the council yard was moved to Horsefair Street, where a house for a foreman could be built; and there the Charlton Kings Fire Brigade was established about 1902. The yard foreman could be contacted by telephone and he rang the fire bell to summon the men. All the firemen were volunteers who were paid a retainer of 30 shillings a year with an extra payment for every fire attended. They wore handsome brass helmets (very like Cheltenham's) and these were kept at the yard. As they were expected to deal mainly with chimney and rick fires, they had a hand truck with a manually operated pump to which they could fit standpipes; for a house fire they could call up Cheltenham Brigade which had a horse-drawn engine.

Two episodes are especially remembered. The first was a fire in Cirencester Road in a yard behind the house called Laureltyne. A corn chandler from Andoversford had sheds and outbuildings there where he kept straw and grain, and during the 1914–18 war they caught fire and were burnt down. Mrs Midwinter, then living at Brunswick Villa, heard the bangs when the corrugated iron roofs blew up with the heat and was convinced it was bombs! Charlton Kings Fire Brigade was there but could do little about it.

The second occasion was in 1924, when the Fire Brigade tackled two fires in one night. A very fine early seventeenth-century barn at East End Farm caught fire – it was timber-framed and stone roofed. Against the south end of the barn a brick cottage had been built about 1700, and to light it a gas pipe had been taken through the length of the barn from the main in the road. The cottage caught alight during the night. The late Frank Neather (who had taken his father's place in the Brigade about 1920) used to tell how he heard the fire bell and looked out of his bedroom window in Horsefair Street. Already he could see the flames up at East End, and by the time the Brigade got there, the stone tile roof had fallen in and they hadn't a chance of saving the walls, for the gas pipe through the barn had fractured with the heat. They couldn't even get hold of anyone to turn off the gas for there was no one on night duty at the gasworks! So they concentrated on saving the cottage, which they did. They also tried to save the magnificent oak tree near the north end of the barn but the great heat had damaged the roots and it died in the course of the next twelve months. Coming back up Church Street after that fire, about seven in the morning, the firemen saw smoke coming from the thatch of a cottage behind The Merry Fellow. In the cottage they found a mother in bed with a new baby; the father had gone out to work and some small children left on their own had tried to see what would happen if you pushed a lighted candle into thatch! That time they saved the house.

In 1925 the Charlton Brigade was disbanded and Cheltenham took over; the fire bell was hung at the cemetery and for a long time was tolled for funerals. It still exists in private hands.

A Public Cemetery

By 1900 the extension to the churchyard secured in 1854 was almost full and the need was felt for a public cemetery to supplement it. The New Cemetery, managed by the Urban District Council, was consecrated by the Bishop of Gloucester in January 1909; the land was one of the plots which the owner had refused to sell for this purpose in the 1850s.

A Playground

At the beginning of the century the 'Rec' owned by the Workingmen's Club was available to many Charlton children, and it was still safe for others to play in the road (as George Ryland recalled in 'Four till Bedtime').[4] But then the 'Rec' was taken over by the school, road traffic increased, and the need for a playground was obvious. In 1928 Mr A. W. Martyn of The Hearne offered eleven acres at The Beeches for a playing field, as *The Echo* reported on 12 December. But the Chairman Mr Harris hesitated to accept:

> He pointed out that they would be faced with a certain amount of expenditure which they would be bound to meet when the field became their property – they would have to pay something like £200 to put the land in decent order. Some of the people in the parish had as much as they could do to find food for themselves and from his point of view it was fleecing people to the extent of a 2d rate for the benefit of the children who lived on that side of the parish. In addition the field was waterlogged half the year.

In spite of this, the Council decided to accept the offer but to do nothing immediately; it was not until June 1931 that the Council applied to the Ministry of Health for sanction for a loan of £1250 for levelling and draining the land and erecting shelters; to the Unemployment Grants Committee for a grant of 63 per cent towards the cost of labour; and to the Playing Fields Association for a grant (they received £125 from this source in June 1932). Everyone agreed that the site was not ideal but that it was (and is) the best available.

16

The Health of the Community

There were a number of smallpox epidemics in the late seventeenth and early eighteenth centuries, and Charlton suffered accordingly. Between September 1682 and January 1682/3 the parish register marks fourteen burials 'SP' – deaths from smallpox. Bridgeman, collecting material about Charlton Kings, found evidence for other epidemics in 1690, 1702, 1712, 1720–2 and 1727–8; the Overseers of the Poor wrote 'smallpox' against names for 1720 and 1722;[1] and Rudder in *A New History of Gloucestershire* (1779) remarks: 'In the 10 years from 1700 there were 125 baptisms and 152 burials. In four of these years there was a great mortality in the Parish which carried off 88, being 40 more than died in four common years.'

But setting epidemics aside, Charlton seems to have been remarkably healthy. Our water supplies came from wells or springs and were reasonably unpolluted – we did not have to drink from streams or ponds. It was generally believed that the chalybeate found in much Charlton water promoted longevity and we could certainly boast of centenarians like Henry Ussell (buried 1 November 1683 aged 100) and Mary Harding widow (buried 10 January 1709 aged 101), possibly James Cleevely (buried 1 October 1734, apparently the James who had been baptised 24 August 1634); and nonagenarians like Thomas Cherington (buried 12 April 1702 aged 97). Infant mortality was high between 1538 and about 1580, but after that it fell to a very low level – of the 165 babies baptised in the decade between 1635 and 1644, only thirteen died before the age of 5.[2] Considering the sewage disposal problem, we were lucky to escape cholera in the nineteenth century but somehow we did.

One contributory factor to our relatively clean bill of health may have been the amount of help available for the sick from charity money, so that death from malnutrition was rare.

By 1875 this parish, like most others, was divided into Districts, each with a Visitor whose duty it was to report cases of sickness and need. The Sick and Aged Fund raised £42 4s 9¼d in the year from Easter 1883 to Easter 1884 and this money was at the Vicar's disposal. Then in 1883 the clergy and District Visitors formed themselves into a Nursing Committee, drew up rules and engaged a parish nurse who was to attend non-infectious cases (infectious cases were visited only on the order of the doctor and the Vicar). She was not to attend 'cases which properly belong to a Maternity Society' (which suggests that such a Society existed; there was or had been a Charlton Kings Benefit Society). The first nurse was Miss Fletcher, who began her work here in January 1884, having been engaged for six months in the hope that the £80 per annum for her salary could be raised by subscription. The February 1884 *Parish Magazine* reported:

> even during the short time Miss Fletcher has been with us, she has rendered most important service to the sick and afflicted, and already people are beginning to wonder

how we got on without her aid, as on more than one occasion, she (by her trained skill as a nurse) has been the means, under God, of saving life and alleviating much pain and suffering. Her services have been rendered also to others besides the poor, and the question was discussed at the District Visitors' Meeting whether those who can afford to pay for her services should be allowed to do [so]; when it was decided that in no case could payment be accepted. . . . In all emergencies she will obey the call, come it from where it may, rich or poor; but beyond this first visit . . . Miss Fletcher cannot accept the case, as her first obligation is towards the poor in whose cottages the medical practitioner is unable to get his orders skilfully carried out. To secure as far as possible the immediate application of remedies ordered by the doctor, a supply of Lint, Disinfectants, and ordinary requirements of a sick room, has been purchased from the result of the Offertory on Christmas Day; but these stores may not be drawn upon by those who can afford to purchase such things, or by those who are entitled to receive such aid from the Parish.

These medical supplies were kept at the Vicarage. It must be remembered that there was no chemist's shop in Charlton: until Mr Cheshire came in 1922 everything had to be fetched from the town. Miss Fletcher's first six months were paid for out of the Offertory taken at the Harvest Festival in 1883. She obviously hoped for an increase – she had earned more elsewhere – but that was out of the question here and she left in June 1884; parishioners subscribed for a 'pretty little watch' to give her.

The Vicar was assured by the Lady Superior of St John's Nursing Establishment in London that £80 a year was 'not deemed inadequate by those who are qualified to judge',[3] and in September another nurse, Mrs Rudwick, was secured. Alas, 'the Harvest Festival on Thursday the 18th of September was a success in everything except the amount of the Offertory for the Nursing of the Sick Poor', so the parish kept her on until Easter 1885 and then abandoned the scheme 'with extreme regret'.[4]

The Queen's Jubilee Nursing Institute was founded in 1887 (with part of the money from the Women's Jubilee gift), and this led eventually to District Nurses not dependent on occasional offertories. In January 1893 Charlton Kings welcomed Nurse Fenton who was to work under the new rules, charging 5 shillings for attending a childbirth and 9 pence an hour for visiting in sickness (those paying less than £12 rental a year to be attended free). Mrs Bagnall of Bafford House was Superintendent. Since 1893, Charlton has enjoyed the devoted service of many District Nurses, one of the best remembered being Nurse Newdick who worked in Charlton from *c.*1905–33. In the *Parish Magazine* of July 1884, the Vicar remarked that the Parish Nurse 'should have no time to spare for superintendence of a Crèche'. So perhaps the crèche run in Charlton Kings for the benefit of working mothers and their babies started about that time – it is remembered to have been carried on from about 1905 in a house in Copt Elm Road and to have continued until about 1919.[5]

The problem of getting medicine even when entitled to it 'on the parish' is well illustrated by a story told by the late Frank Neather who was born about 1897.

When I was a boy, I used to collect medicine for an old woman who lived in Mill Lane (School Road). There wasn't any doctor or chemist in Charlton then, I had to walk to Leckhampton to the Doctor's, then to the Workhouse for the medicine, and then back to Charlton, and was paid a farthing for doing it. One day, watching the men building the loop, I dropped the bottle and had to do the whole round again![6]

And George Ryland remembers how his mother used to cure septic wounds with applications of Burgess' Lion Ointment:

> In those days there was no Health Service, there was just the patient and the doctor. Unless the patient had to be taken into hospital, the doctor treated him at home. His calls usually cost 5s but this was quite a drain on most workmen's pay. The more thrifty certainly paid subscriptions to 'Clubs' which paid out a pittance during incapacitation. Which ever way you looked at it, illness was a time of major disaster. . . . If the wound did not heal easily, the doctor's method was to open the wound and scrape down to the bone. In those days there was no local anaesthetic and it cannot be wondered at if patients would do anything to avoid the knife. On the other hand, the ointment worked painlessly and drew out the puss – I have seen a cylinder of puss break through almost the size of a cartridge.

Most of these septic wounds were caused 'by handling weights they never should have attempted'. One never sees anything of the sort now.[7] A good deal of the tuberculosis in Charlton in the early part of this century was probably the result of dirty cowsheds and infected milk, again a thing of the past.

Another step forward in health care was the setting up of Charlton Kings Infant Welfare Centre in 1923 'as a place where any mother could get minor advice as preventative to more serious illness' and where a doctor would attend to see any baby recommended to him by the nurse. General R. G. Burton was the moving spirit, the co-operation of Charlton Kings Nursing Association was secured, and Dr Barrett Cardew agreed to undertake the duties of Medical Officer. The clinic was held twice a month. The basic minimum of equipment was bought: a weighing machine at £4 3s 6d, three screens at £1 19s, a fireguard, stationery, bucket, etc. Drugs were to be bought from Mr Cheshire and a drug cupboard was to be placed in one corner of the St Clairford Hall, where the clinic met at first, everything – weighing and examining babies and toddlers – happening in the one room, merely separated by the screens. At the first meeting, only eight mothers and eight infants attended. By the end of the year, there were 62 mothers and 75 infants on the books, and the value of 'the Welfare' was generally recognised. Since then it has met in various rooms and gone from strength to strength, always working on a shoe-string budget.[8] Eventually all voluntary organisations of this kind were taken over by the Health Authority, and Charlton Kings Infant Welfare Centre met for the last time on 26 November 1986.

17

Transport

The Railway in Charlton Kings

Almost fifty years elapsed between the first proposals for a railway line through Charlton Kings and its actual opening. Plans for the Banbury and Cheltenham Direct Railway were deposited on 13 November 1872. The course of the line was to be to the south and east of the village before following the valley of the River Chelt towards Dowdeswell.[1]

The subsequent Act of Parliament enabled the railway company to purchase compulsorily a large tract of land within the village. The Book of Reference attached to the Act[2] lists two houses, six cottages, one beerhouse, five sets of farm buildings, 45 fields, and three plantations. Sir William Russell is named as jointly owning 30 of the 62 items affected. In 1870 Russell had petitioned the London Bankruptcy Court for the liquidation of his affairs. The joint ownership of the lands and properties could imply arrangements with his creditors or, more likely, that full liquidation had not been fully enacted by that date. In several cases the National Bank of Scotland is named as joint owner.[3]

The Banbury and Cheltenham Direct Railway had opened the line from Chipping Norton to Bourton on the Water in 1862 and work on the remaining section commenced soon after the passing of the Act in 1873, the necessary £800,000 being raised by share issue and loan.[4] From Bourton on the Water to Dowdeswell the work went satisfactorily. On inspecting the Charlton Kings section the contractor, Lawrence, suggested a deviation which would avoid steep gradients and considerable earthworks. Parliamentary blessing was quickly received, and so was saved John Wilson's beerhouse and the site of the future reservoir.[5]

Work on the Charlton Kings section was slow and laborious. Eventually the mixture of clay and sand proved too much for Lawrence because in late 1876 he resigned. He was persuaded to start again in July 1877 but ceased almost immediately. Work was now at a standstill for almost two years.[6] Alfred Keen, a local man, worked on one of the embankments. His son recalls him saying, 'When we were building the embankment often the work they put in by day fell away during the night and left the metals [rails] exposed next morning'.[7] Some of the labour was recruited locally, but such was the extent of the excavations that large numbers of navvies must have invaded the area. Their impact would have been quite traumatic, with their capacity for hard work, hard drinking and an almost total disregard for property.

Work on the line restarted in 1879 when a new contractor was persuaded to complete the work for £82,000. This must have come as a great relief to the villagers who had had a long-awaited but incomplete railway on their doorstep for three years.[8] Progress was slow; the clay was difficult when wet and iron hard when dry.

In March 1881 the drama was nearly over, the line was ready for the official inspection by

Col. F. H. Rich. The officer must have been more than somewhat surprised when his train drew into Charlton Kings Station – it did not appear on the official plan! It seems likely that permission for it was never given. Worse was to come, for the station was grossly below standard. The footbridge and staircase were of insufficient strength, a clock was not provided, and because the gap between platform and train was too great, the track had to be realigned.[9] Two further inspections were needed before the railway was deemed safe. Thus it was that on 1 June 1881 at about 7 a.m. the first train steamed into Charlton Kings station.

Within six weeks of the opening of the line through Charlton Kings the Swindon and Cheltenham Extension Railway Act was passed.[10] This railway was to join the BCDR at Andoversford; it soon became part of the Midland and South Western Junction Railway. The BCDR had been operated by the Great Western Railway from its inception whilst the MSWJR was allied with the GWR's bitter rivals, the Midland and the London and South Western Railways. As a result of this enmity MSWJR trains passed through, but did not stop at, Charlton Kings or Leckhampton stations.[11] The situation was resolved in 1899 when it was agreed that the MSWJR could use the village station from 1 April – at no cost to themselves. It was also agreed that the line between Cheltenham and Andoversford would be doubled, thus disposing of the MSWJR complaint that their trains were held up whenever possible.

From 1899 to 1914 Charlton Kings rail travellers enjoyed a very superior service. Not only were there local trains to Cheltenham, Banbury and Swindon, but major expresses began to use the line. Most passed through the village, but many would stop as long as the guard was informed on boarding or the company was advised by letter. Thus it became possible

17.1 Charlton Kings railway station and Urban District Council employees on a day-trip to St Giles's Fair in 1912.[12]

17.2 The horse bus in London Road in 1897.

17.3 The electric tram.

to catch a train to places as far away as Manchester, Birmingham, Swansea, Newcastle and Southampton, journeys which a generation before would have been major undertakings. One could even join the Ocean Express from the north of England at 24 hours' notice, giving access to the liners bound for America, South Africa and the Orient.[13] At this time the station had a full staff consisting of station master, porters, goods handlers and signalman.[14]

With the outbreak of war in 1914 traffic increased but was of a very different nature to that of pre-war days. As an inland route to the south coast the line was of great strategic importance, and millions of men and many, many tons of equipment were transported along it. Almost as soon as the first troop trains had left, ambulance trains began to arrive carrying tragic reminders of the realities of conflict. No doubt many casualties were transferred from Charlton Kings station to the houses and schools commandeered as emergency hospitals.

After the war the railways were grouped into four large companies: the MSWJR becoming part of its rival the GWR. And so began a slow decline – what had been a key cross-country route was reduced in status to a branch line. Few through expresses (with stops by request) were run, most trains stopped at all stations with a consequent reduction in speed. Local passenger traffic was difficult to maintain in the face of the motor coach as many stations were some distance from the villages they served. Some new local traffic came after 1924 when a mineral railway was opened from Leckhampton quarries joining the main line to the west of the station. This branch only lasted until 1926. The GWR attempted to increase passenger services in 1936 by introducing its new high-speed diesel trains. These were not a success and were soon withdrawn.[15]

Just as in 1914, so the outbreak of war in 1939 saw an enormous increase in the volume of traffic. Many trainloads of men and munitions passed through Charlton Kings heading for the army camps of Wiltshire and beyond. Inevitably many ambulance trains made the journey northwards.

In the years after the war, services were yet again reduced, freight particularly so. The iron ore shipments, once so vital to the line, fell to no more than one train per day. Charlton Kings lost all its goods facilities from 1 January 1954 and was reduced to a halt with minimal manning from 6 April 1956.[16]

In the late 1950s railway economics were under serious review and it was all too obvious that the country could no longer afford to subsidise the idyllic branch lines which ran to Swindon and Kingham. It came as no surprise when closure of the former MSWJR line was announced, with effect from 9 September 1961. The Kingham line was closed a year later. Thus it was that the village lost the railway for which it had fought so long and worked so hard.

Road Transport

In the days of coaches, Charlton Kings was able to make use of the services to and from Cheltenham (as listed in Road books) but to catch them people had to walk into the town. When the Birmingham–Gloucester railway came to Lansdown in 1840 it just meant walking an extra mile; then in 1847 St James station was opened and there was a direct route to London.

People wanting to get to local villages not on a railway used the regular carriers' carts – in Charlton Kings the Duke of York was the pick-up place on the London Road and the New Inn on the Cirencester Road. These carts were still working in the 1920s, before the days of country buses. For the town, people might catch the horse bus from Six Ways, which ran in the 1890s.[17] There is a photograph of the bus in 1897 (17.2) coming up on the wrong side of a London Road empty of traffic[18] and another old photograph shows the bus at the end of its run, standing at the top of Copt Elm Road. Electric trams (17.3) came to Charlton in 1903[19] and encouraged house building along Cirencester Road – the tram lines ended outside the New Inn and just below the railway station. When buses replaced trams in 1930 they still followed the same route: up to Six Ways, down Copt Elm Road, along Lyefield Road West, and so up Cirencester Road, though after Bradley Road was cut they halted short of the pub. Now buses in their turn have given way to Metros. But until very recently there were some stalwart Charltonians born in the pre-tram era who always walked into town and back and scorned to claim bus tickets!

One final note – Charlton Kings was the birthplace of the Black and White Coach Company which started in 1926 with two coaches to London a day and two back, operating from a garage in Cirencester Road.

18

Charlton Artists and Poets

Thomas Robins the Elder and his son Thomas the Younger

Charlton Kings was the birthplace of Thomas Robins the elder, whose rococo paintings of gardens and summerhouses have been described by John Harris of the RIBA in *Gardens of Delight*.[1] Since the book appeared there have been exhibitions of Robins's work in London, Bath and Cheltenham; and as a result, other examples of his painting have been recognised. John Harris did not go into Robins's background, beyond mentioning his baptism here on 3 February 1715/16. A book on the family, *The Robins Family of Gloucestershire and London* has been compiled by a many-times-removed nephew John Anthony Robins,[2] and information about Thomas was published in the *Bulletin*.[3] More information bearing on Thomas and his training as an artist came from studying the will of Jacob Portret, a Charlton fan painter.[4] So now we can begin to understand how a place like Charlton suddenly produced an artist of genius.

Most members of the Robins family were connected with the building trades; some of them were carpenters or cabinet makers, and one had been apprenticed to a carver in Gloucester. So a feeling for design and an appreciation of fine workmanship was probably part of the family atmosphere, though William Robins (Thomas's father) had become a maltster in consequence of marrying as his first wife Sarah Holder. Her fortune was used to buy the Moorend beedle messuage and malthouse – it was surrendered to William for life, Sarah for life and her heirs by William or trustees of her will in 1709. This beedle messuage, the only Ashley tenement in the tithing of Bafford, stood on the site of the laundry. Sarah died childless in 1712 and by her will dated 8 August 1712 left the property (after her husband's life interest) to a niece Margaret, daughter of her brother Francis Holder, and to Margaret's heirs. But William remarried in 1713 and in 1718 he paid Margaret Holder £42 for a surrender of the messuage for the use of himself and his new wife. This house was so built that it could be used as a single dwelling or be divided into two – several of the sons in turn shared it with their parents. William and his second wife Anne had seven children, of whom Thomas was the second. All grew up except the last child, Priscilla, who died at the age of five; one of Thomas's children was named after her.

Thomas was baptised on 3 February 1716/17. So far as we know, there were no educational facilities in the village at the time he was growing up, but a fan painter named Jacob Portret was living here – probably a Huguenot refugee since he owned a number of French books – and Thomas may have learned from him the craft of fan painting; one fan painted by Thomas is now in Cheltenham Art Gallery and his exquisite borders of flowers, shells and butterflies, painted as frames to his views of houses and gardens, could be derived from the kind of miniature decoration suited to fans. That there was a link between the two men is certain, for in his will dated 20 December 1742 Jacob left all his best furniture to Thomas, treating him like an adopted son.[5]

Thomas married when he was only nineteen. His wife was Margaret Holder (probably a connection of Sarah) and the marriage took place at Boddington, about five miles from Cheltenham. She was not unprovided for. On 14 July 1742 (GRO D 109/1) Thomas and his mother Anne paid £90 to William Robins maltster for a surrender of a close of meadow or pasture called Grindles Breach at Moorend – this had been part of the land going with the beedle messuage in 1709 and it may be that by this surrender Thomas and his wife acquired his father's life interest in it, though the entry is not precise about that. Anne, wife of William Robins, acted with her son because he was still under age and can hardly have acquired £90 except through his marriage. Incidentally, this entry (and others in the 1750s relating to William and his sister Ann Gardner) is proof that the entry in the register under 2 October 1740: 'Buried William Robins' does not refer to Thomas's father (there were other related Robins in Cheltenham and elsewhere).

Thomas and Margaret had six children all baptised in Charlton Kings, the youngest son, Thomas, not being born until 1748. At first Thomas and his wife may have lived at Moorend with the parents, while the eldest brother Richard was away at Deerhurst. Then in 1750, calling himself 'Thomas Robins of Charlton Kings painter', Thomas bought an

18.1 Mr Prinn's house (Charlton Park) by Thomas Robins the Elder. (*Reproduced by permission of Cheltenham Art Gallery.*)

Ashley copyhold house in Cudnall, with Ryeworth field on the north and east and land late of William Harrison, afterwards of 'Mr Portrat', on the west; so it was somewhere at the Spring Bottom end of the street (which then sloped down the hill from Grove House to the water-splash). Portret's land was presumably what became the garden of the nineteenth-century Porturet House (the use of 'Mr' before the name and the description of the house supplied by the will and inventory suggest a sizeable dwelling). Thomas's new house was next door, and both were on the upper side of the road, pulled down when the new line was cut up to the new 1787 London Road, and the old sloping road closed in 1836. He used this family home as a base from which he travelled round the country, painting the newly laid-out gardens of his patrons and possibly suggesting improvements.

Thomas is believed to have done only one oil painting, that of Mr Prinn's house (Charlton Park) *c.*1748 (18.1). All the rest were in watercolour, which suited his style better. A sketch book with 133 drawings and 22 paintings from it were known when *The Robins Family* was written; since then, others have come to light. From all these a chronology of his travels has been compiled – he worked in Gloucestershire, Shropshire, Staffordshire, Dorset and Berkshire, in addition to the 45 drawings he made which record the growth of Bath. All his views are enhanced with little groups of children at play, cows being milked, girls with sheep, fishing and boating parties. 'Through his floral frames we view a magical world.' It was not until some time after 1760 that Thomas decided to move his family to Bath, and there he died on 12 January 1770 as 'the Limner of Bath'. His work was to a large extent forgotten after his death.

Thomas the younger was 22 when his father died and eighteen months later he married Ann Willings at Bath Abbey. They had only one child, a daughter. Thomas II took as his study the flowers, butterflies and insects with which his father had created frames for his views – already the taste for rococo gardens and garden buildings was passing and flower painting had become a subject in its own right. Like his father he used watercolours to give transparency, with the occasional touch of opaque white. Wilfred Blunt in *The Art of Botanical Illustration*[6] remarks of his painting: 'The drawing is exceptionally sensitive and delicate and the brush work is crisp; the treatment decorative but without sacrifice of Naturalism. . . . in its own way perfect'.

It was perhaps too perfect for Bath visitors. The father had always worked for patrons and had not needed to advertise; the son was obliged to resort to an advertisement in the *Bath Chronicle* of 29 November 1787: 'Mr Robins begs to announce that his pictures of exotic plants and insects may be seen at his apartments in Chandos Buildings and at Mr Rickard's Print Shop, Broad Street.' By 1805 Thomas was in distress for money and though he valued his two volumes of paintings at £100, he was glad to pledge them to the Bath and West Society for 20 guineas, and had not redeemed them at the time of his death in 1806. The Society kept the volumes until 1967–8 when all the paintings in its possession were sold; and then the work of Thomas Robins the younger was appreciated at its true worth for the first time.

Thomas the elder is believed to have represented himself as a slightly comic figure in the foreground of some of his sketches; portraits of Thomas the younger and his intended wife are reproduced in *The Robins Family*.[7]

Meanwhile the Moorend beedle messuage had come into the possession of Henry, the youngest of William the maltster's sons, who lived in Oxenton. He died in 1802 and his son Henry sold it to John Whithorne in 1805. Henry the younger turned his artistic inheritance to good account as a London auctioneer specialising in the sale of elegant furniture, and the business in Covent Garden became nationally and internationally known under his son George Henry.[8]

Briton Riviere (1840–1920)

Though not born in Charlton Kings, Briton Riviere may be claimed as a Charlton artist. His father William came to live here so that his son could attend the College – the 1858 rate book shows him at no. 485, Porturet House, g.e.r. £65. William was an historical painter who had exhibited at the Royal Academy from 1826; and his son inherited his talent, exhibiting at the Academy from 1858. He was 'best known for paintings of lions and other animals, although he himself cared least for these';[9] and in fact in all his paintings it is the animals which catch the attention rather than the somewhat sentimentalised human figures – witness such paintings as 'Sympathy' in the gallery of Royal Holloway College, or 'Circe and the Swine' (where the very lively pigs are said to be Charlton pigs sketched at East End farm). Briton Riviere married Mary Alice Dobell, one of the daughters of John Dobell of Detmore[10] – all the members of that family were interested in art and science, and several of them were good amateur artists. In his will of 24 December 1918 Briton Riviere noted that he had already given an 'imaginative' picture to the Corporation of London, and would like 'an animal work', 'The Bank of an African River', his 'best and most complete work', to find a place in the Guildhall gallery.[11]

Clara Georgiana Mary Burton (exhibited as Clare Burton; d. 1947)

Clare was a daughter of General Edmund Francis Burton, one of a family of nine sons and three daughters (one of the sons being General R. G. Burton of Bafford Grange). Clare was not born in Charlton Kings, but a sister and brother were baptised at St Mary's in 1874. After the General's retirement from the Indian Army, he settled at Hambrook House where Clare had a studio.

At the age of 28 she took herself to Paris to study and had a picture exhibited at the Paris Salon; and between 1897 and 1900 she exhibited four paintings at the Royal Birmingham Society of Art. A painting from that period which is of special interest to Charlton Kings is a study of passengers inside the horse bus: 'Charlton to Cheltenham, all the way for 2d'. Some of her best work was in pastel: sensitive portraits of women and children, among the latter the two young daughters of H. O. Lord of Lilleybrook. Other portraits included several of Indian princes. Examples of her work are to be seen at the Walker Art Gallery, Liverpool, and the Manchester Art Gallery.

She went on exhibiting until 1911, when her eyesight began to fail. She and her mother were then living at The Hermitage (Bridge House), and when she became unable to paint, she threw herself into war work during the 1914–18 War and then into work for the Conservative Party. She died in Cheltenham in 1947.

Sydney Dobell (1824–74)

The poet Sydney Dobell came to live in Cheltenham in 1835 and moved to Charlton during 1840. Though he was not native here, he always regarded Charlton as 'home' above any other place, and his letters are full of local references.[12] When John Dobell first rented Detmore in 1840 it was a very small house, much as Dinah Mulock (Mrs Craik) described it in *John Halifax Gentleman*. That book, which was first published in 1857, was partly written during a visit there. We don't know exactly when John Dobell added the two big sitting-rooms facing south-east with a view of Coxhorne and Red Wood, but a letter of Sydney's dated 1852 suggests that the alteration had already been made; that explains his extreme anxiety as to the effect of a projected line of railway which would have come through Detmore field – fortunately for them the scheme came to nothing.

Sydney helped his father in their wine merchant's business. In 1844 he married Emily Fordham, and at the end of 1848 they took a lease of Coxhorne House for five years. This seems to have been the happiest time of his life. Here he finished 'The Roman' and wrote much of 'Balder', poems which he regarded as his major work – contemporaries thought well of them and Dobell was even tipped by some as a possible poet laureate. Now he is chiefly remembered for his lyrics – in 1900 Quiller Couch included four in his edition of the *Oxford Book of English Verse* and two of those are often found in children's anthologies. 'The Roman' depended for its appeal on the current interest in Italian politics and the Victorian practice of reading aloud.

When Currer Bell published *Jane Eyre*, Dobell was one of the first reviewers to recognise the author's sex and give the novel just praise; he corresponded with Charlotte and invited her to stay at Coxhorne to see apple orchards in flower, a sight she said she had never experienced. One wonders what she would have made of Charlton's meadows and orchards, and the Cotswold hills rising only 900–1000 feet from the plain to level off into a tableland, so different from her Yorkshire moors. She never came, her father's blindness making a visit impossible.

For himself, Sydney Dobell felt: 'I can write . . . under the necessity of the case here in London but every breath of inspiration is of Charlton air. I sit here but I *am* at home.' He was greatly distressed when the inheritor of Coxhorne refused to renew the lease and he had to leave – 'his wife remembers his kissing its gate, his cheek moist with tears, when, for the last time as the gate of his own home he leant on and looked over it'.

Eva Dobell (niece of Sydney and daughter of Clarence Mason Dobell of The Grove) published several small volumes of verse including in one of them a description of the mature garden at Detmore as it was around the turn of the century.[13]

Cecil Day-Lewis, Poet Laureate (1904–72)

Though we can scarcely claim him as a Charlton poet, we can claim Day-Lewis as a resident novelist. He and his wife lived at Box Cottage, Bafford Lane, for seven years from 1931; a plaque to that effect was put on the house by the Civic Society in 1983 and was unveiled by his widow.

Day-Lewis taught at Cheltenham College until 1935 and was living at Box Cottage when he wrote his first detective story, *A Question of Proof*, published under the name of Nicholas Blake (Collins, 1935). The setting was a school which bore enough resemblance to the College to annoy the authorities, and this led to Day-Lewis's resignation, but he stayed on in Charlton for two years after that and continued to write detective fiction.

In May 1935 W. H. Auden stayed at Box Cottage with the Lewises and introduced them to his fiancée Erika Mann (eldest daughter of the German novelist Thomas Mann).

Some Literary and Heroic Links

Sir Nathaniel Wraxall (1751–1831), author of historical memoirs, rebuilt Wraxall House in 1816–17 as his own residence.[14]

Sir Thomas Phillipps (1792–1872), antiquary and bibliophile, married his first wife Harriett Molyneux at St Mary's on 23 February 1819.[15]

Adam Lindsay Gordon (1833–70), best known for his lines beginning 'Life is mostly froth and bubble',[16] was baptised at St Mary's 3 December 1833.

Dinah Mulock (1826–87), who became Mrs Craik on marriage, used Detmore as part of the setting for *John Halifax Gentleman*, first published in 1857.

Alice Liddell ('Alice in Wonderland') stayed with her grandfather the Reverend Henry George Liddell at Hetton Lawn in 1863 and was visited there by Lewis Carroll (C. L. Dodgson, 1832–98) who was staying in Cheltenham. This is believed to have been the start of *Alice through the Looking Glass*.[17]

Mary Colmore, first wife of C. F. Cregoe Colmore of Moorend Park, was the daughter of the Reverend Edward Pryce Owen (1785–1863), who is well known for his etchings of Shrewsbury, and granddaughter of the Reverend Hugh Owen, co-author of the standard *History of Shrewsbury* (1825). She was buried at St Mary's, 20 June 1865.

Robert Burns's granddaughters **Sarah and Annie Burns** and his great-granddaughter, **Margaret Constance Burns Hutchinson**, were buried in the churchyard at St Mary's between 1909 and 1925.

John Samuel Pritchard (d. 1934), the tailor whose story inspired Beatrix Potter's *Tailor of Gloucester*, is buried in Charlton Kings cemetery.[18]

There have been two VCs with Charlton Kings links: Captain Edward Unwin, VC, CB, CMG in the First World War; and Commander David Wanklyn, VC of HMS *Upholder* in the Second World War.[19]

19

Games and Athletics

Over the last hundred years Charlton people have enjoyed various forms of games and athletics though it is not easy to find hard evidence about the clubs and their activities. What follows relies on reminiscences.

Cricket

There was an appeal in the *Parish Magazine* of June 1879 for the use of a field for cricket, and the July issue announced:

> A Parochial Cricket Club has been successfully started by the help of various kind friends. The use of a suitable field has been obtained from Mr Mitchell at Ryeworth [that is, George Mitchell of Ryeworth Farm]. The Captain of the Club is Mr Brice and it is governed by a Committee. . . . The members' subscription is 2s 6d for the season.

A year later, in September 1880, the magazine was able to print the scores of matches played against Leckhampton and other clubs in the vicinity; and from time to time cricket news was put into the magazine as space and funds allowed. An AGM on 21 April 1884 chose W. R. Burroughs of The Endeavour as secretary in place of Mr Peacy; and in April 1885 Mr R. Burroughs was elected captain. The subscription was altered to three shillings for those over 18 and two shillings for those younger; it was hoped that this slight increase would solve the pecuniary difficulties of the previous season.

A problem about the use of the Ryeworth ground arose in May 1899, and after considering a field at Withyholt farm, the influence of the Burroughs family led to the transfer of the Club to a meadow at The Beaches[1] where it has been ever since. So cricket history here goes back over a century, or as George Ryland says: 'Charlton Kings had a side from time immemorial and played regularly against the best sides in the vicinity.' Mr Burroughs himself was a member for many years and his son after him. A large number of people used to turn out to watch on Saturday afternoons, especially to watch Arthur Bee. This was 'Busy' Bee who came to live at The Reservoir Inn about 1912. Bee's son Frank confirms the stories of his father's prowess – he played for both Charlton Kings and All Saints because for a long time he worked as stud groom looking after 25 horses at Mr Lord's Cotswold Hunt kennels in Whaddon Lane. He was a very fast bowler (Burroughs the wicket keeper said of him: 'I see his little arm come over but never see the ball!') and a terrific batsman – on one occasion he hit two separate sixes one-handed on his left side over the two poplar trees on the All Saints' ground!

The transfer of the original Club to The Beaches left Ryeworth rather out of it and about

19.1 Charlton Kings cricket team c.1930.[2]

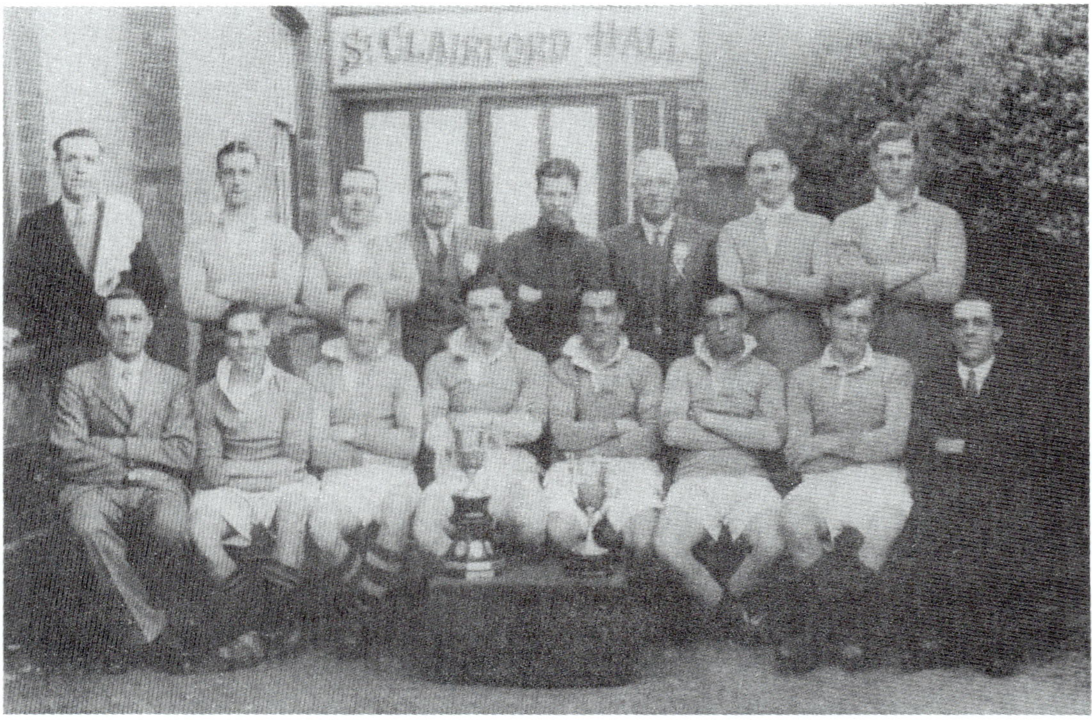

19.2 Charlton Kings football team c.1930.[3]

19.3 Scouts and Cubs at Moorend Park *c.*1930.

80 years ago Ryeworth Cricket Club was started on land belonging to Captain Willis of Glenfall House. Eventually the Club was able to buy the land from Arthur Mitchell of The Glenfall, subject to restrictive covenants to prevent the land from being sold for building, and the Club's facilities now are excellent.

Charlton Soccer and Rugger Clubs

There was already an active soccer club in Charlton Kings in 1884 – the *Parish Magazine* for November 1884 reports a victory over Ryecroft and Cinderford; and a fixture list for 1884–5 was printed in the magizine for January 1885. It is not clear where the team played or whether it was the same as the team called Rangers, which George Ryland recalls playing on a pitch at Greatfield in Sandy Lane in the early 1900s. The Secretary of the AFC was Jack Lawrence who actually lived in Cheltenham in Keynsham Road. The Rangers team died out sometime before 1914.

In the years 1900–6 or thereabouts there was also a rugger team called the Rovers, which played on an adjoining pitch at Greatfield, so spectators could divide their attention between them. But the Rovers never expanded, they only played local games, and about 1906 the team faded away. (This may have had something to do with the Reverend Thomas Hodson leaving the parish in that year: his sons were all keen on rugger.)

Lyefield or Charlton Kings Old Boys

J. F. 'Boss' Fry started an Old Boys' Side called Lyefield Old Boys very soon after he came here as headmaster in 1897. At first they played at Dick Burroughs' place at East End Farm. But then they moved to Glynrosa. In the *Parish Magazine* for May 1899, Hodson remarks: 'Lyefield Boys' School Association Football Club – a successful season, thanks to Mr E. Attwood who so kindly and gratuitously placed his field at the disposal of the Club for the whole season.' Edwin Attwood lived at Glynrosa and the field, two acres, was large enough for a pitch because it came right down to the house (it was shortened in 1911). George Ryland says he played for this team when he left school and did any amount of coaching later. The name was changed to Charlton Kings Old Boys.

Bill Keen used to tell a story about a fellow who broke his leg on the field: they dumped him into Attwood's handcart and wheeled him to the doctor, which must have been excruciating – that cart was much too short for a man to lie in. Fry took a regular interest in the team and Walter Butler was Secretary. Dick Smith (afterwards the Surveyor) was centre forward in the 1909–10 seasons.

The Choir Rugger Team

From 1895 Hodson's sons ran a rugby team on the Grange field behind the Vicarage; they played on Sunday afternoons. To encourage schools the rugby authorities gave out sets of jerseys and masters who were interested organised teams in Cheltenham. There was one at Naunton Park, for instance, and several schools changed to rugger, so there were other teams to play against. After Neale came, the Grange was let and the field was no longer available, so then the Charlton boys played on the 'Rec'. We had a couple of Internationals who played for England as Boys who started there – Bernie Bloodworth and 'Ratty' Smith. 'Ratty' was a wonderful player but went to work on the railway and had to give it up.

Athletics

There was a great deal of interest in walking and running. George Ryland remembers a walking race in 1897 for Queen Victoria's Diamond Jubilee, from Albert Dowler Mitchell's place at Glenfall Farm to the lamp in Clarence Street and back. Harry Attwood used to win these walking races regularly. Among the big clubs was Birchfield Harriers and one of their outstanding milers was 'Soldier' Smith (brother of 'Ratty') who lived in Gladstone Road. Arthur Bee took part in some athletics matches in Charlton Park.

Walking races (but not over so long a distance) continued to be associated with Albert Dowler Mitchell (of Glenfall Farm and later of Ham Court). The course was from the Ryeworth Inn to the Duke of York and back. Mitchell used to start the race by blowing a horn, usually wearing hunting kit or a tail-coat, and those taking part often put on fancy dress too. These light-hearted races went on into the 1950s.

20

Mumming, Visiting and Buff Blowing

There may once have been a Charlton Kings Mummers Play, though it was possibly the same as the one recorded at Leckhampton by Reginald St Johnston in his *History of Dancing*[1] and brought from that parish by Mr Taylor when he settled in Charlton. One nice variant remembered by his daughter, the late Mrs Sallis, was a character called Turkey Snipe (Turkish Knight).

Some houses in the parish were 'visited' on New Year's Day. The custom varied. Sometimes children knocked on the door shouting: 'Old Year Out, New Year In, Coo-ee'; the door would be opened slightly and a coin passed without the occupiers seeing or speaking to the Visitors. Sometimes a boy entered the house by the back door (or by a back window if the door were fastened), walked through the house, picked up a silver coin left for him in the hall and left by the front door. No one was supposed to speak to him on the way. This seems to have been a compliment paid by choir boys to the clergy or to occupiers of houses which had once had clerical associations such as Lyefield Villas (the Vicarage in Mayne's day).

But the real Charlton New Year custom was Buff Blowing. The boys came round very early on New Year's Morning, long before it was light, and chanted a rhyme outside the door to bring the occupiers luck. There were several versions of the words, some adapted to Temperance principles; but Gerry Protherough's version ran:

Buff Blow
Fare Well
God send
Ere well
Apples to roast
Nuts to crack
A barrel of Cider
Ready to tap
On New Year's Day in the Morning –
Choo-ee!

After that they hammered on the door, and if not answered at once would add:

The Old Year's Out, the New Year's In.
Open the door and let me in – Choo-ee!

They expected to be given coppers and apples or mincepies; at some houses the older boys got wine or cider. This custom lasted until the Second World War[2].

So let the Charlton Yarlies have the last word!

References

Abbreviations: GRO – Gloucestershire Record Office; PRO – Public Record Office; WRO – Worcestershire Record Office.
Note: *'Bulletin'* refers to the *Charlton Kings Local History Society Bulletin*. Title deeds, unless otherwise stated, are in private hands and are not generally available to be consulted.

Chapter 2: Settlement

1. *Bulletin* 7, pp. 35–7.
2. *Bulletin* 13, pp. 3–4.
3. PRO E 106/2/3.
4. IPM 1246. (IPM is 'Inquisition *post mortem*', an enquiry by the Crown on the death of a tenant into the land he held and the nature of his tenure.)
5. *Transactions of the Bristol and Gloucestershire Archaeological Society*, vol. 103 (1985) pp. 150–1.
6. GRO D 855 M 68; *Bulletin* 15, pp. 10–18.
7. *Bulletin* 8, pp. 8–46.
8. *Bulletin* 1, p. 5; 13, p. 6; 15, pp. 11, 15.

Chapter 3: Custom of the Manors

1. *Bulletin* 15, pp. 6–18.
2. GRO D 855 M 68.
3. PRO E 106/2/3.
4. GRO: GDR wills 1548/94; *Bulletin* 5, pp. 7–10.
5. GRO D 855 M 10 f.84v.
6. GRO D 855 M 10 f.80.
7. GRO P 76 M 1 1/1.
8. *Bulletin* 13, pp. 9–12.
9. For other examples of the operation of custom before 1625 see *Local Historian*, vol. 15, no. 3 (August 1982) pp. 166–73.

Chapter 4: Roads and Footpaths

1. *The Cartulary of Cirencester Abbey*, ed. C. D. Ross (Oxford: Oxford University Press, 1964) vol. 2, p. 383.
2. GRO P 76a CH 1/1.
3. 29 Geo II (cited in 25 Geo III c.125).
4. 26 Vic c.51; GRO D 3043.
5. 14 Geo III. (cited in 25 Geo III c.125).
6. 25 Geo III c.125.
7. GRO Q/SRh 1784 C/1.
8. GRO SR 1777 A/1.
9. 25 Geo III c.125.
10. GRO Q/SRh 1787 C/1.
11. GRO Q/RUm 97.
12. GRO Q/SRh 1836 D.
13. *Bulletin* 11, pp. 23–9; 13, p. 49.
14. GRO P 76 SU 3/2.
15. GRO Q/SRh 1826 C/2.

Chapter 5: Agriculture

1. GRO D 1252; *Bulletin* 13, p. 7.
2. *Bulletin* 13, p. 7.
3. *Bulletin* 6, p. 27; GRO: GDR wills 1557/230.
4. *Bulletin* 1, pp. 7–10.
5. Gwen Hart, *History of Cheltenham* (Leicester: Leicester University Press, 1965) p. 43; PRO S.C.2/175/3; 175/26/5.
6. *Bulletin* 7, p. 13.
7. GRO D 855 M 12 p. 286.
8. *Bulletin* 5, pp. 37–50; 6, pp. 52–4.
9. GRO: GDR wills 1557/234.
10. *Bulletin* 9, pp. 6–7.
11. Gloucester Library, Hockaday abstracts, vol. 147; *Bulletin* 9, pp. 5–6.
12. GRO D 855 M 68.
13. GRO D 855 M 8 f.83v.
14. GRO D 855 M 8 ff.169v, 182v.
15. GRO D 855 M 12 p 185.
16. GRO: GDR inventories 1695(140).
17. GRO: GDR inventories 1687(129).
18. GRO: GDR inventories 1663(276).
19. GRO: GDR inventories 1664(3).
20. GRO: GDR inventories 1670(36).
21. GRO: GDR inventories 1685(156).
22. GRO: GDR inventories 1698(36).
23. GRO: GDR inventories 1699(235).
24. GRO: GDR inventories 1664(3); and 1684(231).
25. GRO: GDR inventories 1682(122).
26. GRO: GDR inventories 1686(224).

27. GRO: GDR inventories 1682(127).
28. GRO: GDR inventories 1685(156).
29. GRO: GDR inventories 1687(31).
30. GRO: GDR inventories 1684(231).
31. Mrs Rundell, *Domestic Cookery, by a Lady*, new edn, 1867.
32. GRO: GDR inventories 1685(123).
33. GRO: GDR inventories 1684(116).
34. GRO: GDR inventories 1698(36).
35. GRO: GDR inventories 1695(164).
36. GRO: GDR inventories 1684(231).
37. GRO: GDR inventories 1685(156).
38. GRO: GDR inventories 1670(36).
39. GRO: GDR inventories 1686(224).
40. GRO: GDR inventories 1688(31).
41. GRO: GDR inventories 1664(3).
42. GRO: GDR inventories 1685(156).
43. GRO: GDR inventories 1689(235).
44. GRO D 1224 (uncatalogued collection).
45. *Bulletin* 5, pp. 11–19.
46. GRO D 1224.
47. GRO D 109/2.
48. *Bulletin* 13, pp. 8–12.
49. GRO MF 199/14.
50. GRO D 1876/5–6.
51. GRO D 109/1.
52. GRO D 1876/4.
53. GRO D 855 M 68.
54. *Bulletin* 15, pp. 10–18 (1450 rental); *Gloucestershire Historical Studies* (University of Bristol) vol. XII (1981) pp. 73–85 (1557 and 1564 surveys); *Bulletin* 18 (1617 survey).
55. Gloucester Library, Hockaday abstracts s.v. Prestbury.
56. GRO D 85 M 7.
57. GRO D 1224 (uncatalogued collection).
58. Ibid.
59. GRO D 855 M 9 pt 2 p. 103.
60. GRO D 1224 (uncatalogued collection).
61. GRO D 1388 SL 3 no. 57.
62. GRO D 1388 SL 5 no. 90.
63. GRO D 1388 SL 3 no. 24; D 109/2; *Bulletin* 17, pp. 13–14.
64. GRO D 1388 SL 4 no. 102; SL 5 no. 9.
65. GRO D 855 T4.
66. GRO D 1388 SL 5 no. 90.
67. Ibid.

Chapter 6: 'A Bit of Old Chorlton'

1. GRO D 855 M 8 ff. 41v, 114v, 127v, 147.
2. F. E. Witts, *Diary of a Cotwold Parson, Reverend F. E. Witts (1783–1854)*, ed. David Verey (Gloucester: Alan Sutton, 1979) p. 37.

3. *Bulletin* 4, pp. 1–5.
4. *Bulletin* 2, p. 34.
5. *Bulletin* 1, pp. 31–4; 2, pp. 22–4; 14, p. 20; GRO D 2202 II Daubeny and D 1381 acc. 2593.
6. GRO D 855 M 7 f. 83.
7. *Bulletin* 11, pp. 33–42.
8. *Bulletin* 16, p. 16.
9. *Bulletin* 10, pp. 36–9.
10. GRO: GDR inventories 1670(183).
11. *Bulletin* 12, pp. 40–2; 15, pp. 27–8.
12. *Bulletin* 15, pp. 27–34.
13. GRO: GDR inventories 1557(85); *Bulletin* 6, p. 30.
14. *Bulletin* 13, pp. 36–41.
15. *Bulletin* 15, pp. 18–27.
16. An article on Hawthorne's is to be published in *Bulletin* 18; *Bulletin* 13, p. 46.
17. Ibid., pp. 14–22.
18. *Bulletin* 1, pp. 12–15.
19. *Bulletin* 5, p. 33.
20. *Bulletin* 13, pp. 23–5.
21. *Bulletin* 5, pp. 11–19; 7, pp. 45–7.
22. Gyles Ashmead's will is included in the title deeds GRO D 1224 (uncatalogued collection).
23. GRO D 109/1.
24. GRO D 855 M 14 p. 46.
25. GRO D 855 M 11 f. 106v.
26. GRO D 855 M 11 p. 212.
27. GRO D 855 M 16 pp. 109–10.
28. GRO D 109/2 and title deeds.
29. GRO D 109 M 2, under 20 July 1885.
30. *Bulletin* 6, pp. 16–19.
31. GRO D 855 M 7 f. 130.
32. GRO D 109/17: Ashley original surrenders 63, 85; C 59.
33. S. Y. Griffiths, *A Historical Description of Cheltenham* (1826).
34. *Bulletin* 10, pp. 1–5.
35. GRO Ashley manor court book I, under 1748 and 1752, GRO D 109/1.
36. GRO D 109/17: Ashley original surrenders C 117.
37. Ibid., C 11, 103, 101, 127.
38. GRO D 109/2 under 9 March 1829.
39. GRO D 855 M 11 p. 173; *Bulletin* 6, pp. 54–7.
40. GRO D 855 M 5 ff. 39, 47; M 7 f. 100.
41. Ibid., M 11 f. 99.
42. Ibid., M 14 p. 360; M 16 pp. 6–7.
43. GRO: GDR inventories 1685(156).
44. GRO D 855 M 9 pt 2 p. 248.
45. Ibid., M 16 pp. 54–5.
46. Bafford House title deeds.
47. *Bulletin* 2, pp. 3–6; although this account of the Robins family and the site of the laundry is mainly correct it does need revision.
48. GRO D 855 M 15 pp. 205, 215.

49. *Bulletin* 9, pp. 11–32; GRO D 1224 (uncatalogued collection); GRO D 1692/149.
50. *Bulletin* 8, pp. 8–51; GRO D 1224 (uncatalogued collection).
51. GRO D 855 M 10 ff. 131v–2, 168v.
52. J. A. Rawes, *Memorial Inscriptions of Cheltenham*, vol. 1: *St Mary's Church and Churchyard* (Cheltenham (37 Naunton Lane, Leckhampton): J. A. Rawes, 1983).
53. GRO D 855 M 10 ff. 131v–2; 168v; M 11 f. 26; M 12, pp. 219, 227–30; M 13 pp. 157–8.
54. GRO D 855 M 7 ff. 100, 123, 147; M 8 ff. 20v, 38, 115v, 118v; M 9 pp. 22, 44, 50, 210; M 9 pt 2 pp. 102, 176, 273; M 10 ff. 11, 11v, 136.
55. See, for example, Helen Allingham and Stewart Dick, *The Cottage Homes of England* (1909; new edn, Bracken Books, 1984) plate II.
56. GRO D 109/17: Ashley original papers C 112.
57. GRO D 109/17: Ashley original surrenders 9 and 10.
58. Title deeds to Grove House; GRO D 109/1.
59. *Bulletin* 3, pp. 39–41.
60. *Bulletin* 13, p. 9; 15, pp. 36–8.
61. *Bulletin* 3, pp. 34–8; 7, p. 56; 6, pp. 47–52.
62. *Bulletin* 17, pp. 5–29.
63. *Bulletin* 4, p. 11; GRO: GDR wills 1545/3.
64. GRO D 109/17: Ashley original surrenders 119.
65. GRO GBR C 10/3 f. 742.
66. GRO D 109/1; D 885 M 9 pt 2 p. 139; M 13 pp. 267–8; M 17 pp. 32–4.
67. GRO D 1388 SL 3 no. 25.
68. Norden's 1617 survey; GRO D 855 M 51.
69. The history of the Wraxall House site will be the subject of a paper in a future *Bulletin*.
70. For a history of the career of Sir Nathaniel Wraxall see his entry in *The Dictionary of National Biography*.
71. GRO D 855 M 8 f. 66v; M 9 pt 2 p. 273.
72. *Bulletin* 10, pp. 8–15.
73. GRO D 2025/1.
74. *Bulletin* 6, pp. 58–9.
75. For Nathaniel Hartland's pedigree and his expenditure on his house see *Bulletin* 7, pp. 13–34.
76. *Bulletin* 3, pp. 11–12.
77. *Bulletin* 13, p. 8.
78. *Bulletin* 3, pp. 5–10.
79. Griffiths, *A Historical Description of Cheltenham*.
80. *Bulletin* 12, pp. 10–17.

Chapter 7: In the House: Inventories, 1680–1750

1. GRO D 1224 (uncatalogued collection); GDR inventories 1692(149).
2. GRO: GDR inventories 1733(128).
3. GRO: GDR inventories 1688(11).
4. GRO: GDR inventories 1684(231).
5. GRO: GDR inventories 1663(276).
6. GRO: GDR inventories 1741(1).
7. GRO: GDR inventories 1714(148).
8. GRO: GDR inventories 1685(156).

Chapter 8: Places of Worship

1. *Bulletin* 14 and 16.
2. *Bulletin* 8, pp. 55–6.
3. *Bulletin* 9, p. 32.
4. *Bulletin* 13, pp. 9–11.
5. *Charlton Kings Parish Magazine*, 1878.
6. *Bulletin* 12, p. 43.
7. WRO: WDR wills 1537/254.
8. *Bulletin* 4, p. 8.
9. Ibid., pp. 7–12.
10. Ibid., p. 15.
11. *Bulletin* 5, pp. 10–11.
12. *Bulletin* 14, pp. 11–18
13. GRO: GDR wills 1611/6 and 1612/8.
14. GRO D 855 M 68.
15. (a) GDR B 4/1/453; (b) GRO P 76 IN 3/1.
16. *Bulletin* 13 lists the relevant houses in East End.
17. *Bulletin* 14, pp. 21–3.
18. Ibid., pp. 24–32.
19. GRO P 76 ch. 1; *Bulletin* 4, pp. 19–22.
20. GRO F 1/4 C.
21. GDR 208 p. 77.
22. GRO P 76 CW 2/17.
23. GRO P 76 SP 1/2.
24. *Charlton Kings Parish Magazine*, April 1893.
25. *Bulletin* 14, pp. 32–48.
26. F. E. Witts, *The Diary of a Cotswold Parson, the Reverend F. E. Witts*, ed. David Verey (Gloucester: Alan Sutton, 1979) p. 37.
27. *Charlton Kings Parish Magazine*, April 1876.
28. Ibid., May 1878.
29. Ibid., May 1877.
30. Ibid., January 1880.
31. Jesus College, Oxford, archives.
32. Ibid.
33. *Bulletin* 16.
34. GRO D 2970/171.
35. *Bulletin* 10, pp. 20–30; 12, pp. 31–2.
36. GRO D 1381 bundle 32, Dilapidation papers.
37. *Charlton Kings Parish Magazine*, July 1886.
38. *London Gazette*, 25 May and 10 July 1888; GRO P 76 IN/3/4.
39. *Charlton Kings Parish Magazine*, December 1899.
40. GRO P 76 M1 2/3.
41. Ibid.
42. *Bulletin* 16.
43. GRO P 76 SP 3/2 (conveyance of Vestry Hall and land on which it was built); GRO P 76 SP 3/5 (plans); GRO P 76 SP 31 (agenda and minutes of committee set up to adopt old Vestry Hall); GRO P 76 VE 3/3 (correspondence; Vestry Meetings 1835–56); GRO DA 3 100/1–7 (minute books of the Charlton Kings Board of Health, nos 1–7).

44. Holy Apostles Church, *Centenary Booklet* (1966); Steven Blake, *Cheltenham Churches and Chapels, AD 773–1883* (Cheltenham: Cheltenham Museum and Art Gallery, 1979).
45. *Trans. Baptist Hist. Soc.*, vol. 4, p. 208; Hockaday Abstract 66; Edmund Calamy, *An Account of the Ministers, Lecturers, Masters, and Fellows of Colleges who were Ejected or Silenced after the Restoration in 1660 . . .* (1713) vol. II, p. 331.
46. GDR 2052; Parochial list of Dissenting Families GDR 285B; Diocesan Survey 1743 GDR 397.
47. GRO D 2765.
48. GRO D 109/2.
49. GRO 3418/2/5/2–5.
50. GRO D 109/3, 4.
51. GRO D 3418/2/5/6, 7, 10, 13.

Chapter 9: Law and Order

1. GRO D 855 M 10 f. 118.
2. Ibid., M 12 p. 45.
3. Ibid., p. 135.
4. GRO D 855 M 8 f. 78v.
5. Ibid., M 9 p. 265.
6. Ibid., M 5/1.
7. Ibid., M 7 f. 76.
8. Ibid., M 8 f. 126.
9. Ibid., M 9 f. 147.
10. Ibid., M 10 f. 84.
11. Ibid., M 12 p. 243.
12. Ibid., M 9 pt 2 p. 264.
13. Ibid., M 10 f. 33v.
14. Ibid., M 12 p. 70.
15. Ibid., M 10 f. 33.
16. Ibid., f. 109v.
17. Ibid., M 12 p. 70.
18. Ibid., M 8 f. 51.
19. Ibid., M 10 f. 52v.
20. Ibid., M 9 pt 2 p. 265.
21. Ibid., M 10 f. 33.
22. Ibid., M 12 p. 137.
23. Ibid., M 8 ff. 40, 40v.
24. Ibid., f. 40v.
25. Ibid., ff. 159v, 179v.
26. Ibid., f. 179v.
27. Ibid., M 9 pt 2 p. 69.
28. Ibid., p. 171.
29. GRO Calendar of Summary Convictions, September 1810 Q/PC2/29/D 14, 15.
30. *Bulletin* 7, pp. 50–3.
31. *Bulletin* 6, p. 31; 12, pp. 33–5.
32. *Bulletin* 4, pp. 19–22.
33. *Bulletin* 6, p. 15.
34. *Bulletin* 5, pp. 34–5.

Chapter 10: Ale Sellers, Beer Houses and Public Houses

1. GRO D 109/2.
2. *Bulletin* 13, pp. 28–9.
3. Ibid., pp. 26–7.
4. Ibid., p. 33.
5. Ibid., p. 24.
6. GRO D 109/2 p. 420.
7. *Bulletin* 15, pp. 33–4.
8. *Bulletin* 3, pp. 2–4; 15, pp. 1–5.
9. *Bulletin* 4, pp. 38–40; 6, p. 60.
10. GRO D 1224 (uncatalogued collection).
11. *Bulletin* 6, pp. 22–4.
12. Ibid., pp. 1–2.
13. *Bulletin* 2, pp. 12–13.
14. *Bulletin* 6, p. 45.

Chapter 11: Looking After Our Poor

1. GRO P 76a Ch. 1/1.
2. *Bulletin* 10, pp. 18–19.
3. Ibid., pp. 36–9.
4. *Bulletin* 14, pp. 27–31.
5. *Bulletin* 12, p. 42.
6. *Bulletin* 6, pp. 36–45.
7. GRO D 3043.
8. GRO D 1224 (uncatalogued collection).
9. GRO D 3043.
10. GRO D 1224 (uncatalogued collection).
11. *Bulletin* 13, p. 37.
12. GRO D 3043.
13. *Bulletin* 2, p. 34; and 14, p. 27.
14. Cooper-Higgs Charity Trustees' Minute Book, 1882–1957. (Held by the Trustees.)
15. *Bulletin* 1, pp. 22–30; and 3, pp. 42–50.

Chapter 12: Education in Charlton Kings

1. GRO P 76 OV 2/16.
2. *Bulletin* 3, pp. 19–20 and 24–8; and 5, p. 63.
3. *Bulletin* 3, p. 19.
4. *Bulletin* 4, pp. 33–5.
5. Holy Apostles Church, *Centenary Booklet*, pp. 25–6.
6. GRO P 76 SO 3/2.
7. Cooper-Higgs Charity Trustees' Minute Book, 1882–1957. (Held by the Trustees.)
8. *Bulletin* 4, p. 36.
9. *Bulletin* 1, pp. 35–6.
10. *Bulletin* 5, pp. 29–31.
11. *Bulletin* 17, pp. 43–4.

Chapter 13: The Clubs

1. *Bulletin* 15, pp. 33–4.
2. *Charlton Kings Parish Magazine*, October and November 1885.
3. From a brochure about the Working Men's Club published *c.*1904.
4. *Bulletin* 6, pp. 3–4.

Chapter 14: Earning a Living

1. *Bulletin* 1, pp. 8–10.
2. *Bulletin* 10, pp. 39–47.
3. Norfolk Record Office, Walsingham Collection.
4. Cheltenham Natural Science Society, *Proceedings*, vol. 1 (1907–11), pp. 261–2.
5. *Bulletin* 6, pp. 9–12.

Chapter 15: Local Government

1. *Bulletin* 11, pp. 10–20; and 12, pp. 21–7.
2. Charlton Kings Board of Health Minute Books, 1–3 (1862–82); Cheltenham Council sewage documents, box 12 (1862–9); Cheltenham Improvement Commissioners documents, box 4, Charlton sewage papers (1870–80); Cheltenham Town Council Sewage and Drainage Committee minutes, vol. I (1877–83), and Sewage and Drainage Committee minutes, vols. I and II (1852–76).
3. *Bulletin* 5, pp. 31–4; and 6, p. 62.
4. Ibid., 11, pp. 2–50.

Chapter 16: The Health of the Community

1. GRO P 76 VE 2/1.
2. *Bulletin* 10, p. 32.
3. *Charlton Kings Parish Magazine*, July 1884.
4. Ibid., June 1885.
5. *Bulletin* 12, p. 36.
6. *Bulletin* 6, p. 31.
7. *Bulletin* 13, pp. 1–2.
8. Charlton Kings Infant Welfare Centre Minute Book 1, 1923–54.

Chapter 17: Transport

1. GRO Q/RUm 408, Banbury and Cheltenham Direct Railway Plans.
2. GRO Q/RUm 390, Banbury and Cheltenham Direct Railway Plans.
3. *Bulletin* 8, p. 50.
4. GRO RA 33: D. C. Hicks, *The Banbury and Cheltenham Direct Railway* (typescript; 1975) p. 11.
5. GRO Q/RUm 408, Banbury and Cheltenham Direct Railway Plans.

6. GRO RA 33: Hicks, *The Banbury and Cheltenham Direct Railway*, p. 17.
7. *Bulletin* 7, p. 52.
8. GRO RA 33: Hicks, *The Banbury and Cheltenham Direct Railway*, p. 19.
9. Ibid.
10. C. Maggs, *Midland and South Western Junction Railway* (Newton Abbott, David & Charles, 1967) p. 33.
11. Ibid., p. 58.
12. Names of people in the group can be found in *Bulletin* 7, pp. 53–4.
13. Maggs, *Midland and South Western Junction Railway*, p. 111.
14. *Bulletin* 6, p. 62.
15. Maggs, *Midland and South Western Junction Railway*, p. 86.
16. Ibid., p. 106.
17. *Bulletin* 6, pp. 4–7.
18. *Bulletin* 7, p. 41.
19. *Bulletin* 15, pp. 49–51.

Chapter 18: Charlton Artists and Poets

1. John Harris, *Gardens of Delight* (Basilisk Press, 1979).
2. John Anthony Robins, *The Robins Family of Gloucestershire and London* (privately printed, 1982).
3. *Bulletin* 2, pp. 3–12.
4. *Bulletin* 8, pp. 57–9.
5. GRO: GDR wills 1745/80; inventories 1745(1).
6. Wilfred Blunt, *The Art of Botanical Illustration*, 3rd edn (Collins, 1985).
7. Robins, *The Robins Family*, portraits facing p. 9.
8. *The Dictionary of National Biography*, article on George Henry Robins.
9. Ibid., *Supplement, 1901–1960*, article on Briton Riviere.
10. *Bulletin* 5, pp. 19–22.
11. GRO Ashley manor will book 2, no. 139.
12. 'E. J.', *Sydney Dobell, Life and Letters*, 2 vols (Smith, Elder, 1878).
13. *Bulletin* 5, p. 17.
14. *The Dictionary of National Biography*, article on Sir Nathaniel William Wraxall.
15. Ibid., article on Sir Thomas Phillipps; *Bulletin* 12, pp. 1–9.
16. The words quoted are from Adam Lindsay Gordon's poem 'Ye Wearie Wayfarer'.
17. Mavis Batey, *Alice's Adventures in Oxford* (Pitkin Pictorials, 1980); Mavis Batey, 'Alice and Her Wonderful Gardens', *Country Life*, 29 October 1981; *Bulletin* 6, pp. 47–50; 7, p. 56; 2, pp. 30–2.
18. *Bulletin* 13, p. 48.

Chapter 19: Games and Athletics

1. *Charlton Kings Parish Magazine*, June and July 1879; November 1884; January 1885; May and September 1899.
2. Fig. 19.1: *Back row*: ?, Mr Wakefield snr, Arthur Burroughs, Frank Burroughs, Wilf Wakefield, Harry Kilmister, ?, ?

Front row: ?, Billy Simmons (?), George Sadler, Maurice Wakefield, Richard Burroughs, Fred Phipps, Albert Mitchell.

3. Fig. 19.2: *Back row*: Vick Smith, Bert Lawrence, Reg Mobley, Fred Crooks, Dick Smith, Ron Palin, Bill Brewer
   Front row: Jack Palin, Jacky Haines (?), Ted Price, Perrin Prout, Bobbie Roberts, G. Williams, Jack Protherough, Wally Peart.

Chapter 20: Mumming, Visiting and Buff Blowing

1. Reginald St Johnston, *History of Dancing* (Simpkin, Marshall, 1906).
2. *Bulletin* 3, pp. 16–18.

Index

Abbreviations: (BH) = beer house; (PH) = public house. Dates are given in brackets to distinguish between people with the same name. Where house or road names have changed, the alternative names are given in brackets, but index entries will be found under both present and previous names.